THE ALGEBRA OF WEALTH

THE ALGEBRA OF WEALTH

A Simple Formula for Financial Security

SCOTT GALLOWAY

PORTFOLIO | PENGUIN

PORTFOLIO / PENGUIN
An imprint of Penguin Random House LLC
penguinrandomhouse.com

Copyright © 2024 by Scott Galloway

Penguin Random House supports copyright. Copyright fuels creativity, encourages diverse voices, promotes free speech, and creates a vibrant culture. Thank you for buying an authorized edition of this book and for complying with copyright laws by not reproducing, scanning, or distributing any part of it in any form without permission. You are supporting writers and allowing Penguin Random House to continue to publish books for every reader.

Most Portfolio books are available at a discount when purchased in quantity for sales promotions or corporate use. Special editions, which include personalized covers, excerpts, and corporate imprints, can be created when purchased in large quantities. For more information, please call (212) 572-2232 or email specialmarkets@penguinrandomhouse.com. Your local bookstore can also assist with discounted bulk purchases using the Penguin Random House corporate Business-to-Business program. For assistance in locating a participating retailer, email B2B@penguinrandomhouse.com.

Charts and graphics by Prof G Media

Library of Congress Cataloging-in-Publication Data
Names: Galloway, Scott, 1964– author.
Title: The algebra of wealth : a simple formula for financial security / Scott Galloway.
Description: [New York] : Portfolio/Penguin, [2024] |
Includes bibliographical references and index.
Identifiers: LCCN 2023038474 | ISBN 9780593714027 (hardcover) | ISBN 9780593714034 (ebook)
Subjects: LCSH: Finance, Personal. | Wealth—Psychological aspects. | Self-actualization (Psychology) | Success.
Classification: LCC HG179 .G267 2024 | DDC 332.024—dc23/eng/20230919
LC record available at https://lccn.loc.gov/2023038474

ISBN 9780593718322 (international)

Printed in the United States of America
3rd Printing

BOOK DESIGN BY TANYA MAIBORODA

For Alec and Nolan.
Please read this book, and take care of your old man.

CONTENTS

INTRODUCTION
WEALTH — 1
The Algebra of Wealth — 2
Why Wealth? — 4
Permission Slip — 5
The Number — 7
Two Jackets and a Glove — 10
The Hard Way — 12

1. STOICISM — 15
Character and Behavior — 17
Hung(a)ry — 18
Craving Is in Our DNA — 20
You Are What You Do — 21
Ancient Defenses Against Modern Temptations — 22

Slowly	24
Make a Habit of It	25

Building a Strong Character — 27

Working Hard Does Not Equal Character	28
If Money Is the Goal, You Will Never Have Enough	30
Enough	33
Luck	34
Nothing Is Ever as Good or as Bad as It Seems	36
Anger, Indifference, and Revenge	36
Sweat It Out	38
The Algebra of Decisions	39

Building a Strong Community — 41

Don't Be Stupid	42
Greatness Is in the Agency of Others	43
Find Bonds and Guardrails	44
Form a Kitchen Cabinet	45
Tip Well	46
Make Rich Friends	47
Talk About Money	49
The Most Important Relationship	49

CHAPTER REVIEW — 52

2. FOCUS — 55

Balance — 56

Acceptance	57
Flexibility	58
Partner Up	59
Power of Constraints	59

Don't Follow Your Passion — 60

You Don't Know What You Don't Know	61
Passion Careers Suck	62
Work Spoils Passion	63

Follow Your Talent — 63
- "Talent" — 64
- Finding My Talent — 66
- Finding Your Talent — 67
- Can't Always Get What You Want — 68
- Find Your Passion — 70

Career Options — 72
- Some Basics Re: Careers — 73
- So What's the Right Fit for You? — 77
- Entrepreneur — 78
- Academia — 82
- Media — 83
- Professions — 84
- Management Consulting — 85
- Finance — 86
- Real Estate — 87
- Airline Pilot — 88
- Main Street Economy — 89

Best Practices — 91
- Get to a City, Go to the Office — 91
- Desire Is Table Stakes — 93
- Grit — 94
- If You Can't Fix It, You Have to Stand It — 95
- Know When to Quit — 96
- Peaks and Valleys, Not a Ladder — 98
- Be Loyal to People, Not Companies — 101
- Be a Serial Monogamist — 103
- Grad School — 104
- Quick Wins — 105
- Prune and Invest in Your Hobbies — 106

CHAPTER REVIEW — 110

3. TIME   113

The Power of Time: Compounding   115

Compound Interest   115

Inflation   117

Real Returns: Interest vs. Inflation   119

Now   120

Cognitive Errors   120

Time Is the Real Currency   122

   Do the Math   123

Youth's Advantage   126

What Gets Measured Gets Managed   127

Budgeting Your Head Above Water   133

Goals   137

Three Buckets   139

Allocating Your Buckets   141

The Emergency Fund   143

Take the Match   145

Allocation in Practice   146

Debt   147

The Future   149

You Are Not Your Future Self, but You Will Be   149

Black Swans Will Happen, Meteors Will Strike   151

Planning and Advisers   152

CHAPTER REVIEW   154

4. DIVERSIFICATION   157

Basic Principles of Investing   159

Risk and Return   161

The Two Axes of Investing   162

Risk, Part Deux: Diversification   164

Kevlar	167
Random Walk	168

The Capitalist's Handbook — 172

Trading Time for Money	172
The Marketplace of Supply and Demand	174
Capital and the Marketplace of Money	176
Organizing Labor: The Corporation	179
Organizing Capital: Banking	180
The Role of Government	183
Measuring the Economy	185
Valuation and the Time Value of Money	192
Price vs. Value	192
The Basic Valuation Equation	193
Time's Arrow	195

Asset Classes and the Investing Spectrum — 197

The Balanced Approach	198
The Investment Spectrum	202
Stocks	203
Equity	204
Distribution of Profits	206
Financial Statements	207
Equity Valuation	212
Stock Investing	217
Bonds	220
Real Estate	224
Commodities, Currency, and Derivatives	230
Funds	233

Investing's Final Boss: The Taxman — 236

Income Tax	238
The High-Income Trap	243
Payroll Taxes	245
Effective vs. Marginal Tax Rates	246
Defer? I Hardly Even Know Her!	247

Advice from a Lifetime of Investing	249
Zig When Others Zag	249
Don't Trust Your Emotions	250
Don't Day Trade	251
Move	252
CHAPTER REVIEW	254

EPILOGUE
THE WHOLE SHOOTING MATCH   257

ACKNOWLEDGMENTS	259
NOTES	261
BIBLIOGRAPHY	275
INDEX	277

THE ALGEBRA
OF WEALTH

INTRODUCTION
WEALTH

CAPITALISM IS THE MOST PRODUCTIVE economic system in history, and a rapacious beast. It favors incumbents over innovators, rich over poor, capital over labor, and it allocates joy and suffering in ways often more perverse than fair. Understanding—and navigating—capitalism and investing can bless you with choice, control, and human connections void of economic anxiety. This is not a book about what should be, but what is, and it outlines best practices for succeeding in this system.

There are many paths to wealth. Shawn Carter, a high school dropout from Brooklyn's public housing projects, turned his innate feel for lyrical flow into an empire branded Jay-Z, becoming the first hip-hop billionaire. Ronald Read, the first person in his family to graduate from high school, worked his entire life as a janitor, lived frugally, and invested in blue chip stocks. When he died at 92, he left behind an estate worth $8 million. Warren Buffett came from more affluent origins and applied the lessons he learned hanging out as a kid at an Omaha stockbroker's office toward an investing career that's netted him a personal fortune of over $100 billion.

My first piece of advice is you should assume you are not Jay-Z, Ronald Read, or Warren Buffett. Each was an outlier, not just in talent but in good fortune. Less romanticized, but more common, are the frugal janitors and prudent investors whose early trajectory was more consistent than explosive. Outliers make for great inspiration . . . but lousy role models.

When I was in my twenties, I aimed to become an outlier. I wanted the markers of capitalist success and was willing to work for them. In the midst of the striving, I had a conversation about finances with a close friend, Lee. He told me he'd contributed $2,000 to an individual retirement account. At that point, I had no retirement savings. "If $2,000 matters to me when I'm 65," I responded, "I'm going to put a gun in my mouth."

This was arrogant, and wrong. The "swing for the fences" strategy I chose was riskier, less pleasant, and more stressful than my friend's. Ultimately, it worked. Or did I just get lucky? The answer is yes. I've founded nine companies; several have been successful, and their success has led to a media business that is rewarding both economically and emotionally. Economic security is just a means to an end. Specifically, the time and resources to focus on relationships without economic stress. My friend's path to economic security was less volatile and stressful than mine. My path got me there, but a few key principles applied earlier could have put me in the same place sooner with less anxiety.

THE ALGEBRA OF WEALTH

How do you get economic security? There is an answer—that's the good news. The bad news? The answer is . . . slowly. This book distills a great deal of information on markets and wealth creation into four actionable principles.

WEALTH =
Focus + (Stoicism × Time × Diversification)

This is not a typical personal finance book. There are no spreadsheets for you to fill out, no page-long tables comparing the details of ten different retirement plans or mutual fund fee structures. I'm not going to tell you to cut up your credit cards or stick motivational quotes to your refrigerator. Not because that type of advice isn't valuable, or because you should expect to reach economic security without ever making a spreadsheet. But there are dozens of books, websites, YouTube videos, and TikTok accounts teaching these lessons and offering sound advice to get you out of reverse and back on a path. In sum, I'm not trying to beat Suze Orman at her own game—and if you've got bill collectors coming after you, start with her. This book is for those who have their act together and want to ensure they make the best of their blessings. Two people who make the same income today will likely end up in distinctly different places over the years based on their approach to career and money.

We'll discuss how to build a foundation, not only of wealth but of skills, relationships, habits, and priorities that confer advantage. The concepts conveyed here have been tested and supported by science, but above all they are principles you can make your own. The last portion of the book provides a primer on the core concepts of our system of finance and markets. This is an important subject for anyone who lives and works in our system, yet it's poorly covered in schools and glossed over in most personal finance literature. Everything here is based on what I've learned during an up-down-and-up-again career, from founding companies, to hiring and working with hundreds of successful people, to observing generations of young people come through my classroom and graduate to lives that map to every point on the spectrum of success.

WHY WEALTH?

Wealth is a means to an end: economic security. Put another way, wealth is the absence of economic anxiety. Freed of the pressure to earn, we can choose how we live. Our relationships with others aren't shadowed by the stress of money. It sounds basic, easy even. It's not—we live in a globally competitive marketplace with a genius for creating problems that can only be solved by spending on bigger and better things.

This is the first lesson in this book: economic security isn't a function of what you earn but what you keep and knowing how much is enough for you. As the great philosopher Sheryl Crow once said, happiness isn't "having what you want, it's wanting what you've got." It's not about getting more . . . but ascertaining what you need and applying the right strategy to get you there, so you can focus on other things.

My objective for you is straightforward. Economic security is acquiring sufficient assets—not income, but assets—such that the **passive income** they generate exceeds the level of spending you choose for yourself—your **burn rate**. Passive income is money your money makes: interest you make on money you loan to someone else, appreciation in the value of your real estate, dividends paid by stocks you hold, rent paid by the tenant of an apartment you own. I'll talk more about these and other sources of passive income later, but, in short, it is any income that's not compensation paid for working at a job. And your burn rate is how much you spend, day to day and month to month. If your passive income is greater than your burn, you don't *need* to work (though you may want to), because you don't need the compensation to pay your expenses.

That's wealth. There are numerous paths to it; the reliable ones

ECONOMIC SECURITY =
Passive income > Burn rate

take time and hard work but are within the grasp of most people. And reaching for it should be a priority, early. Economic security is control. It is knowing that you can plan for the future, commit your time as you see fit, and provide for those who depend on you.

PERMISSION SLIP

Seeking wealth is not always in fashion. In a society correctly concerned about the acceleration of income inequality, wealth looks like the unfair allocation of a rigged system. "Every billionaire is a policy failure." Maybe. Or maybe not. But it's not relevant here. The urgent issue you face is your own economic security, not the virtues of anyone else's.

"Money doesn't talk, it swears," Bob Dylan said. My experience is that money changes its tone as it grows. It hurls expletives at you when there's not enough and comforts you as it accumulates. But the swearing most of us hear is getting louder. The median home price in the U.S. is six times the median annual income—fifty years ago it was two times—and the share of first-time buyers is barely half the historical average and the lowest on record. Medical debt is the leading cause of consumer bankruptcy; half of American adults would not be able to cover a $500 medical bill without taking on debt. Marriage rates among all but the wealthiest cohort are down 15% since 1980, as people can't afford to tie the knot, much less have kids. Despite record growth in our broader prosperity, just 50% of Americans born in the 1980s are making more than their parents did at the same age, the lowest share ever. Twenty-five percent of Gen Z'ers don't believe they'll ever be able to retire.

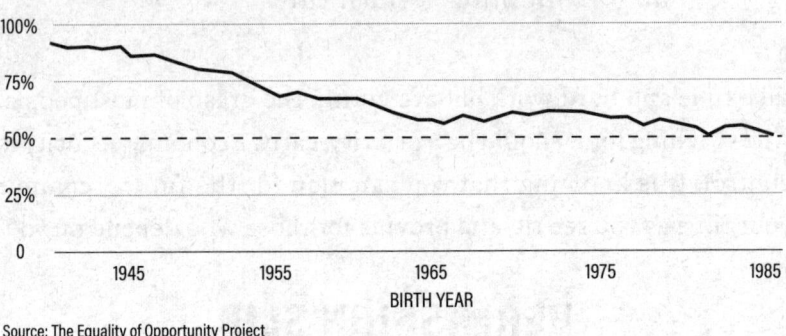

Source: The Equality of Opportunity Project

Divorce, depression, and disability are all moths to the flame of financial strain.

In 2020, Dylan sold his song catalog for $400 million. Money ain't swearing at Bob no more. When he penned that lyric in 1965, an upper-middle-class life got you 90% of what the wealthy had. The wealthiest families had a bigger house than you, had a step up in wardrobe, and played golf at the private club instead of the municipal course. The sixty years since have witnessed the rise of the rich-industrial complex. When the wealthy vacation today, they don't just stay in a nicer room than a regular family; they fly on a different plane (Bob's is a Gulfstream IV), stay in a different resort, see different sights (often after-hours, when the public is not allowed). The 1% go to different doctors, eat at different restaurants, shop at different stores. Wealth used to be a better seat. Now it's an upgrade to a better life.

The key to happiness is our expectations, and unrealistic expectations guarantee unrealized happiness. Yet every time you leave your house or pick up your phone, society and its organizations are either serenading or swearing at you. The difference between the lives of the 1% and the 99% is thrown in your face every day—an entire industry of simulated, flaunted wealth has developed around "influencers." Wealth porn . . . a constant reminder: not of what you've achieved but what you haven't.

The system may need fixing; until then, you have to stand it. Better yet, work it and develop the skills and strategies to increase the likelihood you will prosper within it. What Churchill said about democracy—that it's the worst system except for all the others we've tried—is also true of capitalism. Inequality pricks ambition, incentives drive outcomes, and the wheel turns. If the system suits you, play it the best you can. If it doesn't . . . play the best you can. None of this is your fault. Society faces greater risks than you becoming a millionaire. And until you attain economic security, your time will not be your own and much of your stress will be unproductive. (See above: money swears at you.)

Pursuing wealth doesn't mean you are immoral, greedy, or selfish, and it doesn't require you to be so. Indeed, those qualities only make achieving economic security harder and undermine your happiness once you get there. To overcome the obstacles between you and wealth, you will need allies. You've likely been told to start saving/investing early. Start cultivating allies and fans early, too. In all aspects of your life, you want to have the home-field advantage. You should (and can) be front of mind when people are asked, "Who would be good for this job, this investment, this board?" And the ultimate objective is to enjoy a life rich in relationships, not to die with the biggest number in the bank.

THE NUMBER

Typically, personal finance advice is built around "retirement" (a clear distinction between working and no longer working). It's an outdated construct and not central to our philosophy of wealth. I want you to obtain economic security *before* you stop working. The sooner the better. Once you've achieved economic security, you may decide to continue to focus on work and professional achievement. I have. But the stress surrounding work declines dramatically when it becomes a surfboard instead of a life preserver. We perform better when we are confident. Work is a bit like dating in this regard—the less you need your job, the more it needs you.

You could apply the principles of this book and, with some luck and a lot of hard work, be living on a boat in the Caribbean by age 40, never earning another dollar. Or you could be sitting on boards in your seventies and mentoring CEOs for four figures per hour. Economic security gives you options. And economic security boils down to a number: an asset base sufficient to fund your lifestyle. You may decide to continue to work, as there are numerous studies showing work can extend your life and well-being. What kills you is stress, and much of this stress is a function of not having economic security. Work without economic stress evolves from necessity to purpose.

How big a number *do* you need in your bank account? There's no single answer, but there is an answer for you. Although it's more a goal than an answer, as economic security is not pass-fail. Getting most of the way to your goal will make life easier and more rewarding. Thomas J. Stanley said, "Wealth is not a matter of intelligence, it's a matter of arithmetic." Remember our math: passive income greater than your burn.

So what's your burn rate? Or, more precisely, what's the burn rate you aspire to maintain in perpetuity? This is easier to answer the older you are, as you're closer to perpetuity. But even if you are early in your career or still in school, you can get some idea by building a budget from the ground up, asking family members about their expenses, and researching the typical costs of housing, food, and other items. You don't need to project your spending forty years into the future down to the dollar, nor should you. It's neither possible nor necessary. A rough sketch is a good start; it's something you can refine as your target comes into view.

This exercise is in part financial, but it's also deeply personal. As you gain experience, you'll know yourself better and get a feel for what you need. Everyone's target burn rate is different. For my father, it's not much. Some practical requirements, a studio at the Wesley Palms (an assisted-living facility), a streaming network that offers Maple Leafs games, and a night out (home by seven) that includes Mexican food and a michelada. I'm not cut from the same cloth. My spending burns hotter. Like, supernova hotter. Anyway, whether you like Pabst or Prada, rough out your projected expenses for a year and add them up. Bump it 20% to cover taxes (30% if you expect to live in California, New York, or another high-tax state). That's your annual burn rate.

Now multiply that burn rate by 25. That's (roughly) your number—the asset base you need to generate passive income greater than your burn. Why 25? That assumes your assets produce income at a rate of 4% over inflation. Different financial planners will suggest slightly different numbers, but 4% is in the ballpark, and 25x makes the math easy. This is just a rough sketch. Our tax estimate is simplistic. Your burn rate will rise if you have kids in the house and fall when they move on. We haven't considered social security, which may or may not exist thirty years from now. (I think it will, because old people keep living longer, and they vote, so we're more likely to get rid of schools, the space program, and half the navy before we fail to fund social security.) But any work of art starts with a rough sketch.

If you need $80,000 a year to cover your burn rate, then $2 million is your number. If you hit that in invested assets, then you win—you've beaten capitalism. (Capitalism has some tricks up its sleeve, though: $2 million is your number *today*—if you're planning to accumulate that asset base 25 years from now, inflation will bump your number up to more like $5 million. We'll get to that.)

TWO JACKETS AND A GLOVE

A few years ago, we went skiing, a hobby I endure to trap my boys on a mountain so they have to spend time with me. One afternoon, I'm in our hotel room in Courchevel, using work as an excuse to escape my on-piste obligations. My eldest, who was 11 at the time, comes in, and I know something is wrong. As a rule, both sons reflexively announce themselves whenever they enter a room with a question or bodily function. ("Can I watch TV?" "Where's Mom?" *Belch*.) But . . . silence, until he's in front of me. He's been crying.

"What's wrong?"

"I lost a glove." More tears.

"That's okay, it's only a glove."

"You don't understand. Mommy just bought me these. They cost €80. That's a lot of money. She's going to be angry."

"She'll understand. I lose stuff all the time."

"But I don't want her to buy me another pair—they were €80."

Easy for me to be empathetic here. My son's tendency to lose stuff is inherited. My ex-wife said if my penis wasn't attached, we'd run across it in SoHo on a card table next to secondhand books and a script for *Goodfellas*. I don't carry keys, what's the point?

So, I got this. We agree to retrace his steps. Along the way my mind races: *Is this a life lesson? Would buying him a new pair be coddling?* I look down—he's crying. The ground splits beneath me, and instantly I'm 9 again.

After my folks separated, economic stress turned to economic anxiety. Anxiety gnawed at my mom and me, whispering in our ears that we weren't valid, that we'd failed. My mom, a secretary, was smart and hardworking . . . and our household income was $800 a month. I told Mom, at the age of 9, that I didn't need a babysitter, because I knew we could use the additional $8 a week. Also, when the ice cream truck came by, my sitter gave each of her kids 30¢ and me 15¢.

"It's winter, you need a jacket," my mom said; so off to Sears we went. We bought one a size too big, as my mom figured I could get two, maybe three years out of it. It cost $33. Two weeks later, I left my jacket at Cub Scouts, but I assured my mom we'd get it back at the next meeting. We didn't.

So off to get another jacket, this time to JCPenney. Mom told me this one was my Christmas present, as we wouldn't have the funds for gifts after buying another jacket. I don't know if this was true or if she was trying to teach me a lesson. Likely both. Regardless, I tried to feign excitement at my early Christmas present, which, incidentally, also cost $33.

Several weeks later . . . I lost the second jacket. I sat at home after school, in fear, waiting for my mom to come home and absorb another body blow to our already economically feeble household. I heard the key turn, she walked in, and I nervously blurted out, "I lost the jacket. It's okay, I don't need one . . . I swear."

I felt like crying, bawling really. But something worse happened. My mom began to cry. Then she composed herself, walked over to me, made a fist, and pounded on my thigh several times as if she were in a boardroom trying to make a point, and my thigh was the table she was slamming her fist on. I don't know if it was more upsetting or awkward. She then went upstairs to her room. She came down an hour later, and we never spoke of it again.

Economic anxiety is high blood pressure—always there, waiting to turn a minor ailment into a life-threatening disease. That's not a metaphor. Kids who grow up in low-income households have higher blood pressure than kids who live in wealthy ones.

Meanwhile, back in the Alps, a dad and his one-gloved son have been walking for thirty minutes in 8-degree weather. I attempt to take advantage of his weakened state and break into a song and dance about how *things* aren't important, but relationships are. In the midst of this bad Hallmark Channel scene, my son stops, then sprints to a small Christmas tree in front of the Philipp Plein store. The same store where, the day before, his 8-year-old brother tried to persuade me to buy him a €250 hoodie with a bedazzled skull on the back. On top of the tree, in place of the star, is one electric-blue boy's glove. A good—and creative—Samaritan had found it and placed it within eyeshot of any boy searching for the vibrant accessory. My son grabs the glove, sighs, holds it to his chest, and visibly feels a mix of relief and reward.

We live in an era of innovation in finance, but no cryptocurrency or payment app will offer what I want most—to send money back in time, to the people I loved who didn't have it. The insecurity and shame present in my childhood home will always be there. But that's okay, as it was motivating.

Your pursuit of wealth may be driven by something else. Perhaps validation, or a feeling of purpose. A passion for the good life, luxuries and experiences only money can bring. The desire to do something about the ills of the world. In my experience, noble intentions are a good motivation for hard work, and desire is also powerful—but fear bests them both. What drives you is your business. Find it, nurture it, and carry it with you.

You will need motivation, as there is hard work ahead.

THE HARD WAY

So, how do you reach economic security? There are really just two ways. The smart way is to inherit it. Most of us will have to go the hard way. It's simple. Earn money by working hard. Save some. Invest it. If you maximize your income, minimize your spending, and invest the difference wisely, I can claim with reasonable certainty: you will achieve economic security.

Executing this plan is not as simple as stating it. That goes beyond finance, beyond what you can capture on a spreadsheet. Wealth is the product of a life well lived—hard work, frugality, wisdom. That doesn't mean being a monk—there's room for pleasure, for error, for life. But it does mean hard work, and it does mean a certain amount of discipline. And it's worth it. The Algebra of Wealth has four components:

Stoicism is about living an intentional, temperate life in and out of work. It's about saving money, for sure, but also developing strong character and connecting with a community. This stuff matters.

Focus is primarily about earning an income. As I discuss, income alone won't make you wealthy, but it's the necessary first step. And you're going to need a decent amount of it. So we'll help you plan and navigate a career and maximize the income it generates.

Time is your most important asset. It starts and ends with an understanding of the most powerful force in the universe: compound interest. We'll share how to make it work for you. Time is the real currency, the one asset we're all given at birth, and the foundation of wealth.

Diversification is our take on the traditional personal finance questions, a road map for making sound investment decisions and for being an educated participant in the financial marketplace.

Okay—let's light this candle.

FOCUS

+

(STOICISM

×

TIME

×

DIVERSIFICATION)

1
STOICISM

WHAT KEPT ME FROM ECONOMIC security for much of my life was a stubborn belief that I was exceptional. The market reinforced this. I was starting companies, being profiled in magazines, and raising tens of millions for my start-ups. I was (obviously) on the verge of tens, if not hundreds, of millions as I was (obviously) exceptional. Getting close a couple times only reinforced the belief.

Convinced of my imminent jump to light speed, I ignored the idea of living below my means or saving and investing. The IPO or acquisition would be any day now. I could have easily saved $10,000 to $100,000 per year in my twenties and thirties, but why sacrifice when so much more is right around the corner? Right? Wrong. The dot bomb of 2000, a divorce, and the Great Financial Recession meant that every time the ball looked to be headed for the fence, it would veer foul. And then, at 42, my first son was born.

Angels singing? A Hallmark Channel moment? On the contrary. I was so nauseous I couldn't stand upright. It wasn't the blood and screaming that rendered me useless, but the wave of shame that washed over me. I had fucked up. I could have easily had a few million dollars in the bank, and I didn't. I had failed. Until minutes earlier, I could handle that, because I'd only failed myself. What I couldn't handle was the realization that I had failed my son.

My failure was constructed from poor choices, but it wasn't from a lack of knowledge. I had an MBA, I'd raised many millions of dollars in capital, made payroll every week, and delivered profits every quarter. I *understood* money. I just wasn't any *good* at it. I was not alone in this. A study of UK consumers found that while both financial illiteracy and a lack of self-control contributed to people getting over their head in debt, the data showed "a stronger role for lack of self-control than for financial illiteracy in explaining consumer over-indebtedness."

Economic security doesn't derive from an intellectual exercise; it's the result of a pattern of behavior. How can we avoid the pattern of behavior that leads to over-indebtedness and develop that which leads to wealth? Put another way, how can we align our behavior with our intentions? On the surface, this looks like self-control. But self-control suggests willpower, holding to a plan with white-knuckled grip. That's exhausting, fighting your own impulses constantly. There has to be something deeper that enables some people to align their behavior with their intentions consistently over the years.

The distilled answer: character. In the face of modern capitalism's temptations, human frailty, setbacks, and bad luck, our intended behaviors require durability, and that only comes when those behaviors are rooted in our true character. If durable changes of behavior could arise from intention alone, we would keep our New Year's resolutions and never forget a thank-you note. What we do is an expression of who we are. Contrary to the popular saying, it is not the thought that counts.

This chapter explores the development of our character in three parts. First, I explore the essential mechanics and principles of character building. Second, I describe how I apply those principles in my own life, and then I suggest how you might think about building your own strong character. Lastly, I widen the lens to consider character in the community. Humans are a social species, and we can only achieve our full potential in cooperation (and sometimes competition) with others.

CHARACTER AND BEHAVIOR

Humans have sought to build character throughout history. The good news: we know how it's done. The bad: it's difficult. But it's neither mysterious nor complicated. Character and behavior exist in a self-reinforcing cycle. Just as our actions reflect our character, our character is ultimately the product of our actions. That cycle can be a virtuous circle or a destructive spiral—your choice. This is true for more than mere economic success. Living with purpose and consistency is what it means to live an authentic life, leaving it

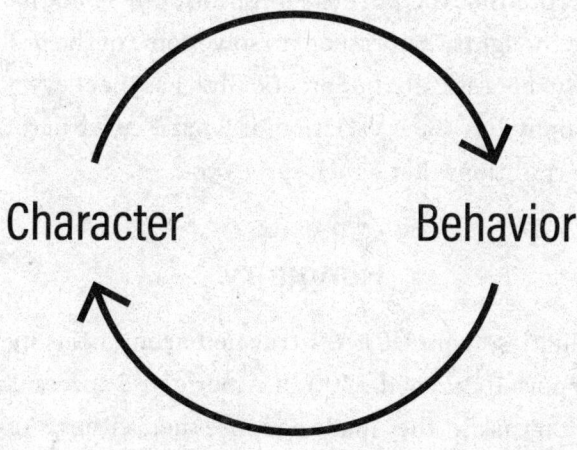

all on the field even if you come up short. The pursuit of wealth, like its cousin, the pursuit of happiness, is a whole-person project.

Humanity has learned the process many times, including through the teachings of Stoicism. Stoicism is a school of philosophy founded in classical Greece that flowered in the Roman Empire and has been reinvigorated by modern interpreters. Stoics regard the development of one's character as the highest virtue, and they have written at length on its pursuit. I call this chapter "Stoicism" because the language of the Stoic philosophers and their modern interpreters resonates with me, and their teachings influence the way I approach my professional and personal life. That said, this section is not an exegesis of Stoic philosophy or limited to its teachings. Marcus Aurelius didn't suggest we "make rich friends," as I do in this section. But I like to think he'd be nodding through most of this chapter.

Around the same time the first Stoic philosophers were contemplating virtue in Greece, the disciples of Siddhartha Gautama were elaborating on his teachings, the emphasis on right intention, right action, and right mindfulness that form the heart of Buddhism. Centuries later, Jesus preached the importance of rightfulness and resistance from temptation, warning us: "The flesh is willing, but the spirit is weak." In nineteenth-century America, Thoreau wrote that the purpose of philosophy is not merely "to have subtle thoughts," but rather "to solve some of the problems of life, not only theoretically, but practically." I suspect every culture and philosophy has some variation of what I cover here. Borrow from these traditions that which serves you.

Hung(a)ry

After graduating from UCLA, I traveled around Europe. At the Vienna airport I changed $300 in American Express Travelers Cheques (don't ask... they made no sense then, either). Anyway, in exchange for three fake Benjamins, converted at 96¢ to the dollar into a foreign currency at an American Express travel office (see above: made no sense), I received several stacks of forints and was now the baller I was meant to be. A short train ride was all that stood between me and the consumer orgy waiting for me in Budapest.

In a store window I saw a beautiful leather travel bag, so I went inside. There I found people shopping for . . . spools of thread and needles. Before I even had the chance to ask about the bag, the woman behind the desk pointed at it and said, "Not for sale." Soon I was back at the travel office with my only slightly smaller stack of forints, getting a lesson in currency exchange and the bid–ask spread.

Thirty-five years of capitalism later, whether you are in Budapest, Hungary, or Budapest, Georgia (yes, this place exists), and you want toothpaste for sensitive teeth infused with olive oil or cereal that tastes like French toast, no problem. Those products exist and can be at your doorstep that afternoon. Say what you will about communism, but it sure made it easy to be frugal.

"The easiest way to make a dollar is to save a dollar" is good advice. Yet every day, hundreds of times a day, we are confronted with messages, arguments, and encouragement to spend. Capitalism harnesses the ingenuity and energy of an entire society toward a singular purpose—to persuade you to spend money. It's what makes the system function. The temptations range from an impulse purchase of gum at checkout to add-ons to your Amazon cart to an upgrade to economy-plus with priority boarding and free drinks. And, by the way, do you want to "protect" your trip (i.e., buy insurance) in case something happens . . . or check the "I do not want to protect my trip" box and feel irresponsible, negligent even? Don't worry, American Airlines (or their insurance partner) can make you feel less negligent for an additional $39.95.

Craving Is in Our DNA

Capitalism has a lot to work with. For 99% of our species's existence, most people didn't live past 35. And the number-one killer was starvation, a lack of "stuff." It's not YOLO ("You only live once") that's being whispered in your ear, but something much stronger: YNSN ("You need stuff now") . . . or you will die.

We are biologically programmed to seek sugar, fat, and salt, because for most of our species' existence these items were in short supply. Just the touch of these substances to our taste buds triggers a cascade of chemical reactions that read as pleasure in our consciousness. Our brains link memories of this pleasure to everything from the color of the packaging of chocolate to the intersection where our favorite burger joint resides. Our brain is trying to help when it does this, mapping us a route back to the ultimate reward, the best feeling: survival.

It gets worse. Once you've checked the "survival" box, another instinctive voice begins screaming at you: propagation. It's easy for me to tell young people to save, invest, etc. However, a twentysomething is tasked with finding a mate. And finding a mate involves signaling and spending. Panerai watches and Manolo Blahniks are nods to your evolutionary obligations, to find a mate stronger, faster, and smarter than you so your genes will mingle with theirs and live forever.

At 23, after my first year at Morgan Stanley, I received a $30,000 bonus. I had, until this point, never had more than $1,000 in my checking account. Finally, a base to build from. A base? Yeah, right. I went out and bought a BMW 320i (hello, ladies). It was navy blue, and I hung swim goggles from the rearview. Why? Because once a week I was (wait for it) swimming. Neither of these actions had anything to do with transportation or exercise but signaled that I was strong and had resources . . . and that you should have sex with me. So . . . yeah . . . easier said than done. Also, there's some logic that a certain level of signaling can be justified: looking good, putting yourself in social situations where there are mating opportunities (e.g., Coachella, clubs, Cancun).

Modern humans are doubly disadvantaged. We live in a world of excess but are built for an environment of scarcity. And we have built our economy on exploiting this disconnect. You are not going to think your way out of this dilemma.

You Are What You Do

Advice on careers, budgeting, and investing is not in short supply. Bookshelves, the Web, and social and family gatherings are bursting with it. None of it matters if it doesn't translate into action. The gap between your intentions and your actions is a decent forward-looking indicator of your future success, emotionally and financially. When we describe people we admire, we call them "courageous," "entrepreneurial," or "innovative." These are all different shades of action, specifically people who are prone to action that foots to their values, words, and plans. As Carl Jung put it, "You are what you do, not what you say you will do."

Unfortunately, we are bombarded with messages that there are shortcuts to closing the gap between intentions and actions. In preparation for writing the classic guide to self-improvement *The 7 Habits of Highly Effective People*, Stephen Covey did not merely study successful people, he reviewed the literature on how to become successful. From the post-WWII period forward, he discerned a shift from what he termed the "character ethic" to a "personality ethic." Older works encouraged readers to build character: foster principles and values in themselves, to build success on the basis of virtues like temperance, industriousness, and patience. The more recent advice, on the other hand, focused on how to change merely your personality: how you present yourself to others. As the title of the grandfather of these self-improvement books puts it, *How to Win Friends and Influence People*.

Covey was working in the 1980s, but any time spent on the internet will confirm that this trend has only accelerated. Social media is littered with "life hacks" (something called mushroom coffee?), dating tips on the best "openers," and other "weird tricks." Every aspect of our lives has a fad diet to better it. What keeps personality ethic advice flowing is that it might give you a momentary boost but it doesn't work over any significant time span or against serious opposition. (A survey of 121 studies found that a variety of popular diets, no matter what theory they promoted or which celebrity promoted them, showed no effect on weight after a year.)

Just as adherents to fad diets inevitably slide back to their pre-diet weight, success tactics are just that—tactics, rooted entirely in a specific behavior—and won't last. If I tell you the secret to success is waking up at 5:30 a.m., taking a cold shower, and running 5 miles, that's not *bad* advice. Likely you will be more focused and productive on days when you follow it. And maybe you'll follow it for a few days, even, if you are highly disciplined, a few weeks. But novelty wears off, and the morning's dark and cold persists. I've spent a lot of my professional life around wealthy people, and some do get up at 5:30, take a cold shower, etc. But that's not *why* they're successful. Those are habits that are the product of living an industrious, disciplined life. Character and behavior are inextricable.

Ancient Defenses Against Modern Temptations

The Stoics identified the four virtues: courage, wisdom, justice, and temperance. I believe these are the keys to resisting temptations—and to much more.

Courage is our persistence, what modern thinkers often term "grit." We have courage when we do not let fear guide our actions: fear of poverty, fear of embarrassment, fear of failure. Instead, we are industrious, positive, and confident. Marketers are masters of exploiting our fears and insecurities. Courage is cheaper than Chanel, and it works better.

Wisdom, as described by Epictetus, is the ability "to identify and separate matters so that I can say clearly to myself which are external and not under my control, and which have to do with the choices I actually control." Or as Annie Proulx put it in *Brokeback Mountain*: "If you can't fix it, you gotta stand it."

Justice is a commitment to the common good, a recognition that we are interdependent. The Stoic emperor Marcus Aurelius believed that justice was "the source of all other virtues." When we act with justice we are honest, and we take the full consequences of our actions into account. We can't build good habits alone, and the latter part of this chapter takes on the ways in which our character is in part a function of community.

Temperance is to me the most important virtue because it is the one most tested by modern culture. Capitalism is fueled by our lack of self-control, our obsession with status and consumption. And not just in the obvious sense of super-sized fries and luxury handbags. Western society encourages indulgence not only in spending but also in emotional outbursts, in victimizing, and victimhood. Temperance is the resistance—or at least the management—of *all* our indulgences.

Slowly

How do we put these virtues into practice? How do we build the character that makes self-control a natural, intuitive way of being rather than a constant battle against impulse? We can start by slowing down.

Perhaps you make a hundred moderately important decisions a day: what to eat for breakfast, whether to go to the gym, how to respond to a pointed Slack message from a colleague, what to do at the end of the day when your time is finally your own. It's human nature to make these decisions reactively—without thinking, based on instinct or emotion. That's the quickest way. In hindsight, we tend to ascribe our response to the conditions—we skipped breakfast *because* we were running late, we wrote a terse response *because* the Slack message was unreasonable.

Recall the Stoic virtue of wisdom—know what you can control. The line is easy to draw, as Marcus Aurelius made clear: "You have power over your mind—not outside events." The psychologist Viktor Frankl observed, "Between stimulus and response there is a space. In that space is our power to choose our response. In our response lies our growth and our freedom." We cannot control our environment, but we can control how we respond.

If you can find that space Frankl describes, between stimulus and response, in just a few of those hundred decisions you make each day, and consider your values, the plan you've set for yourself, you'll build muscle for the next time. Even just once a day, saying, "I control this, my response is my choice," and choosing the behavior you know to be right rather than the one you feel in the moment, is a step on the path to Stoicism.

This doesn't mean never being angry—I get angry often, too often. Nor does it mean never being dismayed, frustrated, or ashamed. Those are normal human responses to setbacks and mistakes. The objective is to acknowledge the anger or the fear—or the greed—but not let it determine your behavior.

Character and behavior can create a reinforcing cycle. Start with just a few chosen behaviors, and you'll build the character to make more.

Make a Habit of It

We can supercharge this cycle by developing habits. Healthy habits harness the brain's tendency toward reactivity and direct it toward the proactive responses we want. The past few decades have witnessed scientific and cultural interest in, as one of the leading popular books on the subject calls it, "the power of habit." It turns out that much of what we do is habitual, and that's a good thing. If we had to consciously process every decision, we'd never get past breakfast.

The key is to train our habits proactively, such that our reactive, automatic response to stimuli matches the response we'd choose if we could take the time to make the choice. The more situations in which we can train ourselves to make the desired habitual response, the more cognitive and emotional energy we have to take the reins on the most important decisions and reactions, and the most difficult ones.

There are several frameworks for intentional habit formation. In *The Power of Habit*, Charles Duhigg describes the "cue-routine-reward" cycle. James Clear, the author of *Atomic Habits*, prefers "cue-craving-response-reward." I'm sure there are others. Like Stoicism and Buddhism, these are similar paths to the same place.

JUST DO IT

On a Thursday night in late 2016, I wrote my first blog post. The team at my newest start-up, L2, had been discussing how to promote the business, and we had the groundbreaking idea of a "blog"—only twenty years after blogs became a thing. I had written a lot through the course of my day-to-day work (letters to investors, pitches to clients, etc.), and I aimed for incision and color. But I wouldn't have described myself as a writer. Nor did I think of myself as someone who would commit to doing *anything* week in and week out. I was always more of a "when it strikes me" kind of guy. Anyway, the first post was easy enough: I criticized Zuck and made fun of Silicon Valley CEOs' dating habits, and my team added some good charts. We called it "No Mercy / No Malice," and emailed it to our client list of a couple thousand people. Even got some positive feedback.

Then, as happens every week, it was Thursday again. Which meant I had to write another post. Less novelty, more work. But I did it, and we sent it out. And then the next week, another one. You can get a hint of my mood on the third Thursday night by the title of that post: "I Hate Myself Less and Less Every Day." It was no longer fun. But it was increasingly rewarding as the blog grew in relevance and we put something decent out . . . every week. My brain connected the writing sessions to the satisfaction I got when people read my work and responded. Thursday nights became a cue, and while the writing itself did not get easier, the decision to sit down at the computer and get those first words out—that became a habit. A year in, then two, I was someone who could meet deadlines and produce something of consistent quality. My habit had become my identity. I was a writer.

Today, *No Mercy* is longer, more analytical, and better. It won a Webby award in 2022, and it goes out to over 500,000 people every week. It leverages a key tenet I hold to—greatness is in the agency of others. There's a team of people at Prof G Media who work across all our channels, including *No Mercy / No Malice*. But still, every Thursday night, I sit on the couch with my dogs and Zacapa and get to work. Because I'm a writer.

This book, my fifth, feels almost impossible to me. Impossible that the first ever happened. That I actually conceived, wrote, edited, and got a book published. I could so easily have never written an outline, or pitched an agent, or given up my weekends and late nights—just not done it. Yeah, it was a good idea, but that's about 10% (max) of the value. The other 90% happens every Thursday night. It's a worthwhile question every person should ask themselves: What are you due to just *do*? What should you start *today*? Clear, whose book *Atomic Habits* has sold approximately 8 billion copies, put it this way: "Your identity emerges out of your habits."

BUILDING A STRONG CHARACTER

Those are the mechanics, the basic principles. How we apply them—or don't—is personal but it needn't be private. I'm not (yet) a paragon of virtuous behavior and good habits, but over the past fifteen or so years, I've figured a few things out that work for me. It's no accident that those have also been the years of my greatest economic success, as well as the richest in relationships.

It wasn't always that way. I spent the first forty years of my life chasing some form of Western relevance so I could register more dopamine surges. See above: I was exceptional (I believed), I wanted more and always more, and yet I always fell short. My first marriage and the focus required by two of my successful start-ups provided ballast for a time, but when I was 33 I got divorced and stepped back from active management in both firms. Not just from my companies. I had consciously decided I wanted to *disengage*: from my marriage, from my community, and from our friends. There was insight in this impulse—what I had then obviously wasn't working for me—but it was buried under a metric ton of selfishness.

I moved to NYC to be all about Scott. Work a little bit, make fake friends (more partners in partying than friends), and not be reliant on, or reliable for, anybody. I was an island living on an island. Tom Wolfe said, "One belongs to New York instantly." I found I also took to being alone instantly. Maybe it was being an only child or slowly becoming more like myself, an introvert. I could go days without interacting with anybody, and it was fine.

Teaching at NYU, partying at Lotus and Pangea, vacationing in St. Barts, and occasionally advising a hedge fund—being selfish came easily to me. I reverted to a caveman status and would only leave my loft for food, sex, or to hunt (make money). It was an empty experience that provided just enough pleasure to keep it going.

My shortcomings *then* are clearer to me *now*. Rather than direct my energies by an internal compass, I reacted to whatever stimulus was most urgent in my immediate field of view. The stimulus that attracted my attention with the most urgency was money, not as a means of establishing economic security, but to feed my addiction: affirmation from others. I wanted nice things and to be able to take care of my mom, but I saw my worth through other people's eyes and believed their criteria for what constituted economic success. And I got those things. I garnered status and found pleasure, but real economic security and lasting happiness eluded me. I didn't know any other way to be.

What changed? The external stimulus was the birth of my first child. But external change is only an opportunity. I still had to walk through the door. The shame and regret I felt was a prompt to take stock and the motivation to make changes. That's when my journey really began. Following are the insights I've had along the way. I'll start with a few things I learned about what *doesn't* work, and then cover some of what does.

Working Hard Does Not Equal Character

From Wall Street to Silicon Valley, this is the big lie of the working world: if you're pulling long hours, that means you're disciplined, virtuous, strong. This false equivalence was my ethos for years. I was disciplined about work. I worked hard, even when I was not creating wealth. I fooled myself into thinking that if I was working hard, then I had character.

When I was in my twenties and working at Morgan Stanley, it was the all-nighter that signified virtue. "How late were you here last night?" was the chest-thumping challenge of the Hermès-suspender-wearing silverback we presented to the world. Now it's hustle porn and meal-replacement shakes that save you the three minutes it would take to make a turkey sandwich.

In the next chapter, I'm going to tell you to work hard, and I believe it's essential not just for economic security, but for personal fulfillment. "Do hard things" is as good a piece of advice as you'll ever get. But while working hard is *necessary* to personal and professional success, it is not *sufficient*, and more important, **it is not the point**. Working hard by itself is just burning energy into the capitalist void. Get strong so that you can provide for others. Gain power so you can do justice. Working for work's sake is economic masturbation.

Too many people use working hard as an excuse. An excuse for ignoring their partner, neglecting their health, being rude or cruel or exploitative. I said earlier that the pursuit of wealth is always a cover story. Equating hard work with character is shoving your fingers in your ears and singing "Roxanne" to drown out what's really driving you, what you really need to work on.

Hard work is necessary, and it does come with a cost. Are you minimizing that cost, or ignoring it? A good tell is spending. When I look back at my twenties and thirties, I see that I lacked discipline about spending. I *deserved* nice things because I worked so hard (I told myself). I *didn't need* to save because I worked so hard, I would always get more (I told myself). None of the advice I offer in the next chapter, "Focus," will get you where you need to be unless you can also follow the spending and saving advice in the chapter after that, "Time."

The false equivalence of hard work and character hides more important failures than bad spending habits. My bigger sin, in those first two decades of my career, was that I failed to invest in others and in relationships. And hard work was such a great excuse for that. But it all fed on itself—transactional friendships and partners in partying were never going to hold me accountable, and they certainly weren't going to tell me to stop spending. Wealth is a whole-person project.

If Money Is the Goal, You Will Never Have Enough

In the 1970s, psychologists Donald Campbell and Philip Brickman were studying happiness and came across a persistent fact: changes in life circumstances had little measurable impact on happiness as we adjust to the new reality. One of their studies compared people who had won large lottery prizes with people who had been rendered paraplegics. Counterintuitively, the lottery winners were no happier than controls, and the paraplegics were only moderately less happy—plus, they reported the highest level of optimism about their future. Subsequent studies of different groups of lottery winners and different-size prizes have sometimes found measurable increases in happiness, but nothing like the sort of quantum leap you might expect from sudden wealth.

Campbell and Brickman coined the term "hedonic treadmill" to describe what they were seeing in the data: no matter how much apparent progress we make toward our goal, we remain in the same place, spinning the treadmill faster.

Historian Yuval Noah Harari, the author of *Sapiens*, wrote, "One of history's few iron laws is that luxuries tend to become necessities and to spawn new obligations." Lifestyle creep is inevitable, and it's an arms race. From old clothes that make you feel underdressed next to your coworker's designer duds (maybe working from

HEDONIC TREADMILL

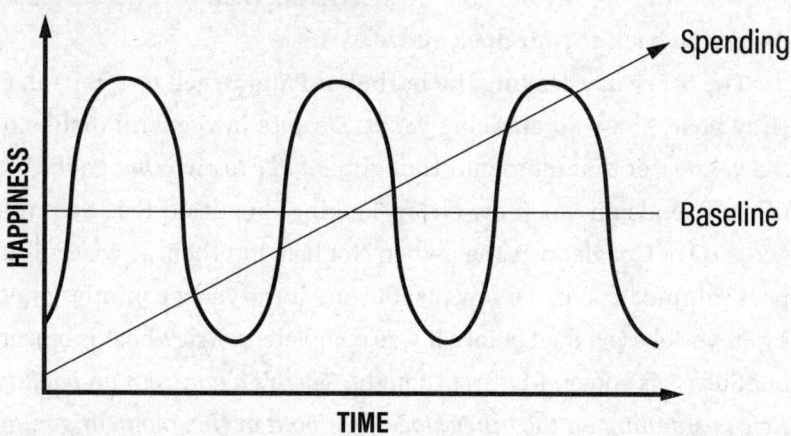

Source: Illustration Concept by TicTocLife

home will save us from that expense) to hiring a tutor for your first-grader because they're competing against kids with two (there is almost no level of income that your offspring won't consume). Each incremental improvement you make to your lifestyle will make every other aspect of your life seem shabby and in need of a glow-up. And each improvement will bring you closer to the next upgrade, which won't seem like such a reach, or so unreasonable. This isn't just a matter of frivolous upgrades, either. You'll likely marry, and possibly have kids, which will naturally make you more concerned about getting the best health care, eating the healthiest food, and driving a safer car. You'll want to insure your income and the nice things you've bought. Increasing your income faster than your mind's ability to normalize at the new level is rare and unlikely.

I'm a member of something called Barton & Gray, which is essentially fractional boat ownership. I would never own a boat as I don't love boating and everyone I know who has one is always complaining about how much it costs, how much of a hassle it is.

Anyway, Barton lets you book a boat and a high EQ guy shows up in a great boat stocked with Zacapa, ice, and cashews. He takes you and your family out for the afternoon, then (the genius part) drops you back at your dock and leaves.

The other day, leaving the harbor at Palm Beach on a Barton & Gray boat, I saw an amazing yacht. Despite my general dislike of sea vessels, at that moment I thought, *I'd like to own that boat*. One of my friends on our (now cheap-looking) boat said Eric Schmidt (ex-CEO of Google) was the owner. Not bad. But then, as we cruised past Schmidt's boat, we saw just beyond it the yacht commissioned by Steve Jobs (he died before it was completed). Eric's boat is bigger, but Steve's is cooler. My first thought: *There's a non-zero probability Eric is standing on the other side of his boat at this moment gazing at the floating Jobs-designed vessel and thinking, "I'd really like to own that boat."*

There's always a better boat, a faster car, a nicer house. But at least there's the potential for satiation or, at least, practical limits. Eventually, you run out of dockage. What's truly pernicious are abstract rewards. There's a great episode of the sitcom *Frasier* (genius show) where Frasier and his brother, Niles, gain access to an exclusive spa only to find there is one VIP level after the next. Finally happy at what they think is the highest level, they discover a platinum door to yet another level, and their experience is immediately devalued. "This is only heaven for the people who can't get into the real heaven," Niles exclaims.

The king of abstract rewards? Money itself. Because money is just a number, and numbers are infinite. And, as such, there's never enough. Luke Skywalker promised Han Solo that the reward for rescuing Princess Leia would be "more wealth than you can imagine." Han's response: "I don't know, I can imagine quite a bit." And that's the rub in a society run on money—we can all imagine more.

Not only is there always going to be more money, but money

has the unfortunate characteristic of becoming less valuable the more you have. Economists refer to this as "diminishing marginal utility." If you have $100 in your bank account, each extra dollar is meaningful, and $1,000 can be life changing. If you have $10 million in your bank account, another $1,000 is irrelevant.

Research into happiness and income levels bears this out. Contrary to what some earlier studies found, the most up-to-date research (at least as of 2023) shows that higher incomes *are* associated with greater happiness, but happiness increases lag income increases, and for some people, there is no correlation at higher incomes. The increase in happiness associated with the jump in income from $60,000 to $120,000 is the same as that associated with the jump in income from $120,000 to $240,000, and then you need to get to $480,000 to see the same jump in happiness again. This is consistent with the well-established concept of diminishing marginal utility. The more you have of something, the less benefit you derive from it on a per-unit basis. The more you make, the less you gain.

Money is the ink in your pen, but it's not your story. It can write new chapters and make some brighter, but the narrative arc is up to you.

Enough

The treadmill does not have to be a trap. You can't get off it, but once you realize how it works, you can stop being its slave. Research suggests that genetics predetermine as much as 50% of our happiness level. That's consistent with our life experience—we all know people who are buoyant and joyful nearly always and others who seem permanently down. Note: both are super annoying. But 50% genetic predisposition leaves 50% under your control. Not the product of circumstance or luck or anything else.

The striving that drives the treadmill is innate, and it's also ... *useful*. The key is to target external rewards such that you have the luxury to focus on internal fulfillment. Young people *should* be motivated by money, but as a means to an end, and be very focused on getting to a certain level of economic security. Beyond that it becomes a personal matter; more money may make you happier and offer new opportunities, but the returns can go negative at some point. An obsession with career and money (beyond what you could ever spend) begins to diminish what is the source of real satisfaction: relationships. The great Roman Stoic Seneca wrote, "There is no enjoying the possession of anything valuable unless one has someone to share it with." Many successful people only realize this when all they have are valuable things.

Luck

When I look at my own success, it boils down to two things above all: being born an American in the 1960s and having someone in my life who was irrationally passionate about my success (my mom). Though she was raised in a household where there was little affection, my mom couldn't control herself with her son. For me, affection was the difference between hoping someone thought I was wonderful or worthy and knowing it.

The most reliable predictor of your success is where and when you were born. Yet Western culture preaches independence and self-reliance, and the implicit message is that outcomes—good or bad—are the result of our efforts alone. When we fail to recognize the huge role that luck (and more generally, forces beyond our control) plays in outcomes, we take the wrong lessons from them and reduce our chances at future success.

Successful people tend to underestimate the contribution luck made to their success, and that gets them in trouble. They can overestimate their capabilities and squander wealth on ventures they have no business entering. This can happen at any level of success, from a $100,000-per-year junior sales executive getting cleaned out through day trading, to a billionaire buying a football team. You are never more vulnerable to a huge mistake than after a big win, when you begin to believe the falsehood that your success is all about you. Yes, you're brilliant and hardworking, but greatness is in the agency of others, and timing (and other features of luck) is everything.

Everyone is different in this regard, but on average, we tend to be quicker to credit ourselves for positive outcomes, and blame external forces for negative ones (sometimes called attribution bias). Consider your last few important outcomes, whether at work or in your personal life. Where you succeeded: How come? And where you fell short: What caused the failure? It's the rare outcome that doesn't have a mix of both, so if you're putting all your causal eggs in one basket, or you note a clear bias in how you explain successes and failures . . . well, that probably means you're human.

Attribution bias aside, ignoring the role of luck is just as dangerous for the unsuccessful. This is the pernicious downside of our "you can do anything you put your mind to" ethos. Because the implication is that if you don't succeed, it must be your fault. The truth is, we all make mistakes, and some portion of most failures is attributable to error. But much falls to fortune, to events outside our control. An entrepreneur whose first venture fails isn't a failure. Hopefully, she's a smarter, hungrier entrepreneur.

I have had so much failure in my life. And my ability to work through it put me in a position to succeed. We focus on the traditional base of success—education, taking risks, making contacts, etc. What I have found is that the most important attribute is, as Winston Churchill said, "a willingness to move through failure without losing your sense of enthusiasm."

Nothing Is Ever as Good or as Bad as It Seems

Following Churchill's advice is a great deal easier if we keep our failures (and our successes) in perspective. Just as we tend to undervalue luck, we greatly overestimate the importance of the present moment. This is especially true when we are young. We extrapolate forward from our current emotional state, when in fact, we will inevitably return to baseline. Develop the strength of character to feel the pain and enjoy the pleasure, but recognize the eternal truth: "This too shall pass."

A survey of senior citizens found that their biggest regret was worrying too much. The things you really beat yourself up about, you'll look back and you'll realize they weren't that big a deal. At the same time, those moments when you absolutely kill it, you'll later realize that (see above) much of that was luck.

Developing this perspective is easier if you can distinguish the event from your perception of and reaction to it. Ryan Holiday put it this way in *The Obstacle Is the Way*: "There is no good or bad without us, there is only perception. There is the event itself and the story we tell ourselves about what it means." Don't get me wrong, events matter—but our immediate perception of them is often exaggerated, reactive, emotional. Modern media makes this worse, with its tendency toward catastrophizing every turn of events. Don't let it cloud your perspective.

Anger, Indifference, and Revenge

I struggle with anger. It impairs me and has been a real obstacle to success and fulfillment. It's an inherited trait. My dad didn't speak much, at least not to me. He was charming, intense, and prone to unpredictable fits of anger. Like many young boys, I was fascinated by my dad. When he'd pick me up for his weekend with me, I'd sit in the passenger seat and stare at him. And he'd begin speaking to himself, except he wasn't speaking to himself. He was speaking to someone else. Maybe someone at work? Whoever it was, the dialogue would escalate and he'd begin cursing under his breath at whoever was on the other end of this imaginary dialogue. He was so angry, always.

If something or someone triggers me, I have trouble getting past it. I carried an imaginary scorecard with me (everywhere) into my forties. Any slight, rudeness, or lack of respect needed to be countered with an equivalent counterpunch to make the world right again. God, what a waste of energy. Don't make that mistake. You don't know what is going on with that person. Maybe they just got fired, filed for divorce, or found out their kid has diabetes. Or maybe they are just cruel. Who cares? You shouldn't. You don't need to respond to every slight, every small injustice.

Easier said than done, of course. Expressing anger has a short-term value, it releases pressure. The weight of unprocessed grievance can be just as much of an encumbrance as raging against it. Anything or anybody who is living rent-free in your head is squatting. That energy and bandwidth could be better invested elsewhere.

The Stoic approach to anger is to cultivate indifference. We can't control what others do, but we can control our response. Some people meditate to clear their mind of everything. I find this near impossible. What I have done, though, is trained myself to cast people into the darkness. My mental darkness, that is. First, I do what financial analyst Lyn Alden recommends: "Don't think of your enemies as enemies, but people. Let them believe you are their enemy, but learn from it and move on." I try to understand what can be learned (e.g., what did I do to inspire this action, could I repair the situation/relationship, etc.?). And then I cast the person into the darkness and attempt to never think about them again.

But I have to admit, it's not always enough. Some people just won't stay in the darkness. That's okay, because I know how to get my revenge. Twenty-five years ago, Hamid Moghadam (CEO of ProLogis) said something to me that has tangibly helped me address my anger, and I carry it with me every day. I was in the midst of a yearslong battle with Sequoia Capital, specifically a partner there who I found incredibly small (see above: trouble getting past things). Listening to me complain, Hamid interrupted me and said, "Scott, the best revenge is to live a better life." Great advice.

Sweat It Out

One of the most important pieces of financial advice I can offer has no direct connection with finance: get plenty of exercise. It might be the single most effective thing you can do for an across-the-board improvement in your quality of life, short and long term. Among the many high-performing people I've worked with or known, there are morning people and night owls, clean-desk neat freaks and scatter-brained geniuses, introverts and extroverts—but by far the most common observable characteristic is that they are committed to exercise. The science backs me up on this. A review of over sixty studies across environments, cultures, and professions concluded, "The scientific proof for the effectiveness of workplace physical fitness activities on productivity is irrefutable." Find a form of exercise you enjoy. It's time well spent on its face, and it will pay dividends in your health and productivity.

In my experience, exercise gives you time back—if you take four hours, six hours a week for physical fitness, you get those hours back because you have more energy, you're more mentally healthy, you're able to work harder. Like so much else, exercise and character form a virtuous feedback loop: the more we exercise, the stronger our sense of purpose becomes; and the stronger our sense of purpose, the more we exercise. The stress of working hard wreaks havoc on our nervous system, and exercise helps us regulate that. It produces mood-improving neurochemicals and helps us sleep better. A review of ninety-seven separate studies concluded that exercise is 50% more effective than therapy or drugs in treating depression. Journalist Steven Kotler, who's made a career out of studying exceptional people performing at their best, puts it simply: "Exercise is nonnegotiable for peak performance."

Anything from a brisk walk around your neighborhood to climbing a mountain can do the trick, but if you haven't been exercising lately, start with the brisk walk. Walk fast enough to get your heart rate up, and it will clear your mind and improve your mood. Build on that base.

I'm a big fan of short, intense workouts and lifting heavy weights. A mythology has developed in our culture around lifting weights. People think it reduces your flexibility (the opposite is true) or that it will make you bulky (only if you train for that). In fact, resistance work improves mood and memory, and has long-term health benefits. I know from experience it makes me feel confident and powerful. (This is where I used to say that you want to be strong enough that when you walk into a room, you should feel as if you can kill and eat everyone in it. Weirdly, people told me that was too much.)

The Algebra of Decisions

Life is an accumulation of decisions, large and small. It's strange that "decision-making" isn't a recognized discipline, a standard high school course. There should be a decision-making section in the bookstore. The second President Bush caught a lot of flak for describing his job as "I'm the decider," but he was saying something profound about the job. The same thing Truman was saying with his THE BUCK STOPS HERE desk plaque. In the White House, there's an apparatus of experts who make all the easy decisions and most of the hard ones. The only decisions that get to the president's desk are the brutal, unwinnable ones. In your life, you get those, too, plus no staff to make the other ones. So it's worth putting some time into thinking about how you make decisions, and how you can make better ones.

That said, you want to make more right decisions than wrong ones. Your instincts are a decent guide to survival and propagation, but a complex world offers exponentially more challenges and rewards. I've learned I need a framework—a set of values that helps define how I want to live my life and serves as a lens through which to filter my thinking.

- For me, the market competition of capitalism is an important principle. What will create the most value? What will be the most successful move, even if it's not the one I think *should* be?
- I've also learned to listen to what my emotions are telling me, but not necessarily follow their instructions. Gut feelings are useful, but you have to distinguish between wisdom bubbling up from your subconscious and your amygdala pressing the panic button. Or the greed (lust) button. That one will really trip you up.
- As I describe later in this chapter, getting input from others is crucial for making big decisions.
- Finally, I try to make the most important decisions in the shadow of death. "Memento mori," the Stoics said. "Remember, you will die." Does that sound dark? It shouldn't. I'm an atheist, and I believe when it's over, it's really over. Frida Kahlo said, "I want my exit to be glorious, and I don't want to come back." Putting myself there, at near-death, helps me sort through life and weigh the decisions that will give me peace. I know at the end I'll be more upset about the risks I didn't take than I will about the fallout from the ones I did.

We're still going to make plenty of bad decisions, however, and part of this essential life skill is knowing how to handle mistakes. When I was younger, I believed I could make any decision the right one through leadership and persuasion. I was more focused on proving my decisions were right . . . because I'm awesome . . . than on making the best ones. Granted, there's a benefit to making decisions quickly; speed can compensate, somewhat, for misdirection. But there's being decisive, and then there's being allergic to course correction. People often mistake this for being principled . . . it's not. **Your decisions are a guide and an action plan, not a suicide pact.** Be open to evolving, changing your mind when presented with new data or compelling views and insights. A step back from the wrong path is a step in the right direction.

A successful small business owner told me recently that, in his experience, it's not the person who makes the *best* decisions who comes out ahead, it's the person who makes the *most* decisions. Making more decisions means you get more feedback, and you get better at it. Each decision you make is an opportunity to pivot, and the more decisions there are the lower the stakes of any wrong decision you make. Accumulating right decisions builds confidence; piling up wrong ones builds scar tissue.

BUILDING A STRONG COMMUNITY

A longtime error that held me back was not appreciating I needed other people and needed to invest in them. Your community is multilayered, from family to mentors to your professional network to the myriad vendors, partners, staff, and random people you will interact with every day. The most successful people I know generate a ton of value through their community, and they give even more back.

An essential aspect of character, and one that contributes to success, is an appreciation for and a belief in our interdependence. In *The 7 Habits of Highly Effective People,* Covey describes three ways we can relate to others: dependence, independence, and interdependence. Independence is interwoven with our American ethos. But independence is, frankly, hard to maintain, and not productive over the long term. It can even be toxic, as it easily mutates into selfishness. *Interdependence* is Covey's term for the kinds of relationships that successful people develop. The Stoic term for this is "sympatheia," the notion that, in Marcus Aurelius's words, "all things are mutually woven together and in sympathy with one another." Therefore, he wrote, "Treat your fellow human beings as if they were your own limbs, as if they were an extension of yourself."

Don't Be Stupid

Our actions affect ourselves and those around us. Aspire to benefit both. In *The Basic Laws of Human Stupidity,* Carlo Cipolla draws a 2 x 2 matrix to capture these two groups and our impact on them.

CIPOLLA STUPID MATRIX

	BENEFIT TO SOCIETY	
THE HELPLESS Contribute even if they're not thriving (e.g., "starving artists")		**THE INTELLIGENT** Channel their intellect for their own and the public good
		BENEFIT TO ONESELF
THE STUPID Destructive to themselves and to society		**THE BANDITS** Not useful to society but canny enough to profit from it

Source: Carlo Cipolla, *The Basic Laws of Human Stupidity*

In the lower left quadrant (note: you never want to be in the lower left quadrant), he defines a stupid person as one who causes damage to others while deriving no gain, or even possibly incurring losses. We invariably underestimate the number of stupid individuals in circulation, as the probability that a certain person is stupid is independent of other characteristics or credentials (e.g., they can have a PhD or be president). We (the non-stupid) are vulnerable to the stupid and their actions, as we find it difficult to imagine and understand—or to organize a rational defense against—an attack that lacks rational structure or predictable movements. As Friedrich Schiller put it, "Against stupidity the gods themselves fight in vain."

Recognize that stupid is a thing, discern how not to be stupid, and, instead, aspire to be "intelligent," which also is a thing . . . and a noble thing.

Greatness Is in the Agency of Others

There's a common caricature of the rich, that they are like Monty Burns from *The Simpsons*: conniving and dishonest, gaining their wealth by cheating someone (or many someones). But in my experience, the opposite is far more common. Most wealthy people are high-character humans. They are typically gracious to others, work hard, moderate their spending and indulgences, and are principled. That shouldn't be a surprise, because it's much easier to be successful when people are rooting for you. Strong character is a wealth accelerant.

There are exceptions to every rule, and some people do achieve great wealth despite, or even with the aid of, low character. But that's no reason to follow their example. Moreover, people who come into wealth without high character often lose their way, and their wealth along with it. Not least because when they start making mistakes, they have no support network, no real friends to be honest with who can redirect them. More likely, they have sycophants. Character doesn't just aid in creating wealth, it's the key to protecting it.

Find Bonds and Guardrails

Look for opportunities to bind yourself to the service of others. For most of us, the most profound and powerful bond is family. Mormon families traditionally tithe a portion of the income (or for some, their wealth) to the church. This is a powerful motivator, as it puts your work in direct connection with a higher purpose. In my experience, the cost of that 10% is made up for by the greater earning power of someone working for that higher purpose. Democracies put leaders in service of the voters and corporations bind CEOs to the interests of the shareholders (in theory and, much of the time, in practice).

This becomes more important the more successful you become. Success in any field brings with it power—the power of wealth, power over other people's careers, the power to make change in the world. And power is a drug that downplays costs and magnifies rewards. People with power are psychologically more inclined to act on their instincts than those without it. This contributes to workplace sexual harassment. Power has an unconscious influence on sexual arousal. A common thread among sexual aggressors and harassers is a belief that their advances are welcomed. Power does, in fact, intoxicate.

The antidote is binding yourself to the service of others. This can be personal (kids), institutional (church), or structural (board of directors). In *Wall Street*, the high priest of selfish greed, Gordon Gekko, tells his protégé, "If you need a friend, get a dog." It's a good line, meant to show what a selfish SOB Gekko is. But it's also good advice. Not because dogs are loyal (they are) or affectionate (also true), but because they need you.

STOICISM

Form a Kitchen Cabinet

As a corollary to the hard stops of our guardrails, develop, over time, the informal guidance of a kitchen cabinet. The term "kitchen cabinet" comes from the presidency of Andrew Jackson, who met semi-regularly with a small group of trusted advisers outside the government. The concept is familiar to nearly any successful leader. It's a group of people outside the formal structure of your organization who give unvarnished, disinterested counsel.

As you build up your career, build a kitchen cabinet of people who can elevate you but also ensure you're grounded (see above: be honest with you). These should be people you trust, people who have your best interests in mind, and people who aren't afraid to tell you when you're being an ass. Your kitchen cabinet will be who you turn to when you need career advice, second opinions on both business and personal decisions, and generally people to bounce ideas off of.

It's best if the members of your kitchen cabinet are themselves smart people with a depth of experience, but that's not their primary virtue. Their greatest value add is that they are *not you*. It's difficult to read the label from inside the bottle, and your kitchen

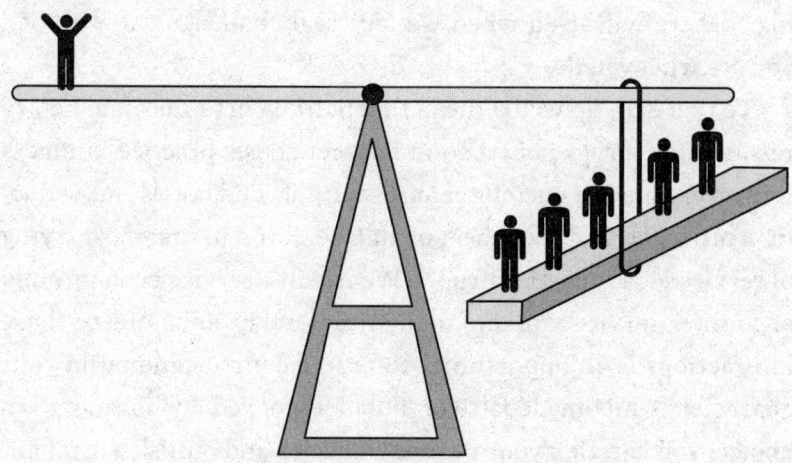

cabinet brings something you can't provide no matter your talent or effort: a different perspective. Asking for advice doesn't mean you have to take it. Often, what's most valuable about advice isn't a recommended course of action but the questions you get in response—pressure-testing your reasoning.

Even at my most selfish, I've always valued (if not always followed) the counsel of others. I collect people I trust and who know me and are willing to tell me what they really think and not what I want to hear. Some of the most valuable advice I get isn't about what to do but what not to do. I've done so many dumb things in my life. But a number of fifteen-car-pileups have been averted because someone said, "Hey, maybe . . . don't."

Tip Well

Often, doing the right thing is hard. Managing your emotional response to a personal betrayal, managing a team through a serious breakdown in productivity—these are crucibles that call on our reserves of character. But much more often, doing the right thing is actually quite easy. So easy that we can overlook the opportunity. But that's a mistake, because doing the right thing when it's easy to do instills the habits of generosity, grace, and understanding that we will need when we face real challenges. Remember, you are what you do.

To that end, tip well. I mean that literally in terms of monetary rewards for service, but also in a larger sense: practice kindness with everyone you encounter at restaurants and hotels, at the doctor's office, behind the wheel of an Uber, even in that most trying of service locations, the airport. We live in a service economy and encounter service workers many times a day. Each one of these interactions is an opportunity to practice virtue and build your character. A mis-made latte or a double-booked appointment is a choice: you can flex your pettiest muscles and punish a stranger for your inconvenience, or you can practice grace and make everyone's day a little better.

Being kind reduces stress hormones and makes you happier; spending money on others can lower your blood pressure as much as a healthy diet; altruism is literally an analgesic. So have another order of French fries, give the fry cook $20, and everyone wins. I love science.

Make Rich Friends

From childhood on, we learn by mimicry. Our subconscious is constantly monitoring how those around us act and modeling our own behavior accordingly. We are heavily influenced by the people with whom we associate. The implication is obvious: give your subconscious the best possible examples to work from.

Our brains are wired to connect what we do with what others do. So-called mirror neurons are specific, biological circuits that fire both when *we* take an action ourselves and when we observe *another* take that action (and some may fire when we merely imagine another taking an action). As social animals, we are constantly benchmarking against others, learning from them, and adapting our own behavior to fit in with our group norms. People even eat more when they are with other people who are eating. Humans are exceptional mimics; it is our primary means of childhood learning, and it persists through adulthood. In fact, there's evidence that adults are *more* prone to mindlessly replicating the actions of others—children are smart enough to mimic only the behaviors that solve a problem or get a reward, while adults will slavishly imitate a teacher, even their mannerisms. And this includes how we act with money. Seventy-eight percent of young adults report consciously modeling their financial habits on those of their friends—I suspect the true number is closer to 100%.

As with so much science, philosophy got there first. Two

thousand years ago, Seneca wrote: "Associate with people who are likely to improve you. Welcome those who you are capable of improving. The process is a mutual one: men learn as they teach."

This is one of my more controversial pieces of advice, and the part that really gets people riled up is the corollary, which is that you should also gracefully move on from personal relationships that are holding you back. To be clear, I am not suggesting that you wholesale write off your childhood friends, or that you cut ties with someone solely on the basis of their bank account. Relationships of long-standing have inherent value that cannot be replicated any other way. True friendship is a gift. But the uncomfortable truth is that even once-strong friendships can become toxic. Not everyone grows out of immaturity, of a life based on taking and selfishness, and nearly everyone has friends who never did. That's not behavior you want to mimic, and you have no obligation to associate with someone just because you happened to be thrown in with them in high school or at your first job. Stoic philosopher Epictetus put it this way: "Above all, keep a close watch on this—that you are never so tied to your former acquaintances and friends that you are pulled down to their level. If you don't, you'll be ruined. . . . You must choose whether to be loved by these friends and remain the same person, or to become a better person at the cost of those friends . . . if you try to have it both ways you will neither make progress nor keep what you once had."

Finding and connecting with wealthy people will give you models of behavior for obtaining and living with wealth. This is particularly important if you grew up, as I did, without much money and without a lot of exposure to it. Rich people also tend to know other rich people, and that network can be invaluable. Too much is often made about connections—they are rarely sufficient to make up for a lack of ability or hard work. But they can increase the number of opportunities you have to leverage those things.

Be wary of what your rich friends say about their investments, however (in fact, this goes for anyone talking about their investments). We are all much more likely to talk about our wins than our losses, so in any conversation about investing, you are likely to think you are the odd one out, the only one without a row of scalps on your wall. Learn from other people's wins, but know they took losses, too.

Talk About Money

Within the relationships you've created—talk about money. Rich people (and employers) perpetuate this notion that people aren't supposed to talk about money, that it's somehow impolite. What bullshit. We live in a capitalist society, by choice or not, and money is the operating system of that society. Of course the people who have the money don't want everyone else talking about it; they might learn something. Musicians talk about music, coders talk about code, golfers talk about golf (incessantly—giving up golf is not a regret). We are all, like it or not, capitalists, so why don't we talk about money? You'll gather intel on compensation, refine your strategies for reducing taxes, benchmark your budgeting acumen, stress-test your emergency plans. Normalize talking about money so you can get better at money.

The Most Important Relationship

The most important economic decision you'll make in your life is not what you major in, where you work, what stock you buy, or where you live. It's who you partner with. Your relationship with your spouse is the most critical relationship in your life; it will have a huge impact on your economic trajectory.

From an economic standpoint, getting—and staying—hitched is one of the most beneficial things you can do. Married individuals are 77% wealthier than single people. Each year you're married, your net worth typically increases 16%. Married people also live longer and are statistically happier than single people. There are many reasons for this, but one that resonates with me is that spouses are a means of accountability, and accountability is key to success. In the same way that CEOs are held accountable by their boards of directors and shareholders, your spouse is the person who will help you get to where you want to go, as they have the greatest stake in your success. In the most successful relationships I know, both parties have embraced the value of living up to their spouse's expectations.

As with any major decision, however, there are risks. One of the worst economic actions you can take is to get divorced. On average, a divorce in America reduces your wealth by about three-quarters—for both men and women.

Getting marriage right is a lifelong project of many dimensions, but money is a bigger one than we want to admit. The greatest predictor of divorce in America for both men and women isn't cheating or parenting decisions or career goals—it's financial disagreement. Money is the second-most-argued-about topic among American couples (number one is tone of voice or attitude). Half of Americans struggling with financial tension say it's had a negative impact on intimacy with their partner. Lack of money is one of the greatest—if not *the* greatest—strains on relationships, which is why divorce rates are significantly higher among lower-income Americans. Marrying someone who is better at money than you can be a great benefit (note: "better at money" doesn't mean cheap). Marrying down in terms of money skills is fine (half of all spouses do it), but know what you are in for. I have a friend who makes an incredible living, and his spouse is pathological when it comes to spending. This person will spend $1,500, no joke, on flowers for a dinner party. They are broken when it comes to managing money. It's a source of anxiety for both of them. Unhealthy relationships with money can come in many forms and will eat away at relationships.

From the outset of your relationship, you have to get real about money. Marriage is many things; an economic contract is one of them. This means talking about it. Treating money as a taboo might be one of the worst societal norms in America. Find a time to sit down and have a broader macro-conversation. What is our approach to money? What are the proof points in our lives that confirm this? (Because the question isn't what we *wish* our approach to money could be.) What is the economic weight class we expect to be in? How are we both contributing to maintaining that weight class? (Some of the most important contributions aren't monetary.) It's especially important to communicate when things are bad. Similar to dealing with a board of directors, bad news is okay. What's not okay is surprises.

CHAPTER REVIEW

ACTION ITEM BULLETS

- **Match your actions to your intentions.** Economic security isn't the product of an intellectual exercise, it's the result of a pattern of behavior. Planning alone won't get you there.

- **Build character for the long term.** The key to matching your actions to your intentions is character. Character is your defense against the weaknesses of our species and the temptations capitalism offers that exploit those weaknesses.

- **Slow down.** Notice a handful of the many decisions you make unconsciously each day—skipping breakfast, responding to a slight. Tell yourself "I am in control, my response is my choice," before you act.

- **Acknowledge emotional responses.** Don't deny anger, shame, or fear; they are natural and healthy. But don't let them determine your actions. Sometimes you'll need an outlet. Find a healthy one.

- **Train your habits.** Identify behaviors you *want* to engage in and use the science of habit formation to make them instinctual.

- **Just do it.** Beware of analysis paralysis. Don't mistake planning for action. You will learn more and make more progress in your initial attempts and early mistakes than you will through theorizing.

- **Seek rewards, don't depend on them.** You need motivation, and rewards such as money and status are powerful motivators. But there will always be a bigger house, a more exclusive club—the more money you make, the less it's worth. Don't expect these rewards alone to bring you happiness.

- **Recognize the role of luck.** Most of us tend to give ourselves too much credit for positive outcomes and unduly blame circumstances for negative ones. Some of us tend in the opposite direction. Be aware of your personal tendencies and take them into account when evaluating your results.

ACTION ITEM BULLETS

- **Sweat.** The correlation between regular exercise and health, success, and happiness is undeniable. Make time for physical fitness and you will net more time in the end, thanks to higher productivity. Lift. Run. Move.

- **Make good decisions.** Be aware of your own decision-making process, review good and bad decisions, and learn from both. At the end, you'll likely regret the risks you didn't take more than the fallout from ones you did.

- **Don't be stupid.** Stupid people take actions that hurt not only themselves but also their communities. Success depends on your network and the health of your ecosystem.

- **Seek out guardrails and advice.** Recognize and value the people and structures in your life that keep you grounded and offer an alternative perspective on your actions. This is especially important as you gain wealth and power, as fewer people will reliably tell you what they really think.

- **Tip well.** You'll get better service, feel happier, and live longer.

- **Make rich friends.** Wealthy people are models for living with money, offer access to opportunities, and elevate your ambitions.

- **Talk about money.** Like it or not, money is the operating system of our society. Normalize talking about money, it's too important to avoid.

- **Invest in your partnership.** The most important decision you can make is to partner with someone and go through life as a team, and your partner is the most important relationship you'll have. Marriage is an economic booster shot, but it requires effort and sustained attention.

FOCUS

\+

(STOICISM

×

TIME

×

DIVERSIFICATION)

2
FOCUS

Our focus defines us. From moment to moment, our brains process vast amounts of data from our senses and our subconscious. Consciousness—our sense of self—is the ruthless disregard of nearly all of it. In each moment, we pursue just one train of thought, we monitor a narrow stream of stimuli. Focus is choosing what to pay attention to.

From week to week, year to year, society offers us an array of temptations and terrors, greener pastures and forks in the road. Our life is the product of the choices we make. We can wander without aim, stumbling into prosperity one year, losing our way another. Or we can choose a path, deliberately, with foresight and flexibility. We can be conscious. We can focus.

Building economic security requires sustained effort over decades, and that's not something you can maintain without focus. My success is a function of many things, most of which were outside my control. The one thing I could control is the same thing you can. I worked hard, really hard . . . and with focus. Working hard is horsepower. It moves the object of your career forward. Without focus, you could just burn fuel spinning in place.

It's not enough just to be told to focus, so this chapter is about how to achieve and direct your focus—mainly in your career, where I believe you will need to direct much of your energy. It's advice drawn from my successes and considerable mistakes, and what I've seen work for colleagues, clients, students, and friends. It proceeds somewhat chronologically, starting with advice about how to choose a career direction, followed by insights more appropriate as you advance. While careers vary and are in a constant state of flux, I think these principles are relevant across most domains and junctures.

BALANCE

It's been said many times: you can have it all, just not all at once. That's a universal truth, but it plays out differently for different people. My life has been sequential: I have a lot of balance now, as a function of the lack of it in my twenties and thirties. From 22 to 34, other than business school, I remember work and not much else. Hours at the office, days on the road, canceled plans, and forgone experiences. My lack of balance as a young professional cost me my marriage, my hair, and arguably my twenties. All that came at a very real cost. For me, considering the course my life has followed, it was worth it. There are things I would do differently. Working less isn't one of them.

For many people, this is the path. In fact, I don't know anybody who wasn't smart enough to inherit money who didn't work hard and not do much else for at least twenty years. A recent study of 233 millionaires found that 86% of them worked more than 50 hours a week.

Okay, but not everyone can or wants to devote this much of

their time and energy to their career. And while I don't believe there's a (legal) way to create economic security without a lot of hard work, there are levers you can pull to get the most out of your time. Indeed, that's what the rest of this chapter is about—whether you work 30 hours per week or 60, you want those hours to be efficient. But if you're closer to 30 hours, then it's crucial you get the absolute most out of them.

Acceptance

There will be practical limitations on the time you can devote to work due to choices and factors outside your control. Don't compound those with psychological limitations. What I mean by this is that you need to accept the primacy of work in the critical years (for most people, from the early twenties through your forties, but these aren't bright lines). You are going to be spending *a lot* of time working—do you really want to be resentful throughout?

As I discuss in this chapter, accepting the role of work is easier if you're doing work that you're good at, if it's financially rewarding, and if you are cultivating passion for the growing mastery of your craft. That's the virtuous circle of focus. If you resent the seizure of your hobbies and indulgences by the late nights and the weekend work (and even more, by the emotional and cognitive energies you have to deploy), you will not do your best work, you will not do the work well, and worst of all, you still won't enjoy the rest of your life, because resentment colors everything. Remind yourself that the future version of you may not feel real to you now, but they will be grateful for your sacrifice.

Likewise, don't pretend to be someone you're not, or resent your own limitations. You will meet people who have strong relationships, are fit, donate time to the ASPCA, have a food blog, and are ballers professionally. Assume you are not that person (most likely they aren't, either—you never know what sacrifices they are making behind the scenes or what support they're getting). I figured out early I was not that person. I'm talented, but not talented enough to be economically successful without working for it, and (realistically) neither are you. Be okay with your limitations.

Flexibility

You can work more hours if you can allocate them around your other obligations and move them at will. Technology is making knowledge work more flexible across the board, but that flexibility is not distributed equally. Fixed commitments are more common in collaborative work, management roles, and jobs within large organizations. Anything involving clients, patients, or direct contact with customers is inherently less flexible. The less time you have to devote to your career, the more flexibility will benefit you.

Flexibility can be earned through reputation, but be careful, because this will be organization specific. After five or ten years at a company, a high performer will have earned (good) management's trust and can usually get an accommodation to adjust their schedule. Leave to go to another firm, however, and they have to build that reputation over again.

As you get more senior, good management can earn you flexibility. There are few better feelings at work than handing off a complex task to your team with the total confidence that they will deliver. (Management is a skill, not a personality trait, and it can be learned.)

Accordingly, if you want to maintain nonnegotiable time commitments outside of work, bias your career trajectory toward individual performance, build up a reputation for getting your work done, and (if you do work within an organization) get really good at managing and delegating.

Partner Up

The most important lever you can pull to maximize your efficiency is finding the right partner. A team of two can get more done than two single people, because a household requires a fixed minimum of time and attention to run well. You want to share that burden with someone. This is especially true if you have children, of course, but people underestimate the career acceleration marriage itself provides.

Most really successful people I know are part of a team in which the partners have different roles vis-à-vis home and career obligations. Just as balance is something you should seek over the course of your life, not your day, most successful couples find balance jointly, not independently. Don't assume that you'll be the career partner, or the household manager. This is in part a function of flexibility: One of my founding partners at L2 was able to devote herself fully to her career (in television news) when her children were young because her husband was starting his own business. The obligations on his time were immense, but they were also flexible—so when someone needed to pick up a sick kid at school, or meet a vendor at the house, she didn't have to leave the studio.

Power of Constraints

Even with other priorities, don't underestimate how much you can work, and how much you can get done. I saw this firsthand after I started Prophet, a brand strategy consulting firm. From the outset, our business was supply constrained. I could find clients, I just couldn't attract enough good people to scale as fast as we were capable of. The reason was obvious: experienced consultants didn't need to come work for a 26-year-old fresh out of business school.

Our (unplanned) solution was to hire new mothers who wanted back into the workforce. The big firms were inflexible in their demands and could afford to be. We were unknown and needed to be more creative. So these sharp, experienced consultants worked for us because I told them they could leave early or even work from home (gasp!) a couple days per week.

They were some of our most productive and valuable employees. They were managing a lot: clients, teams of junior people, the cognitive work itself, plus their obligations at home. So they had no choice but to be efficient. Their colleagues who missed deadlines didn't have nearly as much going on, but that turned out to be a liability, as they believed they could take a long lunch, manage their fantasy football team from their desk, and then just stay late to get their work done. It proved the saying "If you want something done, give it to a busy person."

It all comes back to focus. Focus is saying "no." Steve Jobs held that the most important thing he did as CEO was to say no. Elon Musk's mantra when he built the best car ever made was "The best part is no part." Figure out how to simplify and streamline your life so you can focus on what matters. Then do that.

DON'T FOLLOW YOUR PASSION

If someone tells you to follow your passion, it means they're already rich. And typically, they made their fortune in some unglamorous industry like iron ore smelting. Your mission is to find something you're good at and apply the thousands of hours of grit and sacrifice necessary to become great at it. As you get there, the feeling of growth and your increasing mastery of your craft, along with the economic rewards, recognition, and camaraderie, will make you passionate about whatever "it" is. Nobody grows up saying, "I'm passionate about tax law," but the best tax lawyers in the country are financially secure, have access to a broader selection of mates, and are—because they are so good at it—passionate about tax law. It's unlikely you will ever be great at something you dislike doing, but mastery can lead to passion.

You Don't Know What You Don't Know

Maybe the worst aspect of the advice to follow your passion is that for most of us, it's just not actionable. Stanford psychologist William Damon found that only 20% of people younger than 26 can articulate a passion that guides their life choices. So four out of five of us can't follow our passion even if we want to, because we don't know what it is. And even when we can "articulate a passion," it's often socially determined, reflecting what our culture expects of us, not anything inherent to us. Researchers studying the aspirations of young people have found that their "passions" turn out to be "highly malleable and susceptible to influence" by factors such as how a topic's classroom is decorated. For most of us the kind of passion that guides us, a lodestar-on-the-horizon kind of passion, is not a birthright. It's something we find through hard work.

Author Cal Newport wrote an entire book, *So Good They Can't Ignore You*, debunking what he calls the "passion hypothesis." He starts by looking at perhaps the most famous purveyor of this myth, Steve Jobs. In 2005, Jobs gave the commencement address at Stanford and urged graduates to "find what you love" and make a career out of it. That speech has been viewed over 40 million times on YouTube. But as Newport points out, Jobs's own career contradicts the advice in the speech. Before starting Apple, Jobs had numerous passions: meditation, calligraphy, fruitarianism, going barefoot. His initial interest in technology was in building a gadget that made free long-distance telephone calls (if that makes no sense, ask your parents). When he finally found his calling, it was none of these things. It was promoting a hobby computer built by someone else (his friend, Steve Wozniak). Jobs didn't find what he loved, he found his talent. He *became* passionate about marketing consumer computers—what he would later call "bicycles for the mind"—because he was so good at it.

Passion Careers Suck

Believing you have to be passionate about something before embarking on the uphill journey to mastery will lead you to careers where the supply of eager workers far exceeds the demand—activities better suited to be avocations than careers. Only 2% of professional actors make a living from their craft, the top 1% of musicians garner 77% of their income from recorded music, and half of all visual artists obtain less than 10% of their earnings from their art. Digital media was supposed to democratize this, but it's only reinforced a winner-take-most economy. The top 3% of YouTube channels receive 85% of all views on the platform, and even if a creator reaches that threshold (about a million views per month), their passion generates just $15,000 in annual revenue.

In entertainment and other careers that look desirable from the outside, casting directors, producers, senior vice presidents—aka the tiny group of people with power—know raw talent is cheap and always flowing in. They have little reason to invest in or mentor anyone who isn't already a bankable star. Investment banking, sports, music, and fashion all suffer from this problem. A former client of mine, Chanel, is among the strongest brands in the world, commanding price points in the thousands at gross margins of 90+%. The family that owns Chanel are billionaires. And they had unpaid interns. Billionaires who decided they couldn't pay young (mostly) women who dreamt of being in fashion $7.25 an hour. Why did they do this? Because they could. "Follow your passion" is Latin for "Prepare to be exploited."

This advice holds even if your passion maps well to a potential career, at least early in life. Law school is full of people who grew up watching *Law & Order* and dreamed of being attorneys but who will be out of the profession after just a few years, regretting their choice. What a job looks like from the outside (or worse, on TV) is rarely what it's like on the inside. That's not to say it's worse, just different. Professional athletes, especially in team sports, love to compete, but when they step away from the game, what they most often talk about missing the most isn't the victories, but the camaraderie, the moments of selfless focus, the bond of working hard with others on the practice field—stuff we fans hardly see.

Work Spoils Passion

Following your passion isn't just bad for your career, it's bad for your passion. Work is hard, and it comes with setbacks, injustice, and disappointment. If you got into a field because it's your "passion," that passion may wilt. As Morgan Housel put it, "Doing something you love on a schedule you can't control can feel the same as doing something you hate." Jay-Z followed his passion and is now a billionaire. Assuming you are not Jay-Z, follow your passion on the weekends.

FOLLOW YOUR TALENT

In contrast with passion, talent is observable and testable; it can be more readily converted to a high-earning career, and it gets better the more you exploit it. Passion for something might make you better at it—talent absolutely will. Economists refer to "match quality" as the fit between a worker's talents and the job. And studies repeatedly show that people perform better, improve faster, and make more money where they have high match quality. Doing what you're good at creates a virtuous circle. Your accomplishments come faster, they reinforce your confidence, and encourage further focused effort. Your brain works better as well, as the flow of rewarding neurochemicals improves memory and skill development. The entire experience is something more pleasurable than grueling, making it easier to return to day after day, year after year.

"Talent"

I define talent broadly. A good general definition: What comes easily to you that's difficult for other people? Incidentally, this is also the root of business strategy: What can you do that others can't? We tend to think of "talent" as things like playing an instrument well or being really good at math. But a much broader set of skills factors into career success.

One of the first people I ever hired was Connie Hallquist, a consultant at Prophet who had been, before she joined our firm, a French scholar, a professional tennis player, and a currency trader. Those are all paths that leverage distinct and obvious talents. But what Connie was truly good at, she realized at Prophet, was managing people. I've rarely seen anyone so skilled at putting a plan together, motivating a team, and driving everyone toward a common goal. She had to be, because from the first week she was on board, my strategy became to sell the largest and most ambitious project I could and then turn to Connie to get it done. And she did. She went on to found her own business and has since been recruited to a series of CEO roles. Unlike tennis or trading, "managing people" is amorphous and hard to identify as a talent. But when identified and cultivated, it's arguably the most valuable one a person can have. People often assume if someone is smart and a good person, they are a good manager. That's not true. It's a distinct skill and trainable, but like most skills, flowers best in those with a natural talent.

An inspiration in my life is another Scott, Scott Harrison, who founded a unique and compelling nonprofit, Charity: water. I knew

Scott in his prior life when he was a New York club promoter. Scott made a living by being dialed in. He knew where to go and who was there. Scott was, and is, cool. Turns out, that's a talent. And when he reached a point in his life when he wanted it to mean more than just a series of amazing nights out, he leveraged that talent into fundraising. He built the donor base that underpins Charity: water just as he'd built the guest list for downtown after-hours parties. Scott has many other talents, and Charity: water is innovative and admirable in a lot of ways, but none of it could have happened if Scott hadn't cultivated his talent for making connections.

Talent is *anything* you can do that others can't or won't. In my first job after college, I worked as an analyst at Morgan Stanley. Most of my colleagues were better prepared than I was on the subject matter. They had earned the job. I slid in—the head of the department also rowed crew in college and decided that was an indicator I'd be a great investment banker. My colleagues were more comfortable with finance and the culture of Wall Street, had more in common with our "master of the universe" bosses, and, critically, had a better sense of why they were there. I was never going to be a better investment banking analyst than Chet from Falls Church or Shannon from Greenwich. But the VP who hired me was right about one thing. College crew meant getting up at 5:00 a.m. and rowing until I puked: I'd learned to endure pain. So I leaned into that. When Chet and Shannon left the office at 2:00 a.m., I was still there. When they came back at 8:00, I was still there. I kept a spare shirt in my drawer and used it. I worked 36 hours straight every Tuesday, starting at 9:00 a.m. I got known for that. And in that environment, that had value. If this sounds messed up, and like hustle porn . . . trust your instincts. My advice isn't "work all-nighters for the sake of working all-nighters." If I could have competed with Chet and Shannon and gotten more sleep, I'd have done it.

The key is to figure out what you can do that others can't or are unwilling to do. Hard work is a talent. Curiosity is a talent. Patience and empathy are talents. For wrestlers and boxers, making weight is a talent. If you're a jockey, being short is a talent. The point is to cast a wide net and consider not just your *skills*, but your advantages, your differences, what you can tolerate, what makes you unique. This requires time, flexibility, and self-reflection.

Finding My Talent

It took me a lot of years and many false positives before I found my real talents (beyond soaking up pain). I jumped from consulting to e-commerce to hedge funds to whatever I thought would impress other people. Never really finding my axis. Those career paths were near misses, because they all touched on what I'm genuinely gifted at, which is communicating. It's obvious in hindsight but wasn't at the time.

I got closer when I joined the NYU faculty at 38. That's really when my career started. Standing in front of fifteen, then fifty, then three hundred second-year MBAs trying to distill the principles of marketing in twelve 140-minute sessions honed that communications talent. Then I started writing a weekly newsletter (*No Mercy / No Malice*), produced a weekly YouTube show, wrote my first book, began giving paid speeches, and launched two podcasts. Somewhere along the way, my talent flowered into my true career, something that's kept me working long after I'd achieved economic security. It has become—and this is as clumsy to write as I imagine it is to read—my passion.

Taking the long way around to finding my talent had advantages, the biggest of which is that those years of experience as an entrepreneur and consultant have given me something to communicate about. But it was also a luxury, and not the most efficient path. You can be much more intentional about identifying your talent.

Finding Your Talent

So how do you go about finding your talent? For most of us, school dominates the first two decades of our lives, but our educational system focuses on what we can produce, not who we are. Talents rarely emerge unless called upon, and the classroom triggers only a sliver of the talents that you can leverage in the workplace.

Put yourself in different contexts, positions, and organizations. Volunteer work, student government, jobs, sports—environments reveal talent, so explore several, early. Again, figuring out what doesn't work and what you are not good at is part of figuring out what you *are* good at. This sort of exploration is most useful in school and early in your career because you have the time. It's useful to think of your twenties as workshopping, your thirties for getting good at your chosen field, and your forties/fifties for harvesting.

Prepackaged personality frameworks can help direct this talent search. I'm not a passionate advocate for these sorts of systems, and the science behind them is limited and controversial, but the time commitment to try them out is negligible, and even a minor course correction or nudge early in your career can pay massive dividends. Billionaire hedge fund manager Ray Dalio swears by personality tests, and he uses them at his firm, Bridgewater Associates. Using something he calls "baseball cards," Bridgewater asks employees to evaluate one another along various dimensions, including "creativity" and "extroverted," to better understand their talents. I believe this is a bridge too far, but Dalio can point to more than 200 billion reasons (Bridgewater's assets under management) why I'm wrong.

The best-known tool is Myers-Briggs. Using a battery of questions, Myers-Briggs maps your personality along four dimensions. I don't think many people are *surprised* by their Myers-Briggs score, but the process of both answering the questions and reading the results is illuminating—go beyond the labels and read the capsule summaries of your four-letter category. Another tool to consider is Gallup's CliftonStrengths, which is more explicitly aimed at identifying talents. It identifies thirty-five strength areas and you take an assessment test to narrow that down to your top five.

Beyond formulaic questionnaires, look for evidence that reveals your real talents. What roles do others ask you to take on? Where have you had success, where have you struggled? It's important to look below the surface at these experiences for deeper talents that are transferable to your career. Ask *why* these experiences have played out the way they have. If you throw great parties, that doesn't (necessarily) mean you should be a party planner. But it might reveal that you are creative, organized, good at promoting and selling, have entrepreneurial skills, or have an ability to get people to do what you want (come to your party). Some people refer to this as leadership. In sum, look to your successes (and failures) and disarticulate the skills it took to pull them off. Rate yourself on each of those skills. Which drove your success or lack thereof? (Knowing what you are *not* good at is the other side of the self-awareness coin.) If you have something you are passionate about, interrogate that relationship. What specifically do you enjoy about it? I bet it's the aspect where your talent comes out. What else can you do with that talent?

Can't Always Get What You Want

It's unfair, but our talents rarely match up with our early ambitions. Not just in the childhood "I want to be a starting pitcher for the Dodgers" sense. Even into our early careers, we tend to form ideas about who we *want* to be based on minimal data. What our parents did or valued, what our friends are excelling at, what's valued in whatever job we happen to get after college. It can be hard to accept, or even realize, that our talents likely lie elsewhere.

Sometimes people bang their head against a wall when there's a door right next to them. Another early hire of mine at Prophet was a young man who joined us after a few years in finance. Johnny Lin was naturally comfortable with numbers and quantitative analysis the way a musician picks up an instrument and knows how to make it sing. You could throw any mismatched set of data at him, ask him any question about it, and he would convert it into answers supported by a clean, logical spreadsheet. The only person who wasn't impressed by Johnny's gift was Johnny. He wanted to be a "strategy guy," weaving narratives from PowerPoint slides. He went on to a career in retail, where one company after another promoted him to management roles on the basis of his facility with numbers—eventually he made peace with his talents and learned how he could use them to undergird a broader role as the chief marketing officer and then president at various retail companies. Along the way, he worked hard to shore up his weaknesses, and he's become a comfortable communicator as well. The advice is to follow your talent, not to limit yourself to it.

The delta between the way we saw Johnny's talent with numbers and how he perceived it is a common one. We tend to downplay our own talents (while seeing other people's more clearly) *because* we are so good at them. If something comes easily to us, then we don't value it. Whereas when we see someone else do something that's difficult for us, we are amazed at their talent. Most likely, they are observing something in us the same way.

All sorts of things can confound our ability to identify our talents. Our editor in chief at Prog G Media, Jason Stavers, was a successful lawyer, and now he's an outstanding writer and editor, but he insists he should have been a programmer. Why didn't he go down that path? Despite being fascinated by code and taking to it naturally as a kid, he shied away from it because it wasn't cool. "It's embarrassing to admit this," he told me, "but when I was thirteen, despite living literally in Silicon Valley, I didn't have the self-confidence to be seen in the computer lab, I was too worried about being popular." The world is a noisy place, and it can be hard to tune it out and listen to what makes your heart beat.

My fine print, before I crush all of your dreams: there are some people (<1%) who demonstrate so much early talent in a "passion category" (sports, the arts, etc.) that it may make sense for them to pursue this as a career. If you have the proof points that this might be you, by all means go for it. But put hard metrics on it so you can evaluate, early on, whether this really is where your talent lies and (more important) whether the world is recognizing it. Making a living in most passion categories requires you to be in the top 0.1%. In other careers (anything a 5-year-old does *not* say when asked what they want to be when they grow up), you can make a solid living just by showing up. Put another way, the non-romance careers are a thousand times easier to make a good living at. Achieve economic security and follow your passion on weekends.

Find Your Passion

The happy ending to the search for talent is that it will lead to passion. Not the puppy love of childhood ambition, but the durable passion of a meaningful career—what you'll need to get through years of hard work. That passion comes from mastery, the feeling and activity of doing something difficult really, really well. In *Designing Your Life*, a book based on their hyper-popular Stanford course of the same name, professors Bill Burnett and Dave Evans put it this way: passion is the result of good life design, not its cause.

(Talent + Focus) → Mastery → Passion

It's hard to overstate the value of mastery, and even harder to communicate it to young people who have not yet had the time to develop it. In my experience, very few people under 25 or even 30 have achieved mastery over a complex pursuit. Even elite athletes, who have typically devoted their youth to their sport, are "rookies" when they sign their first professional contract, and usually play like it. It takes years, even as adult professionals, for them to master their craft. Malcolm Gladwell popularized the notion that mastery requires *10,000 hours* of practice.

The path to mastery in our talents mirrors great product design. Innovation is incremental. The key is to ship something and begin improving on it. The first thing produced by every company I've started looked nothing like it would two years in. I'm irrationally obsessed with being successful on television and have been trying to master it for years. The first YouTube video we produced was awful. But—and this is key—we did it. And did it again and again. Over the years, we made hundreds of small improvements: lighting and sound, a unified design language, how we prepared and scripted the content, etc. Eventually we made it good enough that Vice offered me my own show in 2020. We made the first episode (i.e., we signed our first professional contract), and I showed it to my wife. She cried (and not in a happy-tears kind of way). We were rookies. But we got better. Two years later I was asked to host my own show on Bloomberg (didn't happen; long story involving me shirtless), then a year after that I hosted my own show on CNN+, which was immensely better than what I'd done before. When CNN+ closed down, BBC offered me a show on their new streaming network, and it would have been better, too, only the media market corrected and the network never launched. And that's okay. Each show has gotten better and, as a result, we now get regular overtures from networks to do a show.

The point is to attain mastery. I have yet to conquer TV, but my wheelhouse is standing in front of a crowd and communicating about business and issues that I care about. When I do that, I'm in a flow state, which is the signature sensation of mastery. The term "flow," coined by psychologist Mihaly Csikszentmihalyi, refers to a state of intense focus, where we lose our self-consciousness and even our sense of time in total immersion in our activity. Flow isn't just a performance-enhancing state, it's where we learn best as well. And it's enjoyable, producing a rush of neurochemicals we crave after they're gone, pulling us back toward the thing we are mastering. And that's the trick at the heart of a successful career: find your passion, cultivate it up to mastery, and your passion will follow. "Follow your passion" isn't wrong so much as backward.

CAREER OPTIONS

After a false start in investment banking, I chose entrepreneurship, or, more truthfully, it chose me, because I didn't have the skills to prosper in a company. I was too insecure to work for other people, and I wasn't particularly good at it. Turns out, I'm not alone. Researchers surveyed a group of traditional workers and entrepreneurs and found that entrepreneurs scored significantly lower on "agreeableness" (one of the so-called Big Five personality traits) than traditional workers. Shocker. There's also evidence that entrepreneurship correlates with risk propensity and is genetic. The takeaway? Knowing who you are can and should inform your career choice.

Once you have a sense of yourself and what your talents are, how do you match that against a career? It might help to start with elimination—avoiding a career for which you are ill-suited is probably even more important than finding just the right path. I started in investment banking and found I didn't like the work, the people, or the clients.

Be careful you don't write something off for the wrong reasons, however. Bill Burnett encourages people to talk to others who are further along in various careers. "It's like time travel," he says, because you can jump ahead to what a career might be like once you're well into it—and that's often not what it's like at the entry level. If you are early in your career, you want to base career decisions on where you will get to, not where you start. As Burnett puts it, "Do you want your 22-year-old self telling your 40-year-old self what to do?" Listen to your future. Many careers require drudgery in the early years, and probably every career has elements that are tedious, especially once you master the basics. Burnett points out that being bored by *tasks* is fine, because as you move up in your career, you will generally move on to different tasks. What you are trying to avoid is being bored by the *substance*.

Some Basics Re: Careers

Your job, your profession, and your industry are all different. A VP of finance at Disney doesn't have the same job as an animation director at Disney. Nor does the Disney finance VP have the same job as a finance VP at a twenty-person start-up. Prosecutors and patent attorneys are both lawyers but have very different daily experiences after law school (and often before). What you actually do (and the talents it leverages) sits at the juncture of industry, domain, employer, geography, and other factors.

When you're evaluating options, upside potential is critical. What's the economic outcome if everything goes your way? If that's not enough to get you where you want to be economically, then either your expectations or your career path has to change.

Speaking of upside potential, some industries scale better than others, as does compensation. You are looking for roles where compensation scales with profits or valuation increases. Finance is the quintessential example—many jobs in trading, at investment banks, and in other investment-adjacent functions share in the upside of the investment business. Sales, especially at growth companies, scales well in good times. Real estate often includes a piece of the action. Software is famously scalable because most of the work goes into making the first copy—what you sell after that is all profit. Products that depend on human labor in the delivery, on the other hand, are hard to scale. A medical or legal partnership can only see as many patients as it has doctors or lawyers. Even if the industry is scalable, your compensation only scales if it's tied to profits, either through a bonus plan or equity. In sum, you want a piece of the action.

Market dynamics trump individual performance. (I realize how awful that sounds.) Someone of average talent at Google has done better over the past decade than someone great at General Motors. Especially early in your career, be thoughtful about the wave you are paddling into; any opportunity you have when you're young to choose among different paths is a profound blessing.

Look for the best beach with the biggest waves. Twenty-five years ago, I chose the e-commerce wave. My first effort (Red Envelope) failed. Even worse, it failed slowly . . . over ten years (see below: "Know When to Quit"). But I'd picked the right wave. I paddled back out and started a firm (L2) that helped other firms develop digital strategies. It took me a while, but the strength and size of the wave kept me moving, carried me forward, and gave people the impression I was a more talented surfer than I am. I was just riding a Nazaré-size wave.

Macroeconomic cycles shape the kinds of opportunities that make good surfers great. Economic downturns are, in my view, the best time to start a business. I've started nine companies, and the only factor I can identify across the successful ones is that I started them in recessions. It's not just me. Microsoft was founded in a mid-seventies recession, and Apple just after it ended. The post-2008 Great Recession produced Airbnb, Uber, Slack, WhatsApp, and Block. There are multiple reasons for this. In downturns, good salaried jobs are hard to find, because nobody is quitting. So good people (and cheap assets) are plentiful. The absence of cheap, easy capital means the concept has to work from day one. Founders in downturns imprint a more disciplined DNA on the company's culture—they have no choice. Clients and consumers are also more open to change than they are during good times, when there's little motivation to do something besides what you've been doing.

Another macro consideration is to look for ways to leverage other people's investments. Extreme wealth creation is easier for a firm that leverages government investment or fallow assets. Their genius is a thick layer of innovation resting on top of massive government investments in research and infrastructure. Or it was hyper-accelerated by favorable tax and regulatory regimes—see, for example, real estate. Silicon Valley is fundamentally the most successful government investment in history. Double-click on any major tech product or company, and you'll find government funding. Apple, Intel, Tesla, and Qualcomm were all beneficiaries of federal loan programs. Tesla would likely have gone under without a federal lifeline. Google's core algorithm was developed with a National Science Foundation grant. Economist Mariana Mazzucato, in her book *The Entrepreneurial State,* calculates that U.S. government agencies have provided roughly a quarter of total funding for early-stage tech companies, and that in the pharmaceutical industry (a sector requiring immense experimentation and a willingness to fail), 75% of new molecular entities have been discovered by publicly funded labs or government agencies. You pay taxes, so those investments are yours for the leveraging.

As mentioned above, passion careers are a trap. The more appealing an industry appears from the outside, the less rewarding it probably is as a career. Moving to LA to become an actor is romantic, but when you get there, you'll find tens of thousands of other people—all the best-looking, most charismatic kids in their high schools, too—fighting for the same hundreds of roles. The problem that creates isn't the competition, it's the exploitation.

The best career path for many people (especially early in a career) is the not-sexy climb up the corporate ladder. The American corporation is still the premier vehicle for wealth creation in history. If you are fortunate enough to get a job at Goldman Sachs, Microsoft, Google, etc., you should probably take it. It's easy to sneer at the safety of the large corporate employer, but you don't have to stay forever, there's a lot to learn, and potentially a lot to earn. See above: U.S. corporations are the greatest wealth generators in history. You'll need the political skills to navigate an organization, find senior level sponsorship, and have the maturity and grace to tolerate injustices, which are a static feature of the corporate world. If you have these skills (or you put in the work to develop them), you can build wealth slowly but reliably.

With fewer and fewer exceptions, a skill that's an accelerant in any career is the ability to communicate your ideas. It doesn't need to be a natural talent, and it certainly can be learned. If there is one skill I will try to ensure my two boys have some command of by the time they enter the workforce, it won't be computer science or Mandarin, but communications. Not the history of communications or linguistics, but how to express oneself in different mediums. I just bought my youngest an Insta360 camera, as he enjoys making videos, and I've been recording podcasts with my older son, who I task with writing and recording two- to three-minute segments where I interview him on a topic. Communicating is a mainly verbal facility, but don't underestimate the importance of visual communication. Design is increasing in currency. It's no accident the CEOs of Airbnb and Snap are graduates of The Rhode Island School of Design and Stanford's Design School, respectively.

Finally, keep in mind that organizations are also cultures, in that the environment tends to coalesce around certain personality types. There's variety among law firms, for sure, but any two law firms have a lot more in common with each other than they do with a movie set or an emergency room. Odds are you've spent too much time around people you hate, and not enough time with the people you love, or at least enjoy being around. Think about the kinds of people who've brought out the best in you.

In the OG job-hunting guide, *What Color Is Your Parachute?*, author Richard Bolles suggests "The Party Exercise" to identify environments where you'll thrive from among six types: realistic, investigative, artistic, social, enterprising, and conventional. The exercise is straightforward: Imagine you're invited to a party. In six different corners of that party are six groups of people, each representing one of those categories. Which group are you heading to first? Who do you want to hang out with? Who do you avoid? The people you work with have the power to make or break your environment. They are, as Bolles writes, "either energy drainers or energy creators."

So What's the Right Fit for You?

I don't pretend to know what translates to success in every career, and you need to dig into the critical success factors for any career you are considering. Don't assume these are obvious or apparent to an outsider. For a general survey of the personality characteristics and other factors that map to success in a variety of fields, check out *Do What You Are*, which uses the Myers-Briggs framework to break down hundreds of career options by personality type. Even if you aren't moved by Myers-Briggs, it's a useful compendium of every way imaginable to make a buck.

I do know some areas better than others, however, and my thoughts on those follow. I'll start with the areas I know best: entrepreneurship, academia, and media. I was a modest success in the first, the second I steadily got better at, and the third has been a late-career surprise. These, and a few others I'll discuss as well, are what I know. They are far from the full scope of opportunities available to you.

Entrepreneur

One of the many things I learned working at Morgan Stanley was that I didn't want to work at Morgan Stanley, or at any large organization. Or, for anybody else at all. I resented people senior to me, didn't take criticism well, took offense at trivial injustices, and was not motivated unless I felt a direct connection with rewards. See above: I lack the skills needed to succeed in a large organization. Fortunately, that's the defining characteristic of an entrepreneur. As a society, we romanticize entrepreneurship.

I've met hundreds, perhaps thousands of entrepreneurs, and I'm convinced the majority did not start companies because they could, but because they had no other options.

Young people seem deflated when I tell them this, but working at an organization or platform offers better risk-adjusted returns. The reason the organization exists is it can pull together resources and be greater than the sum of its parts. Be one of its parts, and it will share that excess value with you. If you have the skills and patience to navigate the obstacles and the politics, and the maturity to endure the guaranteed injustices, you will over the medium- and long-term reap rewards. I started at Morgan Stanley with a colleague who is now a vice chairman. We ended up in a similar place economically, but I'd guess he's endured substantially less stress and volatility.

Our economy benefits from the mythologizing of entrepreneurship as we need people to pull the future forward in ways that challenge orthodoxy and disrupt legacy businesses. But the stories we tell ourselves about entrepreneurship are based almost entirely on the sliver of ventures that became phenomenally successful. Twenty percent of start-ups fail in the first year, and in a way, they're the lucky ones. Over the next ten years, another 45% will be put out of their misery, and less than 15% of new businesses last two decades. Media attention is lavished on outliers among the outliers—consumer apps and products/services that are familiar or understandable to us. Among the exceptions, start-ups that make their founders and investors wealthy, most are in less sexy categories (the highest survival rates belong to companies in utilities and manufacturing) that require industry experience and expertise, not just a good idea and some ambition. Two kids in a garage tinkering with a computer *can* change the world; it's happened a few times, but as a strategy for obtaining economic security, you're better off working at Google and tinkering in your garage on weekends.

Moreover, win or lose, trying your hand as an entrepreneur is signing up for round-the-clock work and stress. The more initial success you have, the more stress. Say your product idea is compelling, and you obtain funding. "Funding" really means money to hire other people. The first morning you walk into your new office (where you probably signed a 24-month lease you have no means of paying to term) and see the fresh-faced, ambitious young people who've bought into your vision, it's a great feeling. The feeling lasts until lunch, when reality sinks in. Not only does your own economic security depend on your crazy idea, but now you've taken on the economic future of other people. And for every new hire, every new customer, the amount of responsibility and stress increases—employees need health insurance and payroll, the new hire you could barely afford goes on disability leave after two days in the office, and the sponsor at your key client gets fired. Oh, and your key employee is displaying signs of what looks like serious mental illness, so you spend the evening debating whether you should call their parents. And your CFO informs you we need to do a board call because your opiate-addicted assistant has charged $120,000 on your credit card at pharmacies all over Manhattan.

Everything in the previous paragraph happened in the same month at the same firm. Yay, entrepreneurship. But if you're still reading, what are the positive qualifications for successfully starting your own business?

Successful entrepreneurs are typically strong communicators: able to motivate a team, persuade investors to step up and clients to get on board. Entrepreneur is a synonym for salesperson, full stop. We sell our vision to investors, employees, and customers—at the beginning, vision is all there is. How do you know if you can sell? You know if you have a knack for this from a pretty young age. Escaping punishment for missing homework, getting your mom to lend you the car, approaching a strange girl or guy and getting their number. All are sales training for youth.

You have to be able to get back up off the mat. Entrepreneurs miss more shots than they hit, and they take a lot of hits. For me it began in high school. I ran for sophomore, junior, and senior class president, and I lost all three times. Based on that track record, I decided to run for student body president, where I—wait for it—lost again. Amy Atkins turned me down for the prom, and I was cut from the baseball and basketball teams. Then I was rejected by UCLA, the only school I could afford (as I could live at home).

However, I never lost my sense of enthusiasm. I appealed the rejection, UCLA admitted me, and by my senior year of college, I was president of the Interfraternity Council. Weak flex, I know, but it felt important at the time. I graduated with a 2.27 GPA, but that didn't stop me from getting a job in the analyst program at Morgan Stanley (applied to twenty-three firms, one job offer) or getting into graduate school at Berkeley (applied to nine schools, rejected by seven).

In sum, the secret to my success is . . . rejection.

When you're running a small business, cash flow is so important. If you aren't willing and able to watch what comes in and, more important, what goes out, every day, you'll go bust. If your obligations get out ahead of your opportunities, you'll go bust. If you're in tech, and it's a boom phase of the cycle, there will be venture capitalists willing to dump large chunks of cash into your business. Don't be fooled, it's not out of kindness. The more you spend, the more you need, and eventually your funders will own the company, and you'll go from being an entrepreneur to an employee. Make your business work off the money your business makes as quickly as possible. Product is important, market fit is essential, culture and talent retention are critical . . . but cash flow is your company's lifeblood.

Finally, founders have to simultaneously hold two diametrically opposed views of the world. They have to be irrationally optimistic about their ultimate success. That's essential to the salesmanship and the resilience to failure, of course, but it's even more fundamental. If your start-up idea is rational, Google or GE is already doing it. The only reason the market leaders have left you an open lane is that your idea is probably irrational. You have to have the optimism to see past that. At the same time, day to day, you have to be the harshest pessimist in the organization and worry about *everything*. Is a client account tenuous? Might key employees leave? Are you one bad month away from not making payroll? The answer is yes.

The upside to entrepreneurship is similar to that of parenting. You conceive something, care for it, love it, and nothing in your career will likely cause as much stress or deliver as much joy. When things work, there is a real sense of achievement that you started something that is working. People recognize how hard it is and show a level of appreciation and respect that's close to what it feels like to be loved. In addition, there is no ceiling on what you can make. Employees, even the CEO, are somewhat range-bound by what "seems fair or reasonable" to pay you. In the years I sold firms I started, I made tens of millions of dollars. No employer, however good I was, would ever have paid me so much.

Academia

First, a modest disclaimer. I'm a clinical professor at NYU Stern, and I'm proud of the affiliation. But I'm there to teach, not to do research and advance the boundaries of knowledge. My job is to translate the experience of my professional life into domain expertise that provides students with currency in the marketplace. As such, my path to academia involved a twenty-year detour through entrepreneurship and professional services. It's a great gig, but it's not my career the way it is for many of my (brilliant) colleagues. It is, by the way, a great career. The campus environment is wonderful, your schedule is flexible, and your job, at the end of the day, is to become the most knowledgeable person in the world on a topic—no matter how narrow. The pursuit of that goal, even if the knowledge doesn't have commercial application, is intellectually nourishing.

Compensation *can* be rewarding, but it varies widely. If you come up through academic ranks, there are years of laughably low pay in all but a few disciplines, where it's only insultingly low. Professors do better and can do quite well in fields where there's heavy competition from the private sector (applied sciences, law, medicine, business). The real money comes on the side. Universities are great platforms to make money elsewhere (e.g., books, speaking, consulting, boards, etc.)—again, in fields where there's private-sector money. In academia, as in everywhere else, the rich get richer.

Academics in those public fields can do well if they have skill in communications, specifically an ability to transfer knowledge via mediums in a compelling way. Jonathan Haidt (a role model of mine) is blessed with unique insight into societal issues. However, it's his ability to write arresting long-form articles (he penned the most viewed article in history for *The Atlantic*) that pays off financially. Adam Alter writes books that, unlike 99% of academic research, find their way on to bestseller lists. Aswath Damodaran and Sonia Marciano are likely two of the best (in-classroom) teachers in the world. Jeffrey Sonnenfeld at Yale owns a six-minute segment on cable news like nobody else.

The rest of the iceberg, however, toils in much more obscure circumstances—though that can be a boon. If your talents don't encompass getting along with people less brilliant than you, nobody cares about that as long as you can push the bleeding edge of knowledge. You'll need to be self-motivated, however, as there isn't a lot of structure. So, a bit of a lone wolf (research is a lonely journey), genuinely curious, structured, and a disciplined thinker who can drill down and exhaust a narrow area. Being a great student is a leading indicator, but it's not everything—how well can you keep up the focus when the guardrails of assignments and grades are removed? My NYU colleague Sabrina Howell describes academia as a good career for very smart people who are entrepreneurial but lack management or sales talent.

Media

There are a lot of careers within media, and in general, they are overinvested and difficult ways to make a living. At the risk of sounding like a broken record, I'll just say that it's a volatile business that can feel exploitative. Media—publishing, television, journalism—is where people end up who follow their passion, and a case study in why you shouldn't. Jobs in sexy industries offer lower ROI on your efforts, as they are overinvested, which drives down returns. You don't want to do the weather at 3:00 a.m. on Sunday? Okay, we'll find a dozen other people who think this is their path to anchoring the evening news.

The line of people waiting outside to get into the media store is way too long. There's a reason #MeToo's ground zero was the media industry, and it isn't because men in media are different from men anywhere else. It's because the power dynamic is so completely out of whack that those few with power could get away with abhorrent behavior for so long. Eighty-seven percent of journalism majors regret the choice; 72% of computer science majors do not.

Professions

Professional careers are those like doctors, nurses, lawyers, architects, and engineers—where advanced training and apprenticeship is required, and a specific set of skills, often ensured by licensure, is practiced. Professional careers are typically good for people who are good at school. You have to be good at school to make it into most professions, because there's so much school required. The formal, largely written skills of learning, thinking, and communicating continue to be at the heart of most professions. A trial lawyer has to be persuasive and eloquent in court, but for every day spent Perry Masoning a witness, they spend weeks poring over documents and case law, preparing written briefs, and doing what looks to me a lot like homework. Doctors similarly employ various physical and emotional skills, depending on their specialty, but that work sits on a deep foundation of study, memorization, and structured thinking. If your idea of being a doctor is having a great bedside manner and a passion (there's that word again) for helping people, you might make a great doctor someday, but if you aren't also really good at grinding out long hours in the library and working your way through dense textbooks, that day will never arrive.

In sum, these are generally good careers, as there is a (relative) scarcity of professionals due to the certification requirements. It takes seven years of postsecondary education to become a lawyer, and the better part of two decades to become a cardiothoracic transplant surgeon. As a result, there aren't that many, and they can charge a great deal for their services. If you are blessed with the opportunity to pursue postsecondary education, going into professional services is a solid plan. In addition, the professional services industry is great training, as it is demanding and uses a lot of different muscles (client, research, sales, etc.). Many in the services industry transition to the client side and thrive, as they've been through the bootcamp of being on the other side of the client–vendor relationship.

There is an economic downside to professional careers: they are often salary-driven with limited upside. And as I discuss in "The High-Income Trap" in Chapter Four, our income tax system takes the largest bite out of high-income earners, those in the mid-six-figure range. If you find yourself in this income band, the lessons of this book around temperance, saving, and long-term investing are essential to protecting you from a career of long hours that never produces real economic security.

Management Consulting

Consultants are, largely, professionals without credentials. Anyone can hang out a shingle and call themselves a consultant—I did at 26 with only two years of relevant work experience. And I've been some form of a consultant for most of my career. It is interesting, can be great training (sort of an extension of graduate school), and calls on many skills—analytical, client, creative, presentation, etc. It's also a way to advance your career while figuring out what you "really" want to do as you'll be exposed to a variety of sectors and roles. It pays well, even extremely well, though it's not a path to extreme wealth, because it's cursed with the same problem as any business where you're selling your time: difficult to scale. In addition, it's a young person's game as it involves being a servant to someone else's (i.e., the client's) priority and calendar. It takes a toll on you physically, and mentally as you are often away from your family, even if you're in the same city. Unless you love this business, this is an onramp to something else. Generally speaking, consulting is a career for the elite and aimless: talented people who haven't figured out what they want to do. Which is Latin for "people in their twenties."

Finance

Another close cousin to the professions is finance (which in some subfields also requires certification). There are few industries that offer more opportunities for outsized (crazy) compensation than finance. Money suffers less friction than any other substance. As a result, nothing scales like the money business. Growing my first consulting firm from ten to a hundred people was really challenging. When raising money for activist investments in the aughts, going from $10 million in capital to $100 million wasn't easy, but it was much less difficult than scaling a services business 10 times. We will look back on this age and wonder how so few earned so much for so little. It's a demanding job, but there's nothing that matches the ROI on grit and talent like finance.

You will need to be smart, hardworking, and comfortable with numbers. However, more than anything, you will need to be fascinated by the markets. If you aren't intrigued by stocks, interest rates, earnings, and how they relate to one another, you are unlikely to be successful in finance. (The test will be Chapter Four of this book—if it's your favorite chapter, you may have found your calling.) There are different sides to the business (investment banking, trading, consumer finance). You will need to be able to endure volatility and stress. Entire banks may withdraw from a region or close a division overnight. There are no careers in finance, just a series of jobs and platforms where you try to distinguish what you can control from what you can't. Again, if you're built to withstand the stress and volatility, there is no business like show business . . . if show business were finance.

Real Estate

There are few better ways to build wealth than real estate. The asset class is arguably the most tax-advantaged in America. There are few assets that you can finance 80% of and then write off the interest on that leverage/debt. It is also, with a 1031 exchange, one of the few assets that can grow tax-deferred indefinitely, even as you trade in it.

You will likely be at least a part-time real estate investor at some point: if you buy a house. Equity in your home will make up a large portion of your wealth and, ultimately, retirement nest egg. Owning your own home calls on many of the features of the algebra of wealth, as it is a form of forced savings (mortgage) and requires a long-term mindset. America has a severe shortage of housing, and it's unlikely, if you can hold for a decade or more, that you will lose money in residential real estate.

A variation on the entrepreneurial career is building up a portfolio of rental properties. Buying houses or apartments, or commercial properties, such as small retail or self-storage, can be a lucrative career *eventually*. I came to this field late and skipped the lengthy process of starting small and adding to my portfolio by virtue of wealth and timing. I have been in start-ups, tech, hedge funds, and media. The best investments I have made are in real estate.

After the 2008 crisis, real estate values in Florida collapsed. I found myself in Miami, fleeing New York's private school system, which left us without a school for my 3-year-old, who was speech delayed. (Note: he made Head's List last semester.) Anyway, after moving to Delray Beach in 2010, I saw FORECLOSURE and FOR SALE signs everywhere. So I started buying condos that had gone into foreclosure. My in-laws had moved to the area and are competent and handy—condos require upkeep, tenants expect you to fix the air-conditioning, there's always something. However, the returns have been impressive. If you are interested in real estate, take basic finance courses, begin getting a feel for property in your (or an adjacent) area, and begin saving for your first down payment. If I could do it all again, I'd try to save more as a young person and put it into rental properties I could fix and borrow against so I could then buy more.

A decent strategy for economic security is to buy a home that needs fixing up, spend two years living in it while improving it (thoughtfully), then sell it (shielding up to $500,000 [for married couples] in gains from taxation), and do so again. Wash/rinse/repeat. Expand your capital base, your skill set, and your network, then move on to more than one house at time. This is *not* a no-brainer; you need to understand the local market, be disciplined in your approach, and have a feel for what types of improvements would have the greatest ROI. Also, you'll need to be able to manage vendors, and you'll do far better if you are handy yourself. This is not a desktop investment strategy.

Airline Pilot

(Didn't see that one coming, did you? Stick with me.) I'm fascinated by aviation. For any plane flying overhead, I can likely tell you the manufacturer and model. Some people browse for shoes, others for vacation spots. I browse jets and spend free time reading about jet engine thrust and avionics. When I bought my own jet, I effectively became the manager of a tiny airline (customer: me). Not surprisingly, I'm often asked if I'm interested in learning to fly.

No way. See above: don't follow your passion, follow your talent. And the gulf between my passion for planes and my potential talent for flying them is vast. Flying is in part a physical skill—even with the aid of technology, pilots need strong spatial awareness and good eyesight and hearing. But that's not what keeps me out of the pilot seat. Being a pilot is about not making mistakes in two very different circumstances. First, staying sharp in the routine environment of route planning and checklists. An immunity to boredom. That's not me. I crave novelty, not competence. Second, and this is the real crux, on the very rare occasions when the routine is upset by crisis, what separates good pilots from dead pilots is the ability to follow protocols, to apply that same checklist mentality, even as the situation deteriorates. A lot can happen in the air—while I was working on this book, I read about a pilot in South Africa who discovered a five-foot-long Cape cobra slithering up his shirt in midflight. Our hero located the nearest airport, arranged for an emergency landing, landed the plane, and got his passengers off safely, all while a venomous stowaway explored the cockpit.

The role model is Iceman, not Maverick.

Main Street Economy

The last category I want to discuss is not one I have direct experience in (except as a customer), but it has enormous potential and is often overlooked. What I call the Main Street economy is likely the most underinvested part of our labor market (as in people are not entering the field), meaning there is huge opportunity relative to the investment required. This encompasses the trades (electricians, plumbers, and other skilled workers) and small/regional business ownership (often of enterprises in the trades).

Over 140,000 Americans make more than $1.5 million per year, and most are neither technology founders nor lawyers or doctors, but the owners of regional businesses: car dealerships, beverage distributors, etc. Small businesses (<500 employees) create two-thirds of the net new jobs each year and account for 44% of GDP. It's not all car dealerships and dry cleaners, either. A study of innovative businesses found that smaller firms—those with an average of 140 employees—produced 15 times more patents per employee than companies with tens of thousands of employees. In light of increasing concerns about fragile global supply chains, opportunities are increasing for domestic specialized manufacturing.

At an even smaller scale, demand for skilled trade labor is intense—ask anyone who's tried to get solar panels installed or renovate their kitchen in a hot housing market. The job market for electricians is projected to grow 40% faster than the overall job market (and green energy projects are primarily *electrification* projects), and we're projected to be half a million plumbers short of what the market will require by 2027. Yet only 17% of high school and college students are interested in pursuing careers in construction trades.

Those of us who make our living in a field that demands certification from an elite school sometimes look down on these careers. We've decided that if our kid does not end up at MIT, then Google, we've failed as parents and a society. Too many of us have fetishized the information and tech industries to such an extent that we have shamed an entire generation into believing a trades job means things didn't work out for you.

If you have access to capital, there is an increasing opportunity on Main Street for acquisition, as baby boomers retire and look to sell their electrical contracting businesses. These are real paths to wealth not covered by CNBC. The U.S. Small Business Administration, a cabinet-level federal agency, has a range of programs, including financial support for starting and growing these businesses. It helps if you actually want to *live* on Main Street, of course—half the nation's GDP is generated *outside* the twenty-five largest metro areas. Most of my examples and advice (including the next section about getting to a city) are colored by my lived experience in the knowledge worker fields. But the core message of this book, and the path to wealth, can apply to any career path, and the Main Street economy is an economic engine for millions of Americans. Don't overlook it.

BEST PRACTICES

Get to a City, Go to the Office

Early in your career, you need training, mentors, and challenges. A virtual presence can't replace surrounding yourself with smart, creative humans building something. The more opportunities to socialize, explore your interests, gain mentors and potential mates, and make connections, the better. Like tennis, when you rally with someone better than you, you improve. Being in a city forces you to rally with the best. This doesn't have to be New York, though I do think NYC is the best place for young people (those in their twenties and thirties) in professional careers, but it should be a place that presents you with these opportunities and competition. The conveniences of work-from-home pale in comparison to the opportunities—personal and professional—of being in the same space. Pundits have probably been predicting the death of cities since the first two-story building. Complexity thrives in large cities, which produce more patents, more research, and are home to more innovative firms. Over 80% of global GDP is generated in cities.

Also, cities are *fun, interesting, and social*. You will meet people from backgrounds you've never imagined, with views on life that will change your own. While you are in a city, try new things, put yourself in novel situations—you'll learn about your most important subject, yourself. City life can be expensive, but that's okay. Your early career years are important for building economic security, but mostly because that's where you are finding the right career, building the skills to succeed, and forming relationships. As I discuss in the next chapter, the money you save is less important than building your saving muscle, and it's fine to live life while you are unencumbered. Get the cheapest apartment you can stand, don't furnish it, never spend any time in it, and practice saying "yes."

Get to the office, ideally HQ. The office is where you'll build relationships and find mentors. And mentors are the people who become emotionally invested in your success—a key in any organization. When deciding who to promote, it's the person who has the relationship with the decider who will get the nod. Yes, relationships can be formed remotely, but they will be less intimate. Proximity to the office (i.e., your presence there) is directly correlated to your trajectory. A 2022 survey of C-level executives found that over 40% of them believed that remote employees were less likely to be promoted—and studies confirm it. Conversely, if there are layoffs, those without champions or high profiles will over-index on that list. It's easier to fire people you've only met on video.

Is this reality equitable or well designed? Probably not. But your career takes place in the world as it is, not the world as it might be. In sum, while you can, put on a nice shirt and get into the office.

Over time, you'll develop your skills and your network, so the urban setting and even the physical office will have less to offer. And most of us tend to acquire people (mates, children, dogs) and things, and the cost and limitations of megacities become more burdensome. At some point, the arbitrage flips. You can relocate to a smaller city or a suburb, even a rural area, ideally one with low taxes and great schools, while still maintaining the level of focus your career needs at that stage in your professional life.

Desire Is Table Stakes

Whether you're at school, a start-up, or a corporation, everyone wants the same things: success, validation, skills, and economic security. And the universe doesn't care. Desire is necessary, not sufficient.

There's a lot of career and life advice about setting goals. Goals are fine, even necessary, and measurable targets can be important management tools in business. (Research suggests that the simple act of writing down your goals can have a profound effect on outcomes.) But your desire to reach a goal is not going to get you there.

First off, progress isn't linear, it's lumpy. People approach me and congratulate me on my overnight success. Not quite. My "overnight success" took thirty-five years of hard work and getting back up after I was punched in the face. If your motivation for doing the work is your desire for some end goal, you are setting yourself up for a lot of frustration when you're grinding away and not seeing any progress toward the goal. And the bigger the goal, the longer the time horizon before you can achieve it, the greater the opportunity that your desire will burn out before you get there.

Then there's the problem with obtaining your heart's desire. What next? The greater the struggle you've made to get something, the more you've sacrificed for it, the greater your disappointment will be when you win the prize and your life hasn't fundamentally changed. Because you'll still be you, with all your neuroses and fears and regrets, only it's worse because you have the thing you wanted so badly—what will motivate you now?

It's a familiar line: "Life is a journey, not a destination." Or as habit guru James Clear put it, "If you want better results, then forget about setting goals. Focus on your systems instead." Your job is to channel your desire, your ambition, and whatever else motivates you (fear, incidentally, is an outstanding motivator) into building your skills, accumulating credentials and contacts, and working hard, really hard. Find the reward in knowing you did the work, take pride in the improvements and intermediate successes, and the thing you desire will come to pass. Bill Walsh, who coached the San Francisco 49ers to three Super Bowl wins and revolutionized the NFL, later put down his management philosophy in a book, the title of which captured his ethos: *The Score Takes Care of Itself.*

Grit

Talent and desire, matched to the right career, are a good start. What turns these into economic security is years of hard work. There's no secret, no shortcut; it takes toil to achieve. Grit is your ability to step up every day and do the work, even when it's not being recognized, when it's not producing results, when you're exhausted or distracted—that's success, just in its gestation phase.

The guru of grit, neuroscientist Angela Duckworth, defines the trait as "the intersection of passion and perseverance." Her key finding is that this trait factors more into individual success than what our society is so focused on, intelligence. Her measures of grit have been shown to be predictive of success in different environments.

For me, hard work typically meant long hours and near-total commitment. When I was building L2, I was at the office during the day, home for bath time with the kids, then back to the office. On Sundays I worked a half day. If a client called and wanted to meet, I would often get on a plane the next day. Not everyone has the privilege (or the desire) to be that committed. Putting in 110% doesn't guarantee success and working 90% doesn't foreclose it. You can be focused and succeed even if you don't want to be a business Navy SEAL. Figure out how you can contribute more than the next person. Baseball statisticians have a metric, "wins above replacement," that measures how many games a team wins when a star player is in the lineup vs. what the stats say they would have won with a run-of-the-mill player at that position. Find a way to increase your wins above replacement.

Cultivating grit is not easy—it's thought to be a product of genetics and early childhood. But the best thinking is that grit flows from a growth mindset, or an appreciation that, as Steven Kotler puts it, "talent is merely a starting point and practice makes all the difference." Consider your own history of learning and improvement, when something that was initially frustrating and difficult became easier through work ("through work" being the key phrase).

If You Can't Fix It, You Have to Stand It

All our actions take place against a backdrop of forces outside our control. There are plenty of things we can invest time and energy into that we can truly affect, so don't waste resources fighting battles you can't win.

In their book *Designing Your Life*, Dave Evans and Bill Burnett define "gravity problems" as obstacles or contrary forces you can't do anything about. "If it's not actionable," they write, "it's not a problem, it's a circumstance." When you're in the thick of the struggle, it's easy to mistake advice about persistence, grit, and focus as meaning you should never give up, or worse, that if your head hurts from pounding it against a wall, you must be doing something right. But it's important to step back and consider the landscape. Are you ramming a wall that can be breached? Or are you fighting gravity?

There's a saying in the market: "You can't fight the Fed." It means that if the Federal Reserve wants the economy to move in a certain direction, only a fool bets against it. Macroeconomic factors are gravity—so unless you're the Fed chair, you likely can't change them. Gravity exists on a smaller scale as well. Unrequited love, unless you're a poet, is a gravity problem. (S)he's just not that into you. Move on. If your boss only gives choice assignments and promotions to people who they socialize with, and you've got three kids at home and no interest in golf, that sounds like a gravity problem. I left consulting, as it's a relationship business, and I sensed I no longer had the discipline or personality to be friends with my clients.

There are two steps to dealing with gravity. The first is recognizing it. The second is reframing your response so you have a problem you *can* solve. Gravity doesn't mean we can't climb steep hills or even fly. But the solution to those challenges must work within the reality of gravity, not against it. If you are always chasing after romantic partners or jobs or hobbies that don't return your interest, there's probably a mismatch between your passion and your talent. What do you have to offer (and can you enhance it) and what kind of people want that?

Know When to Quit

Persistence should be a feature, not a suicide pact. When you are fighting your way through the jungle, take out your compass regularly and make sure you are headed in the right direction. This is a situation where your kitchen cabinet is invaluable. Don't quit because it's hard, it's supposed to be hard. Quit because the data, or a mentor you trust, or multiple external signs, indicate your time would be better invested elsewhere. There is no shame in this.

In 1997, I started an e-commerce company called Red Envelope. It was great until it wasn't, and it took ten years to finally pull the plug. The worst thing? It failed slowly. Losing the majority of my net worth wasn't fun, but what stung the most was that it took ten years to fail.

Two years after I founded it, Red Envelope was still promising me wealth and glory, and I started an e-commerce incubator company called Brand Farm backed by, among others, Goldman Sachs and J.P. Morgan. The idea was pretty simple: have one infrastructure, one legal department, one technology department, one business development department, one office space, and punch out e-commerce companies. I raised $15 million based on a PowerPoint deck. Six months in, *boom*, dot-bomb implosion. We realized the concept no longer made sense given the economic climate. We shut down the parent business, asked our portfolio companies to cut their burn by 50% to survive the nuclear winter so they could live to fight another day, and we moved on. That was a blessing. Success is the best thing. Failing fast is the next best thing.

Any time you play the odds, quitting should be an option. In tech, we rebrand quitting as "pivoting" to make it more palatable. Great gamblers are great quitters—Kenny Rogers's signature song reminds us we have to "know when to hold 'em and know when to fold 'em." Poker champion Annie Duke wrote an entire book about quitting; she makes a compelling case it's one of the keys to success in business and life. One of her tips: plan your out ahead of time, so when the emotion of the moment takes over, you've got a signal you can count on. Knowing when to quit is essential. It's an art. All successful people have quit. Some, often. Find people you trust who have the backbone and perspective to tell you if/when you should hang in there or fold your cards.

Peaks and Valleys, Not a Ladder

Career progression is not the steady staircase to the executive floor it once was. Rigid expectations of a linear, upward trajectory can blind you to diagonal opportunities. Think of your career not as a ladder to climb, but as a mountain range to cross, with different challenges and environments to master, expanding your tool kit along the way so you can keep moving forward.

Focus does not necessarily translate to linear progression. There's value in variety. One study found that the best predictor of a new CEO's success was how many different jobs they had held before taking the reins.

Successful, wealth-generating employment careers (as opposed to entrepreneurship) typically include strategic job changes that produce jumps in responsibilities and compensation. It's a sad truth of human nature that outsiders will value you more than your current employer—we crave novelty, and bosses are no different. It's a common mistake for managers to view the employee through the lens of when the person first joined the firm vs. a more seasoned executive who is a known commodity.

Even if you don't change employers, market checks can pay dividends. My first year at Stern I was paid $12,000. My value to the school climbed fast (I taught the school's most popular class and I made frequent outside appearances), but my compensation did not. Universities underpay clinical and adjunct faculty to subsidize (too often) unproductive tenured faculty. So every few years I brought them an offer from another university and was transparent: "This is what my market value is, I'd like to stay, and I ask that you match it." They did. Eventually, my other ventures rendered my NYU compensation less valuable (see above: marginal utility), and these days I return my compensation to Stern so I can bite the hand that (doesn't) feed me: I write and speak about the shortcomings of higher education, and it would feel funny to cash their checks as I rage against the machine. But for many years, those raises were a big deal for me. In sum, if you want to grow your compensation at a greater clip than inflation, you will likely either need to leave or demonstrate a credible willingness to do so (see above: offers from other universities).

Be on LinkedIn, maintain your profile, benchmark peers; talk to friends, former classmates, and colleagues about their jobs. There's an incorrect notion that talking about money or promotions is uncouth. Only your employer benefits from your ignorance. If you are in a field where headhunters prowl, take their calls now and then let them buy you lunch and quiz them about the state of the market. Who is hiring? What are they looking for? What skill sets and characteristics are hot right now? Who's struggling to catch on? And most critically, what's your value, and where would it be maximized?

A caveat: explore other opportunities with a healthy skepticism, and actively remind yourself what you like about your current employer. *Every* job has its frustrations, every boss their irritations, and what seems like a dazzling and limitless opportunity will, after six months, likely be just your job.

The nuclear option is to take all this information and actually change jobs. As of March 2023, Americans who had changed jobs in the past twelve months increased their compensation 7.7% in that time, while those who had not changed jobs saw an increase of just 5.7%. The delta changes over time, but job switchers are almost always ahead of those they leave behind. New environments also expand your experience base, making you more flexible and adaptable in a changing economy.

The image of the job switcher is changing, but overall, job tenures have declined only modestly. In 1983, the median tenure for workers 25 and older was 5.9 years. By 2022, that had declined, but

MEDIAN % CHANGE IN HOURLY WAGE

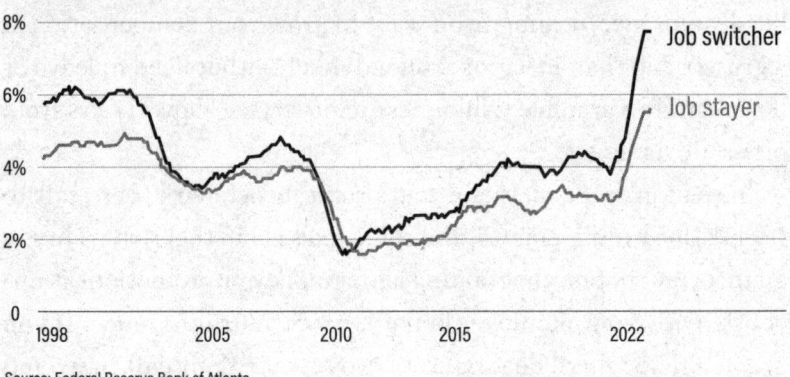

Source: Federal Reserve Bank of Atlanta

just 17% (over nearly four decades) to 4.9 years. Where job switching has accelerated fastest is with younger workers. Twenty-one percent of millennials say they've changed jobs within the past year, more than three times the number of non-millennials who've done the same. Members of Gen Z are switching jobs at a rate 134% higher than they did in 2019, according to LinkedIn data. That compares with 24% more for millennials and 4% less for boomers. And Gen Z'ers plan to keep moving: 25% say they hope or plan to leave their employers within the next six months compared with 23% of millennials and 18% of Gen X'ers.

Changing jobs is a double-edged sword, however, and one to be wielded with care. It often means abandoning investments you've made in learning about an organization and rebuilding a reputation and a network at the new firm. There's significant risk, because no amount of interviewing can ensure you will be a fit at the new organization. And then there's the cumulative effect on your résumé, what message your employment history sends to future employers. If you've had three jobs in seven years, the person interviewing you likely assumes you are the problem. I'm not suggesting you stay at a terrible job solely for CV hygiene. However, if you were at your last job for less than two years and you don't love your current job, I'd think long and hard about what would be required to stay three years plus before switching.

Young people who are comfortable with regular changes of employer shouldn't assume everyone feels the same. For a sense of how we used to view frequent job switchers (and how some still do), in 1974 a Berkeley psychologist coined the term "hobo syndrome" to describe "the periodic itch to move from a job in one place to some other job in some other place," which he thought was an impulse "not unlike that which causes birds to migrate." Hobo syndrome is not a label you want potential employers attaching to your résumé.

So when should you change jobs? When the next move gets you further across the terrain, balanced against your reputation as a serial job switcher. Meaning, when there's strategic value in the change, that it's materially better, not just different. Are you adding a valuable brand name to your résumé? Is it an opportunity to expand your network in a productive way? Most important, will the new position/employer allow you to expand your skill set? This can be technical job-performance skills, like learning new software or analysis tools, but it can also mean softer skills—the opportunity to manage other people, exposure to senior management, better mentors, more direct customer contact. If you can't articulate clear and concrete advantages to the new job, question whether it's just change for change's sake, and whether you'll be looking around again in another year.

Be Loyal to People, Not Companies

Loyalty is a virtue, and it goes both ways. Someone who hires you is saying they believe in your potential. A mentor is saying the same. They are betting on you, and you should reward their loyalty with your own. It will pay for both of you—mentorship has been shown to increase career outcomes for both the mentor and the protégé. At one large tech firm, both parties were at least five times more likely to be promoted than employees who hadn't participated in a mentorship program.

Asking for advice is one of the most powerful bonding things you can do in the workplace. It's an expression of trust—that's why it's intimidating. But trust builds trust and deepens relationships. Seek counsel, and your mentor will be invested in your success.

None of this applies to organizations. They have no advice to offer, no perspective to provide, and *will not be loyal to you*. Your boss might think the sun rises and sets with you, but when your boss's boss screws up and tanks your division's results, the layoff scythe will cut you both down like wheat. Loyalty is a human (also canine) virtue, not an organizational one.

The line between organizations and individuals used to be blurrier. If you worked at IBM for forty years and so did your colleagues, then being loyal to IBM was in effect being loyal to the people who worked there; a distinction without a difference. Today, a generation of shareholder value management strategies and innovation-driven disruptions have sundered us from our organizational affiliations. And that has made our loyalty to one another, as individuals, even more important.

Mike Bloomberg once said, "I have always had a policy: If it's a friend and they get a promotion, I don't bother to call them; I'll see them sometime and make a joke about it. If they get fired, I want to go out to dinner with them that night. And I want to do it in a public place where everybody can see me. Because I remember when I got fired from Salomon Brothers—I can tell you every single person that called me. That meant something. When I was made a partner? I have no recollection of that whatsoever." My friend Todd Benson puts it this way: "Show up when it matters, when it means something. Never miss a funeral. Attend every wedding."

Be a Serial Monogamist

When you are working your way across the terrain of your career, you'll cover more ground if you have your eyes firmly on the destination and the challenge at hand. "Side gigs," in my view, are a distraction, a dilution of the focus you need to be successful. If something is worth doing, make it your main gig. If you have a side hustle, that probably means your main hustle is not what it should be. Would the addition of 10% to 20% of focus and effort result in more upside at your main gig than what your side hustle is providing? Focus is not about what to do, but what not to do.

There are exceptions. If you are a freelancer, taking on multiple clients, then diversifying your customer base and revenue streams is common sense. As a freelancer, you are a business of one, and it's dangerous for any business to be dependent on a single customer or a single product line. But it's equally dangerous to chase every opportunity and spread limited resources across disparate services with little synergy. In the early days of each of my start-ups, the temptation was always to do "stuff for money," and sometimes you have to take on projects that are strategically irrelevant just to make payroll. But it's empty calories. "Stuff for money" projects take just as much overhead and mental energy (sometimes more) as projects in the core business, and they rob resources from expanding the company's skill set and momentum in that core business. Again, it's a judgment call you should discuss with your kitchen cabinet.

The second exception is if you've ignored my warnings concerning entrepreneurship, it can be valuable to maintain a salary/benefits job in the earliest days of your start-up career, for obvious practical reasons. Similarly, maybe you need a day job to fund an asset-building career, like building up a portfolio of rental real estate. If this is your approach, don't think of either effort as a side hustle—evaluate and invest your time in them as a unit, as two lines of business that are complementary. Have a plan and timeline for shifting out of the salary job and into the asset-building career.

Grad School

A tempting side route through the range that most knowledge workers will consider is grad school. Some professions require it, and it forces a level of focus, as two years into residency is *not* the time to figure out you hate medicine. No matter how certain you think you are about a career that requires more school, try to get some inside exposure before you commit years of your life to the entry requirements.

When I earned my MBA at the Haas School of Business (UC Berkeley), the tuition was $2,000 per year—which made it a near no-brainer. As tuition rates have skyrocketed, the bar is higher for what justifies the investment. It's not that business school can't be valuable (I teach at one, and I believe in the mission), but it's not for everyone or necessary for everyone. Business school is an undeniably valuable certification, but so is a job at a top employer. And business school credentials offer rapidly diminishing returns the more you advance—nobody hires a CEO because they went to Wharton—while the $200,000 you spent could be earning compound interest in your portfolio. As I discuss in the next chapter, opportunity cost is critically underappreciated.

Besides the stamp of approval, the most valuable thing about business school for most people is the network. Especially if your background didn't connect you with bankers and executives, business school can go a long way toward leveling the field. What you actually learn is . . . limited, but that's true of most higher education. For both networking and signaling purposes, I don't recommend going anywhere but a top-ten school. (Note: there's probably fifteen schools in the top ten.) Employers say the same thing, but they speak with money: MBAs coming out of the top schools in the U.S. can earn triple what their counterparts from the lowest ranked programs garner in the marketplace.

Quick Wins

"Quick Wins" was a tactic we used in my management consulting days to get momentum with a new client. Consulting projects start with a rush of optimism and energy when a team of fresh-faced MBAs show up at a company with new ideas. The problem is that months can go by, and all the *wunderkids* have produced are meetings, PowerPoint presentations, and six-figure invoices. So we would look for low-hanging-fruit opportunities where we could implement some aspect of our recommendations on a small scale. Pilot projects, simple customer surveys, anything we could do quickly and visibly. The benefits were many: not only did we justify the investment via progress, we made the prospect of implementing our much more ambitious recommendations less daunting, and we learned how the client's organization really functioned.

Creating opportunities for quick wins is a potent technique in numerous domains. In our personal development, it's the key to improving our habits and generating momentum to take on much larger tasks. Personal finance guru Dave Ramsey breaks with doctrinaire economics to advocate for quick wins for people who are deep in debt. He tells his clients to list all their debts in order from smallest to largest. Forget about interest rates or payment terms or anything else, just list the absolute size of the debt. Then pay them off in that order. It's not the soundest approach from a fiscal standpoint (that would be paying off the highest-rate loans first), but as Ramsey points out, he's favoring "behavior modification over math." You might actually pay off that $100 loan from your cousin, even if you could let it ride for years, and that's a quick win. And as Ramsey argues, "You need quick wins to get fired up."

Prune and Invest in Your Hobbies

Recreational activities, from reading romance novels to climbing (real) mountains, keep our bodies and minds active, and can create lasting happiness. And eventually, if you follow the advice in this book, you can expect to have the time and money to pursue them passionately. Indeed, at some point, they will be all you do. And as much as learning a new skill can be rewarding, you don't want to wake up at 70 with no job, a full bank account, and nothing to do. You can surf when you're 70, but it's a lot easier if you learned when you were 25.

The problem you have now, though, is that you need to focus on your career, so your remaining time is precious. How to choose what to prune and where to invest?

Stack rank your recreational activities. (That means list them in priority order, from the most important to you down to the least. No ties.) A recreational activity is anything you do beyond the basic necessities that doesn't earn (or have the legitimate potential to earn) significant income. When ranking, consider these factors:

- Is it a shared activity with loved ones, such that time spent is also invested in those relationships? Be honest—if your spouse comes along to the golf course every Sunday because they love you, but they would rather be doing literally anything than playing golf, this isn't a shared activity. If it is, that's a huge benefit, and should push it up the list.
- Is it exercise? Everyone should have at least one exercise hobby on their list. Mine is CrossFit. I like CrossFit, but I don't love it. Until I find an exercise hobby I like more, however, it's at the top of my list.

- What's the time-cost-to-value ratio? Flying experimental aircraft is probably a thrill, but in a world of limited time and capital, it's pretty far behind "taking a walk on the beach" for most people when the time-cost-to-value ratio is taken into account.
- Can you do it when you're older? This plays out in different ways. For skill-based hobbies, especially physical ones, it's probably a reason to keep doing them now. If you anticipate playing a lot of golf in retirement, it's probably worth developing and keeping your game in at least moderate shape today. If you plan on retiring to Hawaii and longboarding every morning, you should definitely get some wave time in now and then. These are not skills you want to start cold at 65. Cooking, on the other hand, you can probably count on taking up at any age. First-class travel to European capitals doesn't require any practice and is just as easily (perhaps more easily) done in retirement than in your youth.
- Do you have a talent for it? Does it trigger a flow state? Does it bring you joy? The answer to these questions is likely the same, but all are valuable characteristics of a hobby. If you love piano music and imagine yourself dazzling the retirement home with your mastery, but you've got short fingers and piano practice is a daily hour of confusion and distress, you should probably allocate that time elsewhere. Few people can genuinely enjoy something in which they have little skill for very long. Don't follow your passion, follow your talent.
- Is it doing or watching? In my experience, people who sweat are more successful than people who watch others sweat.

Once you've got an idea about what you are getting the most out of, go down the list, and consider how much time each one is taking out of your day/week/month/year. Add it up, and three or four entries in, you've probably maxed out what you realistically have time to do and do well. ("Trying new stuff" is a completely legitimate hobby, and this list shouldn't be static all your life. Just recognize that some time allocation is needed to try new things.) Don't feel guilty for walking away from something you've poured time into in the past. Sunk costs are sunk, and if it was worth doing for all those years, you likely have skills and experiences you can carry forward into your other activities. Competitive sports are the classic example here—the lessons in persistence and hard work I learned rowing in college have stayed with me for life, but I'm at peace with never getting near a crew shell again.

For those items that make the list, don't cheat yourself. That doesn't mean you have to charge ahead—if cooking tops your list because it's a chill activity you can do while listening to podcasts, don't ruin it by feeling you need to take a class every month and cook five-course meals every night. What I mean is: **don't begrudge yourself the downtime or the cost.** If opera is on your list, then go to the best opera you can find and don't feel bad about the expense or the time. That's the virtue of pruning—you can savor what made the list because you are being intentional, and focused.

FOCUS
+
(STOICISM
×
TIME
×
DIVERSIFICATION)

CHAPTER REVIEW: ACTION ITEM BULLETS

- **Consciously direct your attention, time, and energy.** Economic security is created over the long term, through sustained focus on the most productive opportunities.

- **Accept the necessity of hard work.** Nearly all paths to wealth involve time at work, energy spent on work, and sacrifices elsewhere in our lives. Resenting that undermines your current focus and your long-term satisfaction.

- **Don't follow your passion.** Follow your talent.

- **Take the time to ascertain your talent.** Our talents are not always obvious, even to ourselves, and they're often not what we initially think or wish them to be. Push yourself into new contexts and listen to what other people tell you about your particular strengths. Feel for what makes you curious and excited.

- **Focus on mastery; passion will follow.** Sustained, rewarding passion is the product of hard work, not its cause.

- **Iterate.** Try new things, take chances, and don't expect to achieve great success right away. Most "overnight success" stories are the product of years of hard work. Failure is the raw material of success—if you learn from it.

- **Look for the beach with the biggest waves.** Market dynamics trump individual performance, so give yourself the best chance by going where the opportunities are the greatest.

- **Nurture your skill at communication.** Across every career path, the ability to communicate is always a positive, and often essential. Read novels or watch movies you enjoy, learn how to display information visually, listen to how great presenters captivate their audience.

ACTION ITEM BULLETS

- **Make career choices based on culture as well as skills.** It's obvious that you want a job that suits your skill set, but it's just as important that your workplace suits your personality. Work with people who get the best out of you.

- **Look beyond the obvious careers.** If you do well in school, you are inevitably tracked toward an elite college, then graduate school and the knowledge-worker professions: management, technology, finance, medicine, law. These are potentially great careers, but there are also many unhappy law firm partners and senior vice presidents. Look broadly—there are opportunities from architecture to zoology. Don't discount the Main Street economy. Follow your talent.

- **Get to a city, go to the office.** Your twenties and thirties are for learning the way of work, for pushing yourself, for expanding your network and your knowledge of the world. That means being around other people, the more the better.

- **Know when to quit.** Persistence is a virtue, until it becomes a suicide pact. Any time you are playing the odds, quitting should be one of your options.

- **Be loyal to people, not companies.** Organizations are transitory arrangements with no moral compass or memory, and *they will not be loyal to you.*

- **Prune your hobbies.** Interests outside work aren't just enjoyable, they are essential to short-term happiness and long-term satisfaction. But they are also a distraction from your focus, so be thoughtful about what you pursue and let go of pastimes that no longer suit you.

FOCUS
+
(STOICISM
×
TIME
×
DIVERSIFICATION)

3
TIME

THE TWENTIETH-CENTURY AMERICAN POET Delmore Schwartz wrote, "Time is the fire in which we burn." Dark, but he had a point. Time consumes us, inexorably and inevitably. The past is a memory, immutable. The future, a dream. What you have control over, and the opportunity to be present in, is the now. Dwelling on the past or believing the future will unfold positively without action and discipline in the present is a road to regret about what you didn't do, and can't fix, in the immutable past.

You are more agile and talented than the universe. The universe is unable to communicate as fluidly, or to consider nuance. You are the Usain Bolt of the universe: really fast. However, the universe will best everything, everywhere, as it's the master of the most immutable weapon: time. The universe moves at a fraction of a glacial pace, knowing that, eventually, it passes everything else, as it measures change in billions of years.

Time is your most valuable resource, especially as a young

person since you have more of it than anybody else. It's a weapon the young rarely recognize or know how to use. When you've only been conscious for twenty-five years, it's unfathomable to imagine anything will be conscious in another fifty. The ability to grasp this concept—time and patience—may be the delta between people who have the talent to make a living vs. those who have the requisite mindset to build wealth.

Time is one thing you should not be generous with. Squander money, you can earn it back. Squander time, it's gone forever. I'm not saying don't ever relax. Doing nothing is fine, important even, but it should be planned.

When it comes to building wealth, time is our ally over the long term, but in the short term, our nemesis. This has three facets, and they provide the structure for this chapter. First, time's power of compounding. You're likely familiar with this term in the context of "compound interest," and that's a central tenet of financial planning. Thanks to the power of time, small increases in capital can become significant gains.

But compounding is about more than the returns you earn with your money. Investing expenses compound, too, and if poorly managed, they can decimate returns. Inflation compounds, and this makes it your primordial foe, relentlessly eroding the foundations of wealth. This rule goes beyond finance. The impacts of our actions compound across all domains, from the development of habits to the strengthening of relationships.

Second, there is our experience of time in the present. Focus and Stoicism are approaches toward making the most of your present time. Wealth creation requires a clear understanding of how we are allocating our time and spending our money (two ways of saying the same thing), and the skill of making good decisions, large and small.

Third, there is the ultimate question, the trade-off that time presents. Building wealth is a curious notion, because much of it comes down to sacrificing pleasure now, so someone else—your future self—will be happier. We earn money at work so our near-term future self can eat and have shelter. We save and invest money so our long-term future self will have economic security and the rewards of a good life. Visualizing your future self, and what could happen with a mastery of time, is key to accepting the trade-offs between their happiness and your own.

THE POWER OF TIME: COMPOUNDING

Time magnifies small changes into mighty things. Time is how acorns grow into oaks and rivers cut canyons. In economics, and in life, we can see time's power in the phenomenon of compounding.

Compound Interest

The gangster authority on time, Albert Einstein, supposedly remarked that compound interest is the eighth wonder of the world. It's that, but it's also simple math.

INVESTMENT OF $100 AT 8%

WITHOUT COMPOUNDING		WITH COMPOUNDING
$108	YR 1	$108
$116	YR 2	$117
$124	YR 3	$126
$180	YR 10	$216
$340	YR 30	$1,006

Imagine you have $100, and you invest it at an annual interest rate of 8%. In the first year, the investment earns a small return of $8. Your $100 becomes $108. In the second year, however, it doesn't merely earn you another $8. It earns 8% on the initial investment ($100) but *also* 8% on last year's return ($8), for another 64¢. That 64¢ is your acorn. Because now you have $116.64, instead of the $116 you'd get without compounding. In the third year, you are getting your $8 return on the original $100, but also 8% on the first year's $8, the second year's $8, and that 64¢. Combined, these returns on top of returns push your investment from $124 (what you would get without compounding) to $125.97. Your acorn is sprouting. Ten years in, compound interest has turned your $100 into $216—vs. just $180 had you been adding merely 8% of the principal each year. Thirty years of compounding turns your $100 into $1,006, as opposed to just $340 without it—almost 7 times your initial investment from the effects of compounding alone. An oak tree.

Compound interest isn't an optional service your bank provides, it's built into the mathematics of interest. You can calculate its impact with this equation:

FUTURE VALUE =
Present value × (1 + Interest rate)$^{\text{Number of periods}}$

The math gets more complex in many real-world situations (e.g., if you make more than one investment, if the returns change over time), but this is the basic principle.

Here's how that math plays out with real numbers. The following chart shows the growth of your wealth if you invest $12,000 per year at 8% for ten years, then stop and watch your returns compound. If you invest this way from 25 to 35, then you will have

POWER OF COMPOUND INTEREST

Savings = $12,000 a year for 10 years, compounded at 8% annually

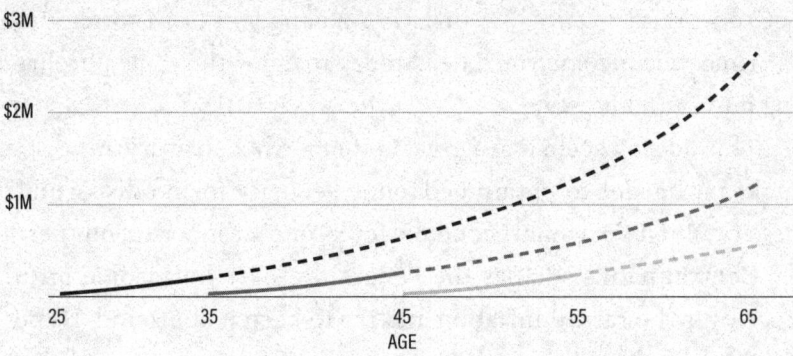

$2.5 million when you turn 65, whereas if you start at 45, you'll have only $500,000. The acceleration in the later years—when you really need it—is astounding. Warren Buffett accrued 99% of his wealth after the age of 52.

Investing is like planting oak trees. The best time to start is ten years ago. The second-best time is right now.

Inflation

Compound interest has an evil twin: inflation. While your returns are compounding and increasing your wealth, inflation is relentlessly using the same compounding power to reduce it. Inflation is a rodent gnawing at the pillars of wealth, the rot in your foundation, a rising tide that never ebbs. It's inevitable but not inescapable. You just have to outrun it.

The mathematics of inflation are identical to those of interest, but in the wrong direction. If the economy is experiencing 3% annual inflation, goods that cost $100 today will cost $103 one year from now. Looking further out, you can probably see where this is headed. Ten years from now, at 3% annual inflation, those same goods will cost $134. Thirty years from now (not an unreasonable time frame when we're talking about retirement savings), what costs $100 today will cost $243. Put another way, if you plan to retire in thirty years, 3% inflation means you need to plan for 2.5 times the income you'd need today to enjoy the same purchasing power and lifestyle.

This doesn't seem like a great system—a tax on everything that makes it harder to obtain economic security for no discernible benefit. But it's a primal economic force, one we ignore at our peril.

Central banks such as the Federal Reserve have some influence over the rate of inflation and try to keep it at around 2% per year, with mixed success. (There are various measures of prices used for inflation; the one you see in the media most often is the Consumer Price Index, or CPI, which aggregates the prices of various consumer goods.) Most of the early twenty-first century has been a period of particularly low inflation, but in 2022 we saw inflation in the U.S. reach 8% on an annual basis, and even higher abroad. Over the past century, U.S. inflation has averaged about 3%, and that's a good number to plan around.

Inflation is not uniform across all goods and services. In particular, education and healthcare costs have gone up faster than inflation for decades: college tuition has increased around 8% per year since 1980. Technology can be deflationary—computers have gotten cheaper over the years, and better, such that price per performance has plummeted. Some categories experience substantial volatility independent of long-term trends: gasoline, for example, has swung back and forth between $2 and $4 a gallon many times over the past twenty years.

The near certainty of inflation means we need to set our goals higher than we would otherwise. When planning for the long term, we need to remember that prices will be higher. An income stream of $100,000 per year might sound like a nice lifestyle today, until you recall that $100,000 thirty years from now will have the purchasing power of $41,200 today. If you are saving money for a newborn's college education, and four years of tuition costs $200,000 today, you will likely need at least $360,000 when the kid goes to college. (And that's assuming tuition increases at just 3%.)

Real Returns: Interest vs. Inflation

I said the only way to escape inflation is to outrun it. If you are anticipating a 3% inflation rate, that means you need to earn a minimum of 3% on your savings to maintain your purchasing power. But you don't want to simply maintain your purchasing power, you want to increase it. That requires a "real" return, which is your return on your investment *above inflation*. You can approximate this by subtracting the rate of inflation from your interest rate: earning 5% on your money in a 3% inflation environment produces a real return of roughly 2%.*

We refer to a financial metric, whether a rate of return or a dollar amount, as "real" if it has been adjusted to account for inflation, and as "nominal" if it has not. If something cost $100 ten years ago, and there has been 3% inflation since then, then we'd say that ten years ago it cost $100 in "nominal dollars" but $134 in "real dollars." In other words, it would take $134 today to match the purchasing power of $100 ten years ago. Sometimes you'll see it termed "constant dollars," or a dollar amount pegged to a specific year, such as "2023 dollars."

Failing to consider inflation is a common but severe oversight in financial planning. (Likewise, taxes, which I discuss in the next chapter, always need to be factored into your planning.) Holding wealth as cash can be comforting—you have access to it, it looks good, and it avoids the risk of short-term pain. Humans will avoid

---

*Subtracting the inflation rate from the nominal rate is a useful approximation, but the proper calculation is: (1 + nominal rate) / (1 + inflation rate)−1. For a nominal return of 5% and an inflation rate of 3%, the real return is 1.94%.

pain, to a fault, but it's not a good idea to have a lot of assets in cash except over the short term, as you are losing wealth each day. Holding cash costs you 3% a year, compounded. Invest, and run faster.

NOW

To secure the 64¢ that grows into hundreds of dollars, or the $12,000 that grows into $2.5 million, takes action now. Life in our present moment is a series of small things, and it can be difficult to perceive their potential. Overcoming our cognitive shortcomings and mastering the present moment is essential to building long-term wealth. Change the time scale of your life, and you change your life.

Cognitive Errors

Despite its power and importance, we are awful at wrapping our heads around time. Our brains are a hodgepodge of faulty heuristics and approximations (one study describes our minds as a "menu of illusions"). A simple experiment: You have a nine-day vacation planned, but at the last minute you are told you have to work one of the days. Bummer. Now reset. You have a three-day vacation planned only to learn you have to work one of the days. Does it hit different?

We perceive time with the same distortions that affect our view of physical distance—we foreshorten it. People asked to contemplate an unpleasant event occurring soon rate it as subjectively worse than the same event scheduled to take place further in the future. When asked to evaluate how close together in time two events are (e.g., two events a week apart, are they "one after another," "somewhat close in time," or "happening far apart"?), we describe pairs of events that are coming up soon as further apart than identically spaced events scheduled for a long time in the future. Just as money you have now is more valuable than the same amount of money in the future (see "Time's Arrow" in the next chapter), we perceive events in the near future as more significant than those in the distant future. (Like many of the cognitive complications in our brains, this is not entirely irrational—events predicted in the distant future are less likely to occur than imminent events—but it clouds our perception nonetheless.)

The passing of time plays tricks on us, and this is particularly true with investing. Our recollection of past performance is positively biased: We are better at remembering successful investments than unsuccessful ones. This echoes into our assessment of the future and makes us overconfident. The exception to this is when we have someone to blame for past failures, those we remember clearly, further distorting our judgment about our own capabilities. (Diligent record keeping, as I discuss below with respect to spending, is an antidote.)

Similarly, we tend to remember high points and normalize our expectations for the future: we anchor off the highs. This is the fundamental mechanism of lifestyle creep, which I come back to later in this chapter—our tendency to continually reset our baseline for what's an acceptable level of material comfort. Once you've stayed at the Four Seasons, you never enjoy a Hyatt the same way again. If we buy a stock at $20, it runs to $100, and then drops to $90, we feel we've lost $10, though in truth we've made $70.

And these issues are just on a single timeline. Finance requires us to consider alternate timelines, but we often fail to do so. I'm talking about opportunity cost—the unrealized gains of the investments we don't make. Young people weighing the cost of grad school make this mistake often. The cost is not just tuition. The money you won't make during your school years, and the compounding effect you won't enjoy on those earnings, can be even greater.

Finally, time is relative, but your lifetime is not. Earning and spending rise and fall in a predictable pattern for most of us. Until our late teens or early twenties, we are almost entirely spenders. In our twenties, earning begins to take off, unless delayed by graduate school, and, ideally, surpasses spending. But both keep rising as we increase our earning power and take on obligations. If we have children, spending typically drops when they become earning adults on their own, and if we've worked hard, been smart, and had some good fortune, our earning continues to accelerate—until we reach a point of diminished interest, energy, capacity, or desire. Earning may diminish gradually, or with the cheers and well wishes of a retirement party. Then finally, there is often an uptick in spending as we face the end, and the attendant costs of postponing it. Your priorities and your strategies will evolve as you travel this path.

Time Is the Real Currency

The richest person in the world and the poorest both get twenty-four hours in a day. The same seconds tick by for everyone. There are no refunds for time spent poorly, and no bank can lend you time. So while it's practical to measure your wealth and opportunities in money terms, the currency that really matters is time.

When I was a kid, my dad used to travel for work a lot. Before my parents split up, my mom and I would sometimes go with him to the Orange County Airport when he left on a trip. From the street, you could walk up a set of stairs to a wraparound balcony, where the bar was. No security. My dad would take me out on that balcony and cover my ears as aircraft engines screamed in anticipation. We'd watch as the pilots released the brakes and the planes made a 5,700-foot transformation from beached seals to soaring eagles. He taught me the difference between a 727 and DC-9 (three engines vs. two), and between the L-1011 and the DC-10 (third engine in the fuselage vs. halfway up the tail). The planes flown by Pacific Southwest Airlines had a smile painted on the nose, grinning at us through the balcony windows. It was time well spent, for both of us.

It also inculcated in me a lifelong love of airplanes. Some people watch ESPN late at night or browse fashion online. I spend hours researching and browsing planes. About six years ago, I realized a dream that began at that balcony bar and purchased my own jet, a Bombardier Challenger 300. Buying a plane and hiring full-time pilots and a management company to handle everything from hangar space to carbon offsets is an expensive and time-consuming process. It cannot be entirely justified as rational.

This is how I rationalized the irrational. At that point in my life, I lived with my family in Miami, but I had to be in New York once a week to teach, and I was on the road giving talks and taking meetings, somewhere across the U.S., also every week. I calculated that if I had my own plane, given my travel schedule, I could spend an additional 13 days a year at home (two major benefits of flying private: it flies on your schedule and from your car to the plane is a two-minute walk—no tickets, no security). So over 10 years I would have an extra 130 days with my family, or over 4 additional months with my boys, who've adopted this terrible habit of growing and, from what I understand, eventually leaving. The cost of the plane after tax benefits is approximately $1.2 million a year. The question: At the end of my life, will I want an extra $12 million in the bank or the memory of 4 more months with my boys? It was a lot of money for me, but it was one of the easiest financial decisions I've ever made.

DO THE MATH

What's thieving your time? Where are you being dollar wise and hour foolish? Take grocery shopping. Most areas have competing grocery delivery services with different models. If you spend 3 hours a week grocery shopping (driving to the store, shopping, bringing it back), that's 150 hours per year, or the waking hours of a two-week vacation. What is that two weeks of relaxation or additional work worth? Answer: more. Especially if the friction of grocery shopping, and the resulting empty shelves, means you order delivered *meals* two or three additional times per week; $25 a week of additional spending on Uber groceries might save you $100 on Uber Eats and still give you back time. That decision is a no-brainer. There are exceptions. If grocery shopping (or cleaning or cooking or washing your car) is cathartic, then knock yourself out.

This is not an argument for being lazy or spending all your money on services. If you pay someone to clean your house and bring you groceries, and then go deeper into your Netflix queue, you're just paying extra for Netflix. The point is to free up your time for what's truly productive, not just for what you'd rather do in the moment. Work, education, relationships. But mostly, when you are young, work.

Social media is likely one of the great wealth destroyers in history. It robs young people of years of time when they need it most—when investing in work and (real) relationships can compound. Pull up the screen time report built into your smartphone's OS. How many hours do you spend on social media? What is your return, other than the dopamine hits from addiction engineered by thousands of programmers, product managers, and behavioral psychologists? Pro tip: they are not on your side. Are you an influencer, such that this is time invested in work? A study of happiness found that social media use ranked dead last, out of twenty-seven different tracked leisure activities, in making people happy. (Try logging out of social apps when you stop using them so you have to make a more conscious decision to open them next time.)

Scolding people about spending too much time on their devices is low-hanging fruit, but work is also a big source of wasted time. Learn to use technology to your advantage: filter email, automate calendaring, use cloud services and tools developed specifically for your sector—there is a universe of productivity tools desperate for downloads. In a few pages, I'm going to get into spending and saving money, but what I'm really talking about is your time.

If your employer provides you with an assistant, invest in the relationship. Initially it will take longer than if you did things yourself, but this, too, is a form of investment. My superpower, if I have one, is recognizing that greatness is in the agency of others and spending the capital (time and money) to attract and retain people, vendors, and relationships that scale my narrow set of skills. This is where it pays to be fundamentally lazy, which I am. Since a young age, I've always wondered: Could someone else be doing this as well or better than me? If so, and the cost is less than what you could reasonably expect to earn with the additional time you retake possession of, then outsource it. As a budding professional, it may be a cleaning service and takeout meals. I hire out my home decor, technology, housekeeping, landscaping, tax planning, editing, wardrobe, nightlife (concierge), vacation planning, event planning, dog walking, physical training (personal trainer), driving, grocery shopping, nutrition, even gifting. So, yes, I'm an incompetent regarding most skills. However, I've reallocated all of this capital into two things: trying to be the best in the world at what I do for money; and doing more of the things I do for joy (e.g., walk the dogs on the weekends, spend a lot of time with my boys).

Technology is an enabler, but time management is a skill that transcends technology. Being good with money means being good with time. Some people have luck with a formal system—*Getting Things Done* by David Allen is a bible for some. Not my jam, but a popular system to adopt. My primary time management tactic is ruthless prioritizing. Emphasis on ruthless. It's been years since I saw the bottom of my inbox, or worried about a task I didn't get to. There are too many demands on my time, and I have the luxury of picking which ones to accept. My job's essential requirement is to be present and focused with 100% of my attention for short bursts of insight—TV hits, podcast recordings, public presentations, and chapters in books. If you engage me to speak at your event, know that at the dinner the night before I will seem aloof and distracted . . . as I am. I'm thinking about the stories that support the charts, the timing of the videos, and where I will slow my speech for dramatic effect. It comes at a price: I will likely forget the name of the hotel, and my assistant will have to remind me to eat that morning.

Youth's Advantage

I write often about the hoarding of wealth by older Americans and the challenges younger generations face building wealth. But there is one source of wealth older people lack and young people have in abundance: time. It's an irony of human perception, however, that many of us only come to appreciate these riches once we've squandered them. If you are young, you are rich in time, and just as the rich in money leverage their wealth, the young can do the same. Most of the time, however, they don't.

If you are young and time-rich, you can afford to have some fun with the money you're working so hard for. There's a disconnect between most personal finance advice, which is often "save to the point of pain," and what economists recommend as mathematically optimal, which is to delay saving, as in our early career years, most of us don't make enough to make saving worth it.

I'm 90% with the economists on this. Enjoy yourself now because the energy, passion, and willingness to take risks *does not last*. Dogs, spouses, kids, and mortgages will rob you of some of the carefree opportunities presented when you're in your twenties. But human behavior is not an economist's algorithm, and yours won't change as easily as numbers in a model. Learn to save now, build that muscle when you are young, so the habit of saving will compound.

The next few sections are about budgeting and saving, which are key to wealth, but if you are in the first decade or so of your career, read them as primarily about *behavior*, not outcomes. You should save, but as a means of creating the base and building good behaviors and character. It's when you move into your higher earning years that practice is over and the bigger game begins. You likely didn't save a lot in your twenties (difficult) and you need to catch up. As Lyndon Johnson said: "It's nut cutting time."

What Gets Measured Gets Managed

It's a trope you'll hear from the rich: "I never worried about money." Bullshit. Every rich person I know is *obsessed* with money. Not necessarily obsessed with obtaining it (some are) but with tracking, managing, and coddling it like Sméagol and his precious. It's a humble brag to say you don't think about money. Because what you're saying is, "I'm just so talented that money pours in and obviates the need to organize or think about long-term planning." To say you think a lot about money is to say you think a lot about sex. There's something uncomfortable and unseemly in admitting what we all know. Money and sex are on everyone's mind. Not necessarily in that order.

For most of my adult life, I've known how much money I had. The times I didn't, when I wasn't tracking spending, always ended with an unwelcome surprise. Not tracking your money, and your spending, is to eventually find out you have less.

When I was young, counting my money was easy: none. But I knew how much I owed my fraternity, what my credit card bill was. Now I talk to my broker every week. Measuring your money like this is a fine line, because you want to be **rationally obsessed**.

What do I mean by that? Maintain focused attention on your income, spending, and investments, without letting yourself become *emotionally* engaged. The trick is to keep it an intellectual exercise, to give yourself the feeling of control, not increase your anxiety.

I built a company on this principle, applied to managing digital businesses. At L2 we helped companies hold themselves accountable for their digital performance. At the beginning of a relationship, we worked with our clients to understand their goals and what it would take to reach them. Then we developed metrics to measure progress. There's an art to this.

"What gets measured gets managed" (attributed to, but possibly never said by, Peter Drucker) is as much a warning as it is a command. Metrics are bright shiny objects, and seeing them move provides positive feedback. But that's true whatever they measure. Measuring the wrong thing distorts action. Measuring something you have no control over creates frustration. The best metrics have an **effect** (what they measure contributes to your goal) and can be **affected** (your actions can change what is being measured).

Not all that matters is measurable, nor is the best measure always obvious. Your stocks may go down, but that should be measured against the performance of the broader market. A focus on just one metric ultimately renders the metric less useful. Only focusing on how much money you have, not your cholesterol or your kids' screen time or your spouse's joy, is a recipe for a financially secure and unhappy person. What you are ultimately measuring is your quality of life, which means having a variety of metrics to roll up to a (hopeful) sense of well-being.

When I talk about managing money, I emphasize the importance of saving and the need for budgeting. I like the *austerity* in those words, the sense that I'm gearing up for something difficult. It makes me feel virtuous. But that might be me. If you're less into macho posturing, replace "saving" with something more positive, such as "building" or "investing." Your goal isn't to save $1,000 this month, it's to build $1,000 of wealth. If "budgeting" sounds overly austere, try "allocating." And be wary of passive vocabulary that connotes weakness or lack of control—whatever you do, own it.

In the early years of wealth building—your twenties and thirties—tracking your savings is less important than tracking your spending. Spending determines savings (it has an **effect**) and it's what you actually do (it can be **affected**). Tracking your spending is not fun, but it's among the most critical behaviors you need to develop. Incidentally, if you want to be an entrepreneur, a gimlet-eyed focus on the money flowing out is a critical success factor. You might as well get started doing it with your personal spending. In life and in business, money has a way of leaking away when you're not paying attention. Capitalism's genius is inventing new things for us to spend money on that feel like needs, not wants.

Because almost all our spending today is electronic, tracking spending *seems* easier than it used to be, but that convenience of having everything on your devices is a trap. When I was a kid, my mother would pay our bills with paper checks, then dutifully record each expenditure, note where we'd spent cash, and "balance the checkbook." While it was a hassle, the benefit of that system was that you were *aware* of the spending in real time. If it's just an app that collects a bunch of numbers you never look at, that's not tracking your spending, that's ignoring it.

In the movie *House of Sand and Fog* (great film), each day Ben Kingsley writes down every expenditure, down to a Snickers bar. Early life goals: be more like Ben Kingsley. That doesn't mean you shouldn't spend money on frivolous things, just track it. As with time spent on less productive pursuits, it's fine as long as it's planned and you know how much you're allocating.

If you're not up for sitting at the kitchen table every Sunday night and breaking out paper checks, find other ways to introduce some friction into your spending, a construct that you'll follow so you can truly keep track. Online budgeting tools are great (e.g., Personal Capital, Rocket Money, Simplifi, YNAB), but they are even better if you use a mobile app to manually enter spending as it happens. Or schedule a weekly update of your budget. Building this habit can be hard, but an accountability partner can help. A spouse is obvious, but a parent, sibling, or close friend can help you commit to tracking your spending. Same concept as a workout buddy. If you're entrepreneurial, treat your personal finances like a start-up: make a plan, have regular reporting, and create a personal profit and loss statement.

The key is tracking what you *actually* spend rather than what you think you spend or what you plan to spend. People consistently underestimate their future spending. And not just in the distant future—one study found people underpredicted their spending for the upcoming week by $100. And then made the same error again the next week, and for the rest of the month. My NYU colleague Adam Alter found that people consistently underestimate their spending because they fail to account for "exceptional" expenditures—which aren't really exceptional at all, since one seems to happen more or less every month. Data > Intentions.

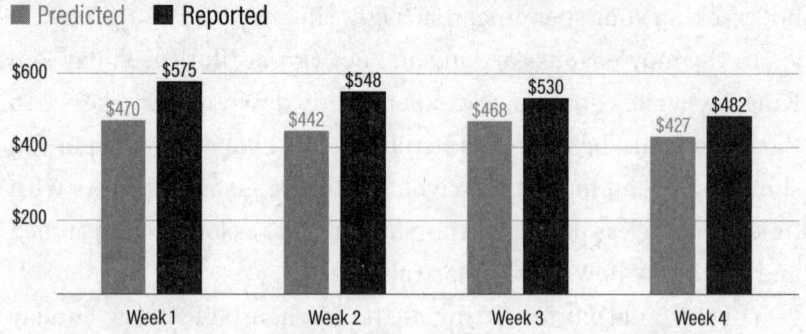

Source: Ray Howard et al., American Marketing Association, *Sage Journal* 59, no. 2, 2022

Measure your spending so you can manage it. But managing your spending is really an intermediate step toward increasing your *savings*. The easiest way to make a dollar is to save it, so you also want to track what you are saving (we'll get to what to do with it soon). Putting even a few dollars or a few hundred dollars a month into savings is a powerful step toward building wealth. As your income increases, especially when you get lump sums like bonuses, you'll need strong saving muscles.

I have trouble keeping weight on (I know, cry me a river) and correspondingly maintaining muscle. Being thin isn't a curse, but I'm vain about being muscular, and the science is clear that strength is strongly correlated with health and longevity. I work out several times per week (my antidepressant), so I'm good there. My diet is where I fall down. Food was not something I was brought up to enjoy—being raised by a single British mother who worked meant that food was (mostly) a punishment. In sum, I could eat one meal a day and be fine. So I have a nutrition app where I enter my goals and everything I eat. It tracks my calories, good and bad, and sends me notifications on progress, recommended adjustments, and so on. Something called the Hawthorne effect kicks in—being observed changes our behavior. If someone is watching me, I strive to impress them. Even if "they" are me. An app, ledger, or spreadsheet can create this feeling of being watched. What gets measured gets managed.

Fitness is a good analogy for managing your finances in another way: you have to do it *frequently*. Totaling up your spending once a month is not much more useful than going to the gym once a month. If you haven't looked at your credit card charges in three weeks, you aren't measuring or managing anything.

Eventually, you will accumulate enough savings that you'll have investments, and real skin in the game. Tracking your investments is where you need to guard most fiercely against emotional attachment. Having money in the markets means there will be volatility and down days, a lot of them. And we are wired to feel the pain of losses more than the pleasure from gains, so it takes fortitude to see your net wealth take a hit and not let it ruin your evening or your week.

There's only two ways to deal with that. You can stop checking. But capital is an active process, not a static entity, and if you aren't keeping tabs, it will surprise you. And money surprises are almost never good ones. Or you can check regularly, not obsessively, and with perspective. The point of investing is not to make money every day. It's not even to make money every year (most years, though). It's to make money over decades. And you will. If you invested $100 in the S&P 500 at the beginning of 2002, fast-forward twenty years and you'd have $517.66 at the end of 2022, a return of over 8% per year (5.7% above inflation). That twenty-year period included some of the worst years in the history of the markets, the most severe financial crisis in a century, and a global pandemic. Again, time and patience are your allies. A single stock's one-day performance is a coin flip. Over a decade, the S&P 500's rise is a near certainty.

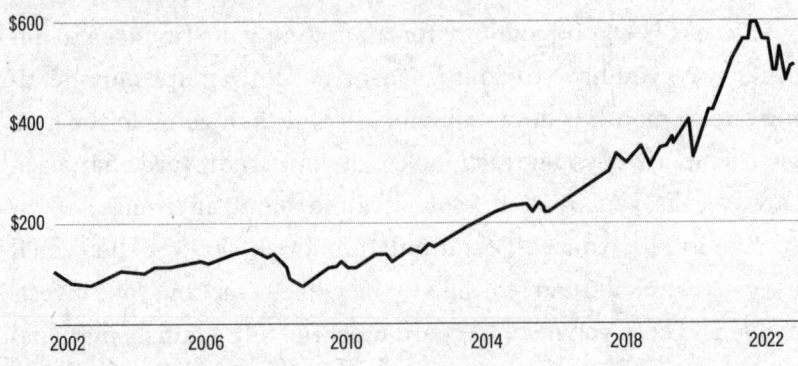

$100 INVESTED IN S&P 500

Source: Prof G Analysis of S&P Performance

Budgeting Your Head Above Water

Once you are measuring your spending, how do you manage it? In part, this happens naturally. Awareness encourages discipline. But to really grab the horns of your financial future, you need a plan. This is not where we spend fifteen pages walking through a personal finance spreadsheet. You can go as deep as you like into budgeting; there are plenty of books and online resources to help. What follows is an approach and a set of principles. Shape them to suit your situation. If you don't have a clear picture of your finances, the path to wealth will be circuitous and frustrating.

When you aren't making much money, budgeting is about being careful—spending with intention and feeling the weight. We lift heavy things to get stronger. This is not about anxiety or shame. If you blow your budget one weekend, or you struggle to fill the savings bucket, take a breath, adjust your plan as needed, then get back in the gym. Learn to throw nickels around like manhole covers, and you begin down the path to wealth. When I was at UCLA, I'd rack up bills to my fraternity for room and board. By the end of the year, I would owe over $2,000 (I miss the eighties). So, knowing I'd have to also come up with a $450 tuition payment in the fall (see above: the eighties), I'd need to make and save $3,000 over the summer.

A group of us would gamify saving and see who could spend the least in a given week. The record was $91 (including rent). I lived for eight weeks on Top Ramen, bananas, and milk. My splurge was on Sunday nights, a bunch of us on the crew team would go to Sizzler. (Steak, Malibu Chicken, and unlimited salad bar for $4.99. The. Eighties.) Six guys all over six feet and 180 pounds walking into a restaurant planning to ingest a week's worth of calories must have felt like an invading army sacking Westeros. In 1996, Sizzler declared chapter 11, and I'm fairly certain we played a role in the chain's demise. I worked, worked out, ate bananas, and attacked a salad bar. What's stranger than this is I look back on that summer fondly. We had a purpose: getting stronger and paying for college. Fortunately, I grew out of my $4.99 all-you-can-eat phase. If you haven't yet, you will, too.

Later, as your income rises and you begin to accumulate wealth, budgeting is more about planning and allocating—filling in various buckets for future expenses such as a new roof or a week in Europe. You progress from pinching pennies to booking hotels, and that means getting your head above water. Getting to the point where you have options, not just obligations. The following approach is how I suggest you get there.

Wherever you are, work out your baseline spending. Figure out your *realistic* monthly minimum spend. Your rent, grocery bill, cell phone, utilities, student loan payments, etc. Include a reasonable allowance for dining out and entertainment, vacations, and clothing. This is not your "I lost my job and the economy collapsed and I need to live on $91 a week" budget. It's a baseline for an actual life. If your social life revolves around going to clubs on Saturday night with your friends and brunch on Sunday, it's not realistic to tell yourself that from here on out, it's Netflix and Top Ramen. It's a best-case scenario for who you are and where you are in life. Your waterline.

Doing this accurately is harder than it sounds, which is why the section on tracking your spending comes before the section on planning it. You need data. Take a few months getting good at getting good data. Even then, you will miss things initially. Scrutinize your credit card bills and bank statements for the past year to catch those annual subscriptions and occasional expenses, and make sure they are included. Spread annual costs out into monthly amounts, so you're prepared when they come around and you face fewer of those "exceptional" expenses. For instance, if you have a professional license you pay $600 per year for, that's $50 a month in your waterline budget.

In this budget, include a line item for "savings." It can start comically small, $10 a month if you have to, but keep that item in your budget. Financial planners talk about "pay yourself first," and it's important to build that muscle. And it's good to have a goal. Budgeting for budgeting's sake isn't motivating. Just make the goal one you can hit *now*. Before you set your sights on being a baller, figure out what you spend on shoes every year. Baby steps.

Once you have a waterline budget, a realistic account of your baseline spend, compare that with your after-tax income. If you make a salary and your employer withholds money for taxes, then your paycheck is probably pretty close to your true income. If your finances are more complicated, you'll need to do some homework. (See the discussion of taxes in the next chapter.) If your waterline budget is more than your income, maybe it's Netflix and ramen after all. Look for easy economies—subscriptions you never use are a ripe target. Avoid encumbering your budget. When young, you should be sleeping, showering, and eating in your apartment, and little else. Live in a small, clean place near work and fun. Your professional trajectory is inversely correlated to how much time you are in your apartment. You're going to need to get your spending under your income eventually. Nobody gets rich by spending more than they make. But don't panic or give up. Above all, don't stop tracking.

Developing spending discipline is where you can apply many of the lessons of Stoicism. It's where the feedback loop of character and behavior pays off. While you are developing greater character, it's hard to white-knuckle spending discipline. Look for ways to jump-start the feedback loop. Life hacks and tactics can get you going. Some examples:

- **Spend cash.** This is about introducing friction into your spending. Counting the bills, seeing the dollars cross the counter, feeling your wallet lighten—all of this makes spending a more felt experience. Spending cash means you have to manually track your spending, but this is actually a benefit (if you do it), because the friction reinforces your awareness.

- **Round up your purchases.** Some banks will do this automatically when you use a card, and there are apps specifically for it as well. It's a simple idea: every purchase gets rounded up to the nearest dollar, and the change is moved into a savings account. This isn't likely to reduce your spending, but it provides quick wins, momentum you can build on.
- **Gamification.** Create a points system for the behaviors you want to encourage. If you want to reduce your restaurant spend by bringing lunch to work, give yourself a point every time you do it—and then track the points with something visible and tangible. Keep a jar on your kitchen counter and a bag of marbles in the drawer. Drop a marble in the jar every time you head out in the morning with lunch in your bag. Or get more elaborate—there are multiple apps, from to-do trackers to apps that score any behavior like a video game. The gamification can be its own reward, but if you choose to give yourself external rewards for achieving milestones, make sure the rewards are consistent with the behavior you are trying to promote. When you fill the jar of marbles tracking your homemade lunches, don't reward yourself by eating lunch out for a week.
- **Spending and accountability partners.** Save and gamify with a friend to get your competitive juices flowing. Easier still, tell someone whose esteem you value what your spending goal is for the day/week/month. Be *specific*, and promise follow up. "Dad, I'm limiting myself to $50 for lunch out this month. I will call you in exactly one month and tell you how I did." Then call him.

The more you measure, the more you manage, and eventually you get to a point—maybe you reached this point ten years ago or it's going to be a few years before you do—where you'll get your income over your waterline. Get your head above water.

Now you can breathe. You know what you need every month, and you know you've got it. How you spend every dollar above that line is a choice.

Goals

It's tempting to start setting ambitious savings goals for yourself, but that can backfire. Research on savings shows two things about goal setting. First, people set overambitious goals for savings in the future. The further out in time we set a goal, the more confident we are about our ability to save—and the more wrong we turn out to be. Set a goal for saving *this month*, and you are likely to be realistic and achieve your goal. Set a goal for saving in *six months*, and you are likely to set an unrealistic goal and fail to meet it.

That's bad, but the second thing research reveals makes it worse. When we set unrealistic goals and then get off track heading toward them, we lose motivation for the goal and may even act contrary to its achievement. Study participants who were asked to make savings goals several months out set more ambitious goals than participants who made savings goals for the next month, but actually saved *less*. Large, longer-term savings goals put your future self in a double bind, first by setting them up for failure with an unrealistic goal, and then by letting your frustration with failing to meet the goal make you worse off than you would have been without it.

Especially early in your budgeting and saving career, focus on your spending, not your savings, and make savings goals that are immediate and doable. Quick wins will build into long-term success. You don't start training for a marathon by running 26 miles on your first day.

As I discussed in "Stoicism," making more money typically leads to spending more money. Lifestyle creep is a force of nature. You will constantly reset your expectations, and the standard of living that seemed luxurious when you made $50,000 a year will be barely adequate when you make $150,000. Your friends will be making more money, and their lifestyle spending will increase. And capitalism will relentlessly find new ways to tempt you. Your consumption bucket is going to grow. What you must do is apply the lessons of Stoicism to keep it growing slower than your income.

I can't tell you how much more you should save each year; there's too many variables and it's too personal. But I can tell you that if your income grew 20% last year, and your consumption grew 25%, you're on the wrong path. A growing delta between your income growth and your consumption growth is the foundation of your economic security.

You will have more success managing the growth rate of your consumption if you avoid two things: **commitment** and **fluctuation**. Commitment is great in relationships, lousy in consumption. Subscriptions, assets that require maintenance (e.g., cars, boats,

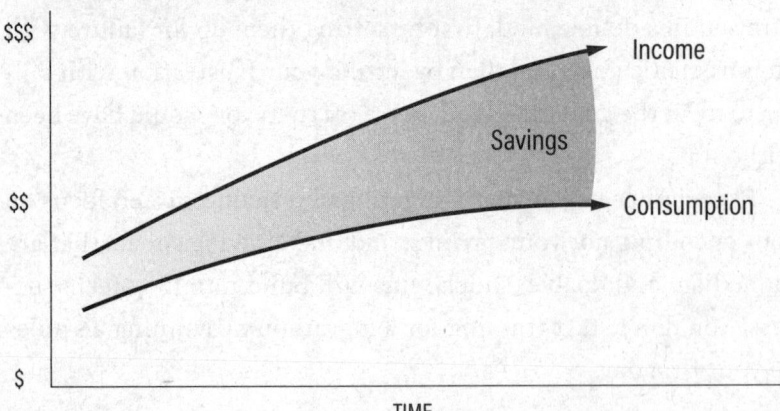

FOUNDATION OF ECONOMIC SECURITY

houses, houseboats—seriously, don't buy a houseboat), anything purchased on a payment plan (aka "buy now, pay later")—all of these make it harder to keep your future consumption under control because you've stacked the deck against yourself.

Fluctuation works differently. It undermines your sense of predictability and control, which is critical to managing your budget. The occasional splurge, especially if you've planned and saved for it, is living a good life. Finishing every month with wildly varying spending will keep you from having one.

Three Buckets

Conceptually, you can choose among three buckets for your incremental dollars. (Where you actually keep the dollars and how you invest them, I cover in the next chapter.) Consumption is the easiest (for most people)—that's buying a nicer quality of life right now with consumer goods and services. Consumption isn't all frivolous or optional: you have to eat, you have to have a place to live. Initially, this is almost everyone's largest bucket. The money you've got in your waterline budget, that's consumption.

Consumption expenditures are *not* investments. In regular conversation, we use the term "investing" loosely. Even in this book, I refer to investing in personal relationships. In that sense, paying for college or an advanced degree is an "investment" in your career. But when you are considering how to allocate your capital, you need to be more rigorous. An investment in this context is something that you expect to generate a direct financial return—once the transaction is complete, your capital will have *increased*. Formally, spending is called consumption because you are consuming goods and services in the economy. But you should think of it as describing how your money is consumed by the transaction: never to be seen again.

The distinction is not always clear with expenses that won't

INCOME ALLOCATION

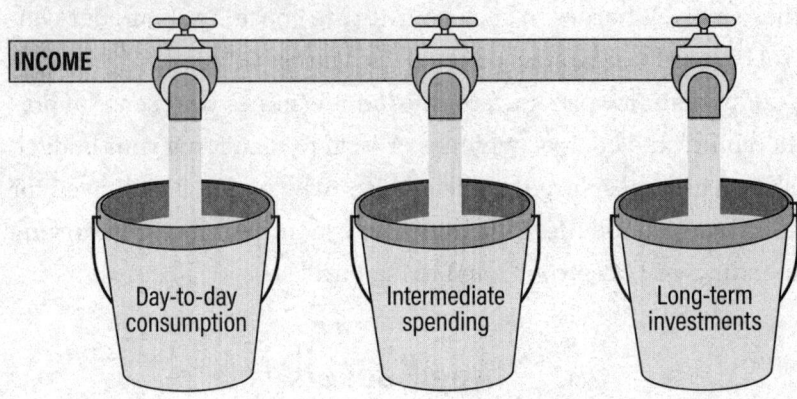

generate a direct financial return, but which you can reasonably expect to increase your income or reduce your expenses. Higher education is the classic example: your degree *might* increase your earning power, so the expense has some flavor of investment about it. You can't sell your diploma, however, so tuition is not an "investment" in the strict sense that matters for financial planning.

I emphasize this because it's tempting to justify consumption by rebranding it "investing." New shoes before a job interview, a membership at a swankier gym, these are things that might improve your economic situation, but they remain consumption, not investment. Some types of consumption are perhaps more noble than others—buying gifts for other people, donating to charity—but the money is still gone once you spend it. Think of it as making yourself less rich. Don't get me wrong, I *love* consumption, and you deserve a nice life. But every dollar is a choice.

Beyond your consumption bucket, there are two buckets for money you will invest. The long-term budget is for "retirement," as my generation calls it, though that's a term that's fading in relevance. Call it wealth building, long money, the foundation of your economic security. It's the $2,000 my friend Lee contributed to his

IRA. It's what's going to get you to a beach with a mai tai, watching your grandkids play in the surf, or whatever your future self desires.

The third bucket, intermediate spending, is the gray area between short-term consumption and long-term investment. Large, anticipated expenses (and some not-so-anticipated): down payment for a car or house, graduate school tuition, buy-in to a professional partnership, major medical bills.

To be clear, the distinctions between the intermediate and long-term buckets and the subcategories of intermediate expenses ("emergency fund," "kids' college savings," "house down payment") are what's known as mental accounting. They are conceptual categories, and they can be useful, but they are not "real" (money is money, however you label it), and relying on them too much can distort your decision-making. Use them, but don't be bound by them.

Every dollar above the waterline is going to go to one of these three places. Your job is to put enough into consumption so you don't resent your choices (that will require less than you think) and to fund your intermediate and long-term investments at the rate that will get you to economic security. I'll cover what to do with the money in the intermediate and long-term buckets in the next chapter.

Allocating Your Buckets

Early in your career, unless you are extremely fortunate, your long-term bucket is not going to get much love. That's okay. It's crucial that you put *something* into it, however. Habits matter. You are building your savings and investing muscles for when you have more money to put to work. As long as you are doing that, you're doing your job. Your twenties won't last forever (a good/bad thing) and you deserve a nice life now for all that hard work. If you're into your peak earning years, however, you want to push harder on the savings pedal, because you've got the horsepower in reserve.

Ideally you'd sink all your savings into the deep dark of your retirement plan, where it can put down roots and provide the foundation of your future economic security. But there's a complication: you will need some of the savings sooner. This is the intermediate bucket. The purpose of this bucket is to ensure that when the time comes for large expenses (anticipated or not) you have enough cash to cover them. The intermediate bucket is a metaphor to help you manage two factors: **liquidity** and **variability**.

Liquidity refers to how easily you can convert an asset into something else—either another form of investment or for use as consumption. Money in your savings or checking accounts is very liquid. Publicly traded stocks and bonds are liquid, as are most other assets traded on exchanges (more on this in the next chapter). A house is much less liquid. You can get the money out by selling the house, or less dramatically with a home equity loan or by refinancing your mortgage, but it takes time and carries transaction costs. Money in a traditional IRA or 401(k) is also accessible, but you'll pay taxes and, unless you are at retirement age, a 10% penalty. Equity in a private company is highly illiquid. Obviously, liquidity is more important the sooner you expect to need the money.

The other factor is variability. I'll get more into this in the next chapter when I discuss risk and diversification, but the key point for planning is that the prices of some assets hold steady, while others go up and down. Cash doesn't vary at all (it declines in value due to inflation, but a $10 bill will always cost $10). Stock in high-growth tech companies is highly variable, and all stocks are at least moderately variable. Recall the performance chart of the S&P 500 over the past two decades: over the long term, it averages out to 8% growth, but returns vary from year to year. You don't care about variability for your long-term investments, because you will hold the asset through the down phases and can time your sale to avoid them. But it poses a risk for shorter term planning because you may be forced to sell in a down phase.

Simply put, the closer you are to needing a sum of money, the more liquidity and the less variability you want. If you are shopping for houses and you plan on making a $200,000 down payment, having $200,000 in your IRA (illiquid) is unhelpful and having $200,000 in a single growthy tech stock is unwise (variable). If you plan on buying a house in five years, however, you can afford more variability and don't need to be as liquid. The distinction between the "long-term" and "intermediate" buckets is not precise—these are metaphors, not real tin buckets.

Intermediate planning is about aligning your liquidity and variability with your anticipated (and unanticipated) expenses, in the context of your overall financial situation.

The Emergency Fund

How do these principles apply to the sacred cow of personal finance books, the emergency fund? First, if you have no liquid savings at all, building up a small, liquid, non-variable emergency fund is a great early goal. It's practical—emergencies will happen—and it's good training for your saving muscles. From zero, a $1,000 emergency fund is a good target. Why $1,000? It's a round number, it's enough to cover many unexpected expenses you may face, and it's achievable for most people. This should be an early goal in your savings project—$1,000 in a savings account, used for emergencies. (Note: it's okay to use the emergency fund, that's the point—it's a buffer, to keep your budget on track, not a sacred idol you worship and never touch.) Do that, and you're already ahead of the pack: 56% of American adults don't have even $1,000 in backup cash.

The label "emergency fund" is useful, but don't forget that it's just mental accounting. What it really means to have a $10,000 "emergency fund" is to have at least $10,000 in liquid, low-variability assets. In practice that means: an interest-earning savings account, a money market fund, or highly conservative investment funds. In the years following the Great Financial Crisis, interest rates were so low that it was difficult to get any kind of return without variability. The zero-interest-rate era appears to be over, however, and, at least as I write this, savings accounts are offering 3.5% to 4% interest, which should be sufficient to protect your emergency cushion against the effects of inflation, and possibly even earn a bit of a real return.

A lot of financial planning fetishizes mental accounting and suggests that you need one account for your emergency fund, another account for your house down payment, another for a college fund, etc. Those are training wheels, and once you have accumulated tens of thousands of dollars in assets, you don't need training wheels. Money is money (economists say it's "fungible"), and what you label it is less important than where you invest it. Forecast what your anticipated expenses will be, when you expect to have them, and build in a cushion of liquid, low-variability investments for emergencies. Layer in the additional savings you expect to accumulate over time. If you have no intermediate bucket expenses coming due in the next year, then the only money you need in liquid, low-variability assets is your emergency cushion. For the rest, invest where you expect the highest return (more on that in the next chapter), without regard to liquidity or variability. As intermediate expenses get closer, shift assets out of those more aggressive assets and into more liquid, less variable investments.

Above $1,000, what should your emergency cushion be? The classic personal finance advice is from three to six months of your income. But the real answer is, it depends. And for a lot of people, especially young people, that much isn't necessary. If you have a stable income with an employer that's financially strong, if you don't have unbreakable financial commitments (no mortgage, no kids), if you are mentally and physically well, if your immediate family is prosperous and supportive—then you realistically don't need so much cushion. The less those descriptors apply to you, the more cushion you need.

What's a *realistic* worst-case scenario (i.e., you lose your job), and what would you need to ride it out without severe hardship (accounting for how much you can reasonably reduce your consumption if you need to)? That's what you want to have in liquid, non-variable investments.

And you don't need to maintain your cushion at that level all the time. First, there are actual emergencies—use the cushion when they arise. But also, when the time comes to make a major expenditure, consider reducing your emergency cushion to make it happen, then building it back up. Again, it depends on your circumstances, but don't make major life decisions based on an arbitrary dollar figure that you want to keep in an "emergency fund" (or any other mental accounting bucket). If you find the ideal starter home, and you need another $20,000 to make the down payment, don't pass on it because a financial planning book told you to keep a $30,000 emergency fund at all times. Drop your cushion to $10,000, buy the house, then be disciplined about rebuilding your cushion. Money is fungible, and you are saving it so you can use it, not to make the green numbers go ever upward.

Take the Match

I'll cover investing and taxes in more detail in the next chapter, but there's one aspect of that discussion that's relevant to bucket allocation and too important to wait. That's the use of retirement funds: 401(k), IRA, and Roth. Short version: use them. They combine forced savings with tax minimization and the power of compounding; they can be the bedrock of your economic security.

How to use them? Highest priority is if you have an employer match in your 401(k), max that out. You will never get a better investment than an immediate, tax-deferred 100% return. Fund this up to the matching contribution level under almost any circumstance.

Contributions beyond the match level are likely a good idea but should be determined by your tax situation and liquidity requirements. There is no single recipe for how to make use of these plans, and no plan is "better" than any other in all circumstances. I'll cover these in more detail in the next chapter when I discuss taxes.

Allocation in Practice

Let's look at a hypothetical example of how your money might be allocated over a typical month. Jack is a year into his career post-college, and early in his savings journey. Jack's salary is $60,000 and his waterline budget is $3,000 per month, which is mostly rent, groceries, and entertainment. He's calculated that a $3,000 emergency cushion is sufficient—his job is fairly secure, his lease is month-to-month, and his parents live close enough that in a worst-case scenario, he could move home until he got back on his feet. He has a savings account that pays 4%, and he has managed to put $500 into it so far, on his way toward building that $3,000 cushion in a liquid, low-variability savings account. His job has a 401(k), and he's put 5% of his salary into it for a year, so there's $3,000 that's his long-term bucket.

At the beginning of the month, after paying his rent and credit card bill, Jack has just $20 in cash and $100 left in his checking account. He'll need most of his paycheck to cover his consumption budget. But that's okay, what matters is that he's got a budget and he's building good habits.

After taxes and his 5% 401(k) deduction, Jack gets two paychecks in the month for $1,750 each, a total of $3,500—and $250 more has gone into his 401(k). Of that, $3,000 stays in his checking account to cover his consumption for the month. Most months, he doesn't quite stay within his budget, either, and this month another $300 gets eaten up by consumption. That leaves $200 in savings.

To get in the habit of building his long-term bucket beyond the 401(k), he opens a brokerage account at Fidelity and puts $20 in there. In the next chapter, we'll see how he can put that to work in higher risk, long-term assets like corporate stock. Twenty dollars isn't much, but it's a start.

The last $180 he moves into his savings account, so now he's got $680 saved up toward his emergency cushion of $3,000. At this rate, it will take Jack another year to fund his full emergency cushion. If he can tighten up his spending, however, and stay within his waterline budget, he could fund his emergency cushion in just three months. He's starting to make a habit of checking his budget every few days and reminding himself that every dollar is a choice. Down the road, he's thinking about business school, and as that gets closer, he'll want more than $3,000 available in his savings account, but for now, once he hits $3,000, he plans to put all his excess savings into his long-term investments.

Debt

There's another bucket, the anti-bucket of debt. Debt is a controversial topic in personal finance, and a personal one. Here's my take: debt is a weapon, but a dual-edged one. Use it with care.

Long-term debt used to finance long-term assets is sensible, even genius. Debt gives you "leverage." Just as a lever and a fulcrum multiply the force you can apply, debt multiplies the earning power of your money. Rich people and corporations *love* debt because of the power of leverage. If I buy a $1 million house with $1 million in cash, and it increases in value to $2 million, I've doubled my money. That's nice. But if I buy that $1 million house for $200,000 in cash and an $800,000 mortgage, when I sell it for $2 million, I pay off the mortgage and keep $1.2 million—I've grown my money 6 times. That's leverage. Yes, I made the same total amount, $1 million, but I only had to tie up $200,000 to do it. Remember opportunity cost: I've freed up $800,000 for other investments by using debt.

Using a mortgage to buy a home you live in is almost always a sound personal finance strategy. (I cover this in more detail in the next chapter when I discuss real estate as an asset class.) Cars are a tougher call. Auto loans are more often used to get into a *more expensive* car rather than to acquire the transportation function of a basic car. The car salesman wants you to ask: "How much car can I afford?" The better question: "How much car do I need?" A car loan is a commitment to consumption spending. If an expensive car brings you joy, then it's worth saving the bulk or all of the cost before buying it. Earn your pleasures; you'll enjoy them that much more.

Short-term debt is the thief in the night: high-interest-rate credit cards, buy-now-pay-later loans, store financing. Even "no interest" loans are still commitments to future consumption, robbing from your future to finance the present. A good baseline principle is that debt should never outlive the asset it was used to acquire. A 30-year mortgage on a home passes this test. Carrying a credit card balance for a year so you can buy shoes you'll wear for a season doesn't. Treat yourself, but don't cheat yourself.

Early in your career, bridging the gap between your income and your consumption with short-term debt is hard to avoid, and in moderation it won't ruin your future. Just be smart about it. Don't get into a car loan if you are carrying credit card debt. *Measure* your short-term debt, don't hide it in five different accounts. Put it at the top of your budget spreadsheet, build payments into your waterline budget, figure out how you will eventually pay it down. And don't let it stop you from building savings muscles. Even if you are paying down an 18% credit card, put $10 a month in your savings.

If debt payments are keeping you from getting your head above water, you need a plan to pay them down. If you are in serious debt trouble—meaning, you can't make even your minimum payments, or your total debt load is increasing every month with no end in sight—you should seek credit counseling. Be careful here: you want to find a *nonprofit* credit counseling organization with *certified* credit counselors. The Consumer Financial Protection Bureau offers a guide and links on its website.

THE FUTURE

While your present self is dutifully budgeting and putting money away, your future self is out there on the timeline waiting to spend it. Your job is to balance your happiness with theirs. Financial planning advice naturally focuses on the needs of your future self, but it really is a balance. A plan that overly deprives you of joy in the present is one you probably won't stick to, and if you do, why? What kind of a person will you be if you get there through deprivation?

You Are Not Your Future Self, but You Will Be

Working hard to earn money and developing the discipline to save it are both hard things. They take sustained effort, and there are setbacks along the way. But planning for the distant future is hard in a different way. It's hard because you can't see the target, you can't even really know if you've hit it until you get there. But it's important that you make the effort because a vision of your future self is both an important planning tool and a motivational one.

Wherever you are in your life, think back a few years and compare who you are now with who you were then. Notice the differences. What brings you joy now that wasn't a priority before? Looking back, I went through some distinct phases (though they didn't feel so distinct at the time). I've always been motivated by a combination of anxiety about money, desire for material pleasures, and a need to please and impress the most important people in my life. The balance of those drives has changed radically over time, as has what I think I need to do to achieve them.

Now look ahead, picture yourself in five years, twenty-five years, or fifty. Do you think the pace of personal change will slow down? Do you think drives and desires that have been so changeable to this point are set in stone? Ask someone twenty or thirty years older than you, "Are you the same person you were two decades ago?" Then ask them, "Are you the person you thought you'd be?" The fallacy that you won't keep changing is known as projection bias, defined as people's tendency to "exaggerate the degree to which their future tastes will resemble their current tastes."

Predicting our individual futures is becoming more difficult for a societal reason as well: the notion of retirement is changing. Twenty percent of "retired" Americans are still working at gig jobs, and the majority say they're doing it because working continues to give meaning to their lives. Getting old is more expensive than it used to be, in part because health care costs keep rising, but also because we live longer. (At least we get something for those health care expenses.) People over 65 have the highest divorce rate of any age group, and divorce is brutal on your finances: men and women who divorce after 65 see a 25% and 41% decline in their standard of living, respectively.

The most important thing to know about planning for your future self is that you won't get it entirely right, because you will change in ways you can't predict. Precision is not a useful tool here. Don't tie yourself to some specific absolute must-have objective. That perfect house on the bluff you go by on your morning jog might never come on the market. Dining at every Michelin-starred restaurant or climbing the seven summits are fine goals, but you'll sacrifice plenty along the way to get there, and once you do, you might regret the choice. Goals like this (even more modest ones) shouldn't become inviolable. If you work ten years to save up enough to start your own graphic design shop but when you are scouting for office space, you get no pleasure from imagining yourself in any of them, it's okay to say, "I've changed, this isn't my goal anymore." It's okay to want the beach house. It's great to put a picture of your dream beach house on your desktop to motivate you, to use the price as an anchor in your financial planning. The trap is equating "rich" with "beach house," so that when it comes time to make real trade-offs, you make the trade-offs that serve who you've become, not who you thought you'd be. Because you don't live the life of your dreams, you live your life.

Economic security is about having options, not closing them off.

Black Swans Will Happen, Meteors Will Strike

Daniel Kahneman says the lesson to take from surprising events is that the world is surprising. Every few years, something is going to come along that knocks your plans askew. A global pandemic, a car accident, meeting the love of your life. Unfortunately, the biggest surprises tend to be negative ones—there are a lot more cancer diagnoses than lotto jackpots. Whatever surprise happens, however, you want to be able to adjust. Roll with the punches.

Accessible savings—the financial planner's beloved emergency fund—is a proof point for yourself that your work is paying off, and it's your first line of defense against the inevitable unexpected. Just as important as your financial defenses against the unexpected, however, are your psychological defenses. This is why building economic security ultimately comes down to character, not math. When your carefully detailed budget plan is blown wide open by life, success comes from taking a break to freak out, then picking yourself up, surveying the wreckage (while reminding yourself that nothing is ever as good or as bad as it seems), and redoing your plan to account for the meteor that crashed into your house. Maybe the crater would make a nice swimming pool?

Planning and Advisers

In the introduction, I provided a quick and dirty way to estimate what you'd need in assets to achieve economic security. Take your desired burn rate—your annual spend, plus taxes—and multiply it by 25 (sometimes called the 4% Rule because it assumes a 4% investment return above inflation). It's a good way to get your planning started, but it's only a start.

As your earning power increases, and if you've applied these lessons, your savings have grown with it, your obligations have likely increased, as well as the overall complexity of your tax and investment needs. That 25x burn number is a useful target, but it's not a plan. If you're über-organized—you make a spreadsheet to go on vacation—and you've developed good budgeting discipline, it's possible to continue on your own. But seriously consider bringing in professionals. Depending on your wealth and complexity, this may mean a tax adviser, an accountant, perhaps a lawyer. But the key figure is a financial planner.

All kinds of people offer their services as financial planners, but you want something very specific. You want someone who is professionally trained and licensed, and—this is crucial—is a **fiduciary**. Meaning someone who is legally obligated to put your interests before their own. You are looking for two formal designations: first, that the company your adviser works for is a registered investment adviser (RIA) and, second, that the adviser personally holds either a certified financial planner (CFP) or a chartered financial analyst (CFA) license.

There are plenty of qualified advisers, so don't deviate from these requirements. Don't hire someone to guide you on the path to economic security because they were in your sorority pledge class or they get great sports tickets. It will be the most expensive Knicks game you've ever been to.

Here's the critical thing about advisers. You aren't paying them for investment returns. Over the long term, nobody beats the market. And if someone does have the secret to above-market returns, they aren't going to be sharing it with you for a fixed percentage. You're paying an adviser for planning, accountability, and confidence. The more wealth you accumulate and the more complex your life gets, the more valuable these services become.

The one person more important to your economic security than your financial adviser is your spouse. No matter how compatible or similar you are with your partner, you won't be identical with respect to money. No two people are. Our relationship with money goes deep, and we often don't perceive the roots or the full complexity of that relationship. You will need to take time, and have many conversations, to pull back the layers and truly sync up your approaches to saving, spending, and planning. A good financial planner can help with this; it's a big part of the job. Always remember, you are building economic security so you can invest time in your relationships and enjoy them. That's the real end game here.

ACTION ITEM BULLETS

- **Value your time above all other assets.** Squander money, and you can earn it back. Squander time, and it's gone forever.

- **Appreciate the power of compound interest.** A small return compounded over many years grows surprisingly large.

- **Beware the power of inflation.** The flip side of compound interest is that money in the future will purchase less than it does today. Your savings goals and investment strategies must reflect this.

- **Be rationally obsessed with money.** Maintain focused attention on your income, spending, and investments, without letting yourself become emotionally engaged.

- **Track your actual spending.** If you only track one metric in your life, make it your spending. Not what you plan to spend or think you spent: the true dollars going out the door every day.

- **Save some money, even a few dollars, every month.** Saving money is a muscle, it gets stronger through use. Get your reps in.

- **Avoid financial commitments.** Commitment is great in relationships but perilous in finance. Be wary of subscriptions, payment plans, and assets that require maintenance.

- **Stabilize your spending.** Fluctuating spending undermines your control, and lack of control over spending *never* results in less spending.

- **Determine your "head above water" budget.** The baseline for your spending decisions should be a realistic minimum monthly budget. Don't forget to plan for annual subscriptions and other infrequent expenses. They won't forget you.

- **Give your future self options.** You'll change in ways you can't predict, so make allowances in your planning for evolving preferences.

ACTION ITEM BULLETS

- **Set achievable, short-term savings goals.** "A million by the time I'm thirty" isn't a plan, and it won't help you get there. But "Five thousand dollars in my savings account by October 1" is something you can use to make daily decisions. Make enough of the right ones, and you'll have that million.

- **Make spending a thoughtful choice.** Unless you are deep in debt, it's neither feasible nor desirable to save every dollar you don't absolutely need to spend. Especially when you're young—life is for living, and many of the best experiences in life . . . aren't free.

- **Organize your expenses into three buckets.** Every dollar above the waterline goes to one of them:

    - **Day-to-day consumption** is food and shelter, clothes, transportation, loan payments, and other regular expenses.

    - **Intermediate expenses** are large and infrequent expenses such as graduate school tuition and house down payments.

    - **Long-term savings** is money you're putting aside for investments, so you can cover your future consumption. This bucket is your future financial security.

- **Keep your intermediate bucket funded with low-variability, high-liquidity investments.** When the time comes to write these checks, you want to have the cash available. Don't tie this money up in real estate or private company stock, or gamble it on high-risk investments.

- **Take the match.** If your employer offers you a matching 401(k) or similar program, maximize the *match* portion ahead of any other spending or investment. A tax-deferred guaranteed 100% return is the best investment opportunity you will ever see.

- **Roll with the punches.** Bad things will happen; you'll make mistakes. These are reasons to adjust your plans, not abandon them. Nothing is ever as good or as bad as it seems.

FOCUS

+

(STOICISM

×

TIME

×

DIVERSIFICATION)

4
DIVERSIFICATION

F EW PEOPLE CAN ACHIEVE WEALTH through income alone. Yes, some do: Fortune 100 CEOs, NFL quarterbacks, A-list movie actors. For the rest of us, income is the foundation. A start, with more work needed. Specifically, we need to convert income from our labor into something more scalable: capital.

Capital is money in motion, money that's being used to build value. It's money at work. Businesses, governments, financial institutions, all operate on a steady supply of capital—and they pay for its use. Similar to greatness, wealth is achieved in the agency of others: leveraging other people's skills (teams, employees, vendors) and capital. It's nearly impossible to build a company or wealth without other people and outside capital. Providing capital for another's use (and getting paid for it) is investing.

Investing is also the bridge between the hard work asked of you in the previous chapters and the economic security promised at the outset. It's also the easiest part of the process. Unlike the requisite personal growth we discussed in Stoicism, the grind of a career in Focus, or the discipline and daily battles in Time, when it comes to investing, someone else is doing the real work—you can sit back and enjoy the fruits of their labor. Congratulations, you're now a capitalist.

Most personal finance books shield readers from the underlying mechanics of capitalism and the financial markets. It's well intentioned and probably the right approach for many people. Finance is a vast ecosystem, with its own language and culture (several, in fact). You don't have to master it to achieve long-term investment returns. Getting into the weeds takes time and cognitive energy that can be spent elsewhere (opportunity cost). It's not the worst idea to leave it to the pros.

I'm taking a different approach. This is the longest chapter in the book, because in addition to coaching you through strategies for investing your capital, I want you to be fluent in the principles that underpin these strategies. The financial system touches our lives every day in ways seen and unseen, and anyone benefits from a working understanding of it. These next few pages just scratch the surface—but they provide more detail than we teach in most high schools and colleges, or around our kitchen tables.

This chapter has five main sections. First, some background principles regarding investing, including why you should do it, and how to think about both individual investments and your investments as a whole. Second, an overview of the financial markets—the marketplace for money, where you put your money to work. Third, a catalog of the major asset classes available in that market, and specific investment recommendations. Fourth, insight into an often overlooked aspect of investment strategy: taxation. Taxes are the price we pay for living in an ordered society. However, our tax *system* is not orderly, and if you don't plan around it, you will pay more than your share. The final section contains some practical advice gleaned from four decades of investing while trying to build a life.

If you work in finance, much of this chapter may be familiar, even rudimentary. Read or skim at your discretion but seeing familiar ground from 20,000 feet can provide a new perspective. If you are new to finance, it may feel overwhelming—it's a lot of information. Finance is a complex landscape, and it's hard to learn about any one piece without having a working knowledge of the others.

Beyond what I cover here, I urge you to make a habit of following the business section of your preferred news sources. Business news has gone mainstream over the past few decades, such that many business stories cross over into general news, but those tend to be the outlier stories, with an emphasis on consumer products and dramatic events. With the basics covered in this book, however, you'll be in good shape to go a bit deeper and follow the markets in more detail.

What will really imprint these principles will be putting them to work with your own investments. As you engage with the financial world, your knowledge will fill in, and what I cover here will come into focus. I promise.

BASIC PRINCIPLES OF INVESTING

I've acquired my own knowledge (which grows daily) from too many sources to count, but the root of it is that I was fortunate as a child—I had a mentor.

When I was 13, I thought I was invisible. Not literally see-through, but socially and intellectually . . . absent. My mom was dating a man who was generous with me, and once I asked him about stocks, which I'd read about in the news that day. He answered whatever my immediate question was, then paused and considered me for a moment. He opened his wallet and withdrew two crisp $100 bills. "Go buy some stock at one of those fancy brokers in the Village." I asked how I would do that. "You're bright enough to figure it out, and if you don't by the time I'm back next weekend, I want my money back." I had never seen a $100 bill before. Terry was kind and took a real interest in my life. He was also married with a family. We were that second family he'd spend every other weekend with that's referenced in TV shows but never the subject of those shows. Anyways, that's not what this story is about.

The next day after school, I marched down to the corner of Westwood and Wilshire and into the offices of Dean Witter Reynolds. A woman with big gold jewelry asked if she could help me, and I told her I was there to buy stock. She paused. Suddenly self-conscious, I blurted out, "I have $200," and showed her the still-crisp bills. Startled, she gave me a clear-windowed envelope, and told me to wait a minute. Sitting, I rearranged the bills in my new envelope so I could see Ben Franklin through the cellophane. A man with curly hair came into the lobby and approached me.

"I'm Cy Cordner. Welcome to Dean Witter."

Cy took me to his office and gave me a thirty-minute lesson in the markets. The ratio of buyers to sellers determined price movements. Each share represented a small piece of ownership. Amateurs act on emotion, pros on numbers. Buy what you know: stocks in companies whose products you like or admire. We decided to invest my bounty in 13 shares of Columbia Pictures, ticker CPS, at $15-3/8.

For the next two years, every lunch hour, I'd go to the phone booth on the main field of Emerson Junior High School and, for two dimes, call Cy to discuss my "portfolio." Sometimes after school, I'd walk to his office to get the update in person (see above: few friends). He'd type in the ticker and tell me what CPS had done that day and speculate why the stock had moved: "The markets were down today," meaning there were more sellers until prices came down and attracted more buyers into the market. "It looks like *Close Encounters of the Third Kind* is a hit." "*Casey's Shadow* is a bomb." Cy also took the time to call my mom. Not to pitch her for business (we had no money), but to let her know what we discussed in the calls and say nice things about me.

After heading to high school, I lost touch with Cy. Then Coca-Cola bought Columbia Pictures, and several years later I sold my Coke shares to pay for a road trip to Ensenada with my UCLA fraternity brothers. However, I retained a couple things. The first was confidence, knowing adults could see me, that I could walk into a downtown financial office and be seen. The second was the demystification of markets. Cy taught me that beneath the complexity of finance, there are basic principles that a 13-year-old can grasp.

Risk and Return

Capitalists put their money to work in myriad ways, from simple bank loans to synthetic derivative securities that the people who design them don't fully understand. But every form of investment distills to the balance between two considerations: risk and return. In a properly functioning market, the greater the risk to your capital, the more (potential) upside you expect to be paid in return. The risk is the price you pay for the return.

A (very) simplified example: betting on a coin flip. If you bet heads on a single toss, there's an even chance you'll win (we say the odds are 1:1) and so you expect a 100% return. Bet ("invest") $1, and get back your original investment of $1, plus a "return" of $1. But if you bet that heads will come up *twice in a row*, that's less likely. The risk you'll lose is three times the likelihood you'll win: of the four possible outcomes from two flips, three of them (tails-tails, heads-tails, and tails-heads) are losses—the odds are 1:3. If you bet $1, you expect to receive your original $1, plus a "return" of $3. Your risk is higher, so you demand a higher return. If someone offers you $2 for $1 on a two-heads-in-a-row bet, that's a bad deal. But $5 for $1, you take that bet every time.

Investing risk and return is more complex. You don't know the risk to a certainty at the outset, as you do with a coin flip, and your objective is to get a positive return, not merely break even, as you would betting the odds on coin flips. Investing outcomes are rarely binary between a payback or nothing, and often returns come as a flow of income, not a single payout. But recognizing an imbalance (less risk than potential return) is still the key to successful investing.

Again, risk is the price you pay for return: nothing ventured, nothing gained.

The Two Axes of Investing

Investing activity can be classified along two dimensions: whether it is active or passive, and whether it is diversified or concentrated. Understanding where an investment falls on these dimensions

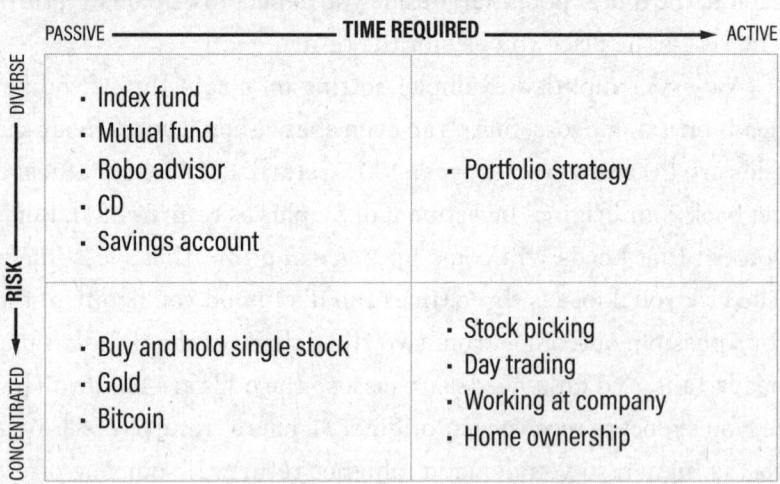

should be the arbiter of when and where you allocate your time and your capital.

Active or passive refers to how much time you put into an investment, and how much influence you have over the outcome. Putting your money in a savings account at your bank is 100% passive: you don't have to do anything other than deposit the money, and it will return whatever the bank offers no matter what you do. Your most active investment, on the other hand, is with your employer. You might not think of your job as an investment, but in fact it's your most important, other than the investment in your relationships, and the most time-consuming. If you own equity, then even more so. Other active investments are owning rental properties (pro tip: get your in-laws to do the active parts) and day-trading stocks.

Because active investing strategies require more of your time, you should expect a greater return on your money than from an equally risky but passive investment. You want a return on your time, in addition to your capital. And because your involvement bears directly on the success, you need to be thoughtful about whether it's an investment that leverages your particular skills. I like art, but I know very little about the art market and am not interested in learning—so bidding against collectors at Sotheby's is not a good active investment strategy for me. But I know more than a grown man should about airplanes, and a few years ago, I made a relatively sizable private investment in a company that services jet engines, an investment that took and continues to require some time to manage, but that I believe leverages some personal domain expertise.

Diversified or concentrated refers to the nature of the investment's risk profile. This is an essential investing concept, so much so that I named this chapter after it. At a basic level, this means not putting all your eggs in one basket. I've owned shares in Apple for many years, and the company has produced staggering returns over that period. But it remains a fairly risky stock (that's how it generates returns—by taking risk), and risks catch up with us eventually: few individual companies stay on top over the long term.

MARKET CAPITALIZATION RANK
U.S. Companies
2003 vs. April 2023

2003		2023
1	Microsoft	2
2	GE	71
3	ExxonMobil	11
4	Walmart	13
5	Pfizer	28
6	Citi	82
7	Johnson & Johnson	9
8	IBM	68
9	AIG	216
10	Merck	20

Sources: Financial Times, CompaniesMarketCap.com

Risk, Part Deux: Diversification

Diversification is a defensive strategy. But as in sports, defense wins championships. Because investing has a fundamental asymmetry. You can absorb infinite upside. But you can't come back from zero. Risky investment assets—growth stocks, derivatives—can go to zero. If you're concentrated in one of those assets, a bad bet can devastate you. Diversification limits your downside. Admittedly, it's also a drag on your upside, but if you go to zero on a single bet, you have no upside. More important, **you don't need to maximize upside**.

This is a profound truth. Contrary to the message of popular media, the objective is not to be the richest person alive. A well-managed, diversified portfolio will generate the returns you need to achieve economic security. You can still pursue step-change, monster wins with a share of your capital. And as you gain experience in the markets, you'll get a feel for opportunity vs. a carnival barker. A safe and steadily growing asset base will give you the confidence to pursue greater opportunities with your more valuable asset, your time. This is the lesson of two paths to wealth I described at the beginning of the book: the best choice is to walk them both.

Focus your time to maximize your current income.

Diversify your investments to maximize your long-term wealth.

Diversification is more than just owning different assets. It's about owning assets with different risk profiles. Remember the example of the coin flip? That's a simplified form of risk, with just one consideration—how will the coin land? Investing risks are not singular like this, they are multifaceted.

Let's take Apple. The company is subject to a variety of different *types* of risks: an economic slowdown could reduce consumer willingness to pay $1,200 for a new phone every two years; China could invade Taiwan and Apple could lose access to much of its manufacturing capabilities and its second largest market; Tim Cook will eventually decide he has better things to do, and his successor likely will lack his management skills. These (and many other) risks constitute Apple's risk profile. We say that Apple is "exposed" to these risks.

My Apple stock likewise exposes me to these risks. If I put all my money in Apple, then I'm highly concentrated, and suddenly my future economic security rests on Xi Jinping or Tim Cook's mood and blood sugar. That's bad. So how do I retain the great returns

Apple provides, but reduce my exposure to specific risks outside my control? (Hint: diversification.)

Notice the risks facing Apple range from very broad (economic slowdown) to something beyond Apple but also a particular risk for the company (war with China) to an entirely Apple-related risk (Tim Cook's eventual retirement). Splitting my capital between Apple and Nike reduces my exposure to Tim Cook's retirement by half, since Cook has no effect on Nike. That's great, but I'm still exposed to China, because Nike is also dependent on Chinese manufacturing and consumers, and exposed to the broader consumer economy, as both firms sell discretionary consumer goods.

In fact, it's difficult to escape exposure to China anywhere in manufacturing or consumer goods. Consider Harley-Davidson, which makes its motorcycles in the U.S. but depends on Chinese manufacturers for many of the parts. Luxury goods designer LVMH still manufactures the bulk of its products in Europe—but depends on China for a quarter of its sales.

A better candidate to offset the risk profile of a company like Apple would be an energy company—most are less tied to the Chinese economy *and* they do relatively well when the economy slows—or a company that is fundamentally national/local in scope such as residential real estate suppliers and managers (e.g., Home Depot, Equity Residential).

If this sounds like a lot of work—it is. Hence the rise of mutual funds and other investment vehicles in which the investor can pay a fund manager a small percentage of their investment (ideally, very small) to do the research and math necessary to provide them a diversified portfolio. The theory behind diversification is known as portfolio theory, and it emerged in the 1950s when economists were able to aggregate enough data to measure the returns of complex portfolios of investment.

Diversification is not just about individual stocks. It's about having a diversified portfolio of investments. Stocks as an asset class (more on this below) tend to move together, and no stock-buying strategy can diversify risks out of your portfolio that are common to stocks generally.

One wrinkle to this story is that the secret power of diversification became less of a secret in the eighties, and institutional investors began investing in all manner of assets in every region. Ironically, this made it more difficult to diversify, because capital flows meant formerly unrelated investments were now linked. When an iron ore stock crashes in Australia, it affects bond prices in Germany, as the investor who took the hit Down Under may need to raise capital (to cover losses) by selling their German bonds. It's still the right strategy, though harder to execute and perhaps less effective than it once was.

In sum, diversification is the art and science of broadening your risk profile so no single failure or global shift can fatally injure you.

Kevlar

Similar to a lot of people, I learned the value of diversification the hard way—being far too concentrated. In the late nineties, the e-commerce company I founded, Red Envelope, was riding the dot-com boom toward an IPO. I was 34 and shopping for private jets; I felt bulletproof. Then the market turned, and the IPO was pulled. The company struggled in the aftermath, we changed management, I disagreed with our venture investors ("disagreed" is me being polite), but I stayed in. The company went public in 2003, and not only did I decline to cash out, I went deeper and invested more, blinded by my emotional involvement with the brand. Five years of avoiding flashing red lights later, I lost 70% of my net worth when the company declared chapter 11 in 2008. And I never saw it coming.

A perfect storm of a longshoremen strike, a mishap at our fulfillment facility, and a credit analyst at Wells Fargo pulling our credit line took the firm down in ten weeks. And here's the thing: perfect storms are rare, but they always happen.

My second lesson in diversification came in 2011, when I made the worst investment decision of my career. I bought a large stake (for a professor, anyway) in Netflix at $12 per share (that wasn't the bad decision). I bought into the company's vision, its management, and felt I had insight into the media landscape and how streaming would disrupt the market. But the market had doubts, and six months later I sold the stock at $10 to take a tax loss at the end of the year. For much of the next decade, I felt physically ill each time I saw that green NFLX ticker show up on my phone screen—the pain peaked at about 50x my investment. But as painful as the bullet to the chest was, I was fine, as I was wearing my Kevlar. My portfolio wasn't limited to Netflix. I also held Apple, Amazon, and Nike, all of which ripped up during that period as well (not as much as Netflix). Selling Netflix for tax purposes was a body blow, but diversification kept it from being fatal. You need to put yourself in a position to survive the stray bullets that, in the world of investing, will inevitably strike you. Nobody is immune. Remember, few people screenshot their losers. But they are everywhere, and everyone absorbs them.

Random Walk

Some years ago, at a Berkshire Hathaway annual meeting, Warren Buffett offered to bet anyone $1 million that a stock market average, the S&P 500 index, would beat any active investor over a ten-year period. (If you aren't sure what the S&P 500 is, for now understand it as an average of stock prices generally—I'll cover it in more detail in the section titled "Measuring the Economy.") An investment firm called Protégé Partners took Buffett's wager. Protégé chose five active funds, and over the course of the decade, swapped some lower-performing funds out in favor of investors they deemed more likely to succeed.

In the first year, each of the five funds-of-funds beat the S&P 500—significantly. The next year, 2009, the S&P 500 won. And again in 2010, and in 2011, and every year after that. By 2017 the S&P 500 had returned 126%. Protégé Partners' returns? 36%. The bet officially ended December 31, 2017, but by that summer, Buffett was so far ahead that Protégé conceded early.

The Buffett story is one Wall Street doesn't want you to know about. Because if you realized that few (if any) can best the market consistently, there would be a lot of stockbrokers, hedge fund managers, and investment advisers looking for work. And that's the market's secret hiding in plain sight: over the long term, no one beats it—no matter how well-educated, capitalized, or staffed. It's certainly possible to beat it in the *short term*. In fact, that's what happened for many people in 2021, who piled into cryptocurrencies and meme stocks that registered upward swings orders of magnitude greater than the broader stock market. My 11-year-old bought Dogecoin and was a genius. Until he wasn't. By 2022, three out of four crypto traders had lost money on their initial investment. Meanwhile, as speculative assets crashed, the stock market kept doing its thing, crawling upward at an unremarkable rate.

Don't take my word for it (or Buffett's)—the data is there. In the past twenty years, 94% of all large-cap funds were outperformed by the S&P 500. In that same period, the average equity fund returned an average of 8.7%, while the S&P Composite 1500 returned 9.7%. One study found that over fifteen years, only half of actively managed U.S. equity funds even survive.

The seminal work on this topic is a book by Princeton economics professor Burton Malkiel called *A Random Walk Down Wall*

Street. Malkiel makes the case that asset prices (particularly stock prices) are subject to the "random walk theory"—that is, they can't be predicted over the long term. Thus, stock-picking is a "random walk" and not worth your time. Malkiel wrote the book in 1973 and it has been reprinted *thirteen times* since. The most recent edition was published in 2023—it discusses Google, Tesla, SPACs, and Bitcoin. And yet the book reaches the same conclusion: long-term, active investing doesn't beat the market. (These discussions focus on stocks, but most of this applies equally to other asset classes—active, individual investors rarely beat diversified passive indexes in any market.)

This should raise two questions. First: What about Buffett himself? Isn't the Sage of Omaha revered as a brilliant investor? Hasn't he been beating the market for years? And second: Scott, why are you telling me to actively invest if I'm certain to lose?

A couple of things. First, putting all your money in the S&P 500 (which you can do with an ETF, as I cover later in this chapter) is not a great strategy, because optimal long-term returns are not your only consideration. The broader market is highly variable. In the years 2000 to 2022, the S&P 500 lost value in seven of those years, including three years when it lost 20% or more of its value. Recall from the last chapter that variable investments are not a good place for money you expect to need within the next several years. If you have $100,000 saved for a house down payment, and you put it in an S&P 500 ETF, there's a decent chance it will be worth less, perhaps a lot less, when you need it.

While you should get your long-term returns from passive, diversified investments, you need to know how to bring down that variability risk for your intermediate bucket capital. And even if you wanted to invest all your money in the S&P 500, you probably won't. Buying a home is a major real estate investment. You may have opportunities to invest in private businesses, such as your employer or a company you start. While broad market indexes offer the best risk/reward ratio, as you garner more economic security, you should look for ways to take on more risk in exchange for a higher potential upside. And getting good with money means understanding money, and that takes more than reading about the financial markets.

Second, if you do make more active investments, you aren't certain to lose. The strong form of the "random walk" hypothesis—that nobody can predict any stock price ever—is controversial, and I think it overstates the case. Market prices are the product of the market as a voting machine, a product of human judgment, which is often irrational and ill-informed. Clear-eyed and level-headed observers can sometimes recognize where prices have diverged from value, and profit from the difference, most often if they're patient and hold assets for long periods. As the saying goes, "Success doesn't come from timing the market, it comes from time in the market."

That's the investing strategy Buffett has pursued his entire career. The point he was making with his $1 million bet was more about highly active investment strategies, where the investor is playing short-term price moves and moving in and out of stocks or other assets frequently. (Also, while Buffett does buy shares in public companies through his own company, Berkshire Hathaway, Berkshire is primarily an operating business—it owns many companies outright and oversees their management. In fact, when you strip away the Nebraska charm and the folksy sayings, Berkshire Hathaway is primarily an insurance company. A very profitable insurance company that diversifies by plowing its profits into other businesses.)

These are the foundational principles of investing: risk and return, diversification, and the futility of trying to "beat the market" (most of the time).

THE CAPITALIST'S HANDBOOK

To properly understand your investment options, and ultimately develop an investment strategy, you need a basic understanding of capital, and the economic system it fuels (aka capitalism). In the next few pages, I sketch a basic but comprehensive overview of the capitalist system. Every concept outlined here is an academic area of study itself. My expertise in these areas varies broadly, as does anyone else's—no single person has an expert-level understanding of the entirety of our economy. But you don't need to be an expert in *any* of these areas to be a successful investor. The complexity and depth of these concepts shouldn't be a barrier to understanding their general contours and, most important, *how they fit together in the system of capitalism*. It's from the 20,000-foot view where the interdependent nature of the system is apparent. To more experienced readers some of this may seem pedantic or reductionist, but too much investing advice overcomplicates and mystifies what's really going on, when in fact what really matters are basic concepts.

Trading Time for Money

All organisms have needs. Plants need water and sunlight, caterpillars need leaves, and humans need all kinds of stuff. One of our economy's competencies is coming up with new things we need. However, our rampant consumerism sits on a bed of real, inescapable needs: food, shelter, companionship. In nature, parents provide for offspring, and some species have evolved cooperative routines, but, for the most part, species rely on their own efforts to secure the things they need.

Humans are different. Blessed with the capacity to imagine and anticipate the future and communicate through complex language, we have developed the means to exchange not just the things we

DIVERSIFICATION

need with one another but also to exchange the real limit on our capacity: time itself. This is how I want you to think about money: it's the means we use to exchange time.

Picture a factory worker clocking an 8-hour shift, a 40-hour workweek. At the end of the week, the factory owner pays the worker a wage. A straightforward exchange of time for money. (Economists will quibble that the owner is paying for the worker's labor, which is true, but time is the essential asset the worker gives up, even if his labor is what makes it valuable to the owner.)

The factory worker takes that money, stops at the bar on the way home, and exchanges $10 for two beers. At least that's what it looks like on the surface. But on a deeper level, he's trading time spent on the factory floor for other people's time at a brewery. He's buying the bartender and barley farmer's time. A sliver of that $10 goes to the janitor who cleans the bar that night and to the city that pays the police and fire workers who protect the bar. The rest, if any, is the reward to the owner who allocated time to opening a bar.

Money—as a means of transferring time—unlocks comparative advantage, the ability to specialize. The power of specialization was famously illustrated by Adam Smith with the example of a pin factory. According to Smith, ten men each making pins could make a few hundred pins per day. Ten men in a factory he visited, each handling one tiny part of the pin-making process, could make over 48,000 pins in a day. The bar is no different. One person working alone could never build, stock, and operate a bar, or a restaurant, or almost any hallmark of modern life. Specialization is a fundamental dynamic of our economy—people spending their time doing one narrow thing very well, like writing books or rebuilding carburetors, then getting money for that time and trading it for the products of other people's time.

Economists have been arguing for centuries over the "true" nature of this exchange and the relationship between the labor that goes into a good and the price of that good. For our purposes, however, you can ignore this debate. Money is how we exchange time, and what gives money value is that others will trade you their time, or the goods they've produced with it, for your money. The rest is noise.

The Marketplace of Supply and Demand

Not all time is valued equally (nor all things). The summer after I graduated from high school, I made $18 an hour installing shelving. Cristiano Ronaldo's contract with football club Al-Nassr pays him about $2.5 million for every hour he spends on the pitch. Relatively speaking, I was overpaid, as I'm bad at installing shelving.

Whenever there's an exchange, there is a price. How many dollars for that cold beer, and how much time on the factory to earn that many dollars? Finding the right price for those exchanges keeps the gears turning in a functioning economy. It's a task of staggering complexity. The price the factory pays for its workers' time needs to be low enough so the factory can produce goods at a price attractive to its customers—which depends on what those customers get paid for their time, wherever they work. Concurrently, the factory workers need compensation for their time so they can buy things they need, and some they want.

The defining characteristic of what we call our "free-market economy" is that we (mostly) rely on the marketplace of supply and demand to thread the needle of pricing. In contrast, a "planned economy" is one in which a central authority (typically a government agency) sets prices. Dreamers are attracted to planned economies, but none has been successful at scale. Maybe someday—but this is a book about the world as it is, and the twenty-first century global economy is (mostly) market-based.

Each transaction requires supply *and* demand. There's a lot of demand for pills that instantly cure cancer, but there's no supply

DIVERSIFICATION

and, hence, no price. If a pill to cure all cancers were invented, but only one could be manufactured per day, the price would be astronomical—likely hundreds of millions of dollars. These high prices would attract competition, and as the supply of cancer pills increased, the price would come down (unless there is regulatory capture—lobbyists swarming DC to restrict supply). If there were tens of millions of pills, the price would collapse. Prices tend to stabilize at the point that balances supply and demand—high enough to encourage manufacturing, low enough to stimulate demand. High enough to capture a profit, but low enough to discourage a swarm of competitors.

This stabilization occurs via markets, which act as a "price discovery mechanism." That phrase captures how market participants bluff and call their way toward equilibrium. Market prices aren't "set" by the market so much as "discovered."

We describe the extent to which prices fully reflect supply and demand as a market's "efficiency." This is largely a function of information: when all market participants have access to full information about one another, they will quickly find the equilibrium price. Markets tend to be more efficient when transaction costs are low and there are a lot of transactions (which create a lot of information about supply and demand) and when the object of trade is a discrete, fungible commodity like gold (which makes it easy to apply data from past transactions to future ones). Markets for nuanced, variable-quality things such as art and labor are less efficient.

Inefficient markets attract "arbitrage," which is when a trader buys goods from sellers who are unaware of the true demand and sells them to buyers who are unaware of the true supply (or who cannot exchange directly, because of distance or cultural barriers).

In the 1980s and '90s, Levi's jeans, especially the classic 501 model, cost much more in Europe and Asia than they did in the United States. Levi Strauss & Co. had successfully marketed the 501 as a fashion item in those regions and kept supply artificially low. The high-demand/low-supply dynamic meant retailers could charge $100 or more for jeans abroad that could only fetch $30 in the U.S. The market for Levi's was inefficient because there was ample supply in the U.S., but that supply wasn't making it to Europe and Asia. And then ... it was. A thriving arbitrage developed, fueled partly by distributors who would divert container loads of jeans intended for the U.S. to foreign markets, but also through what the company called "the suitcase trade": foreign tourists would stock up on Levi's in America and bring them home to wear or resell. Levi Strauss & Co. was one of my first consulting clients, and one of our early projects was to help them understand the volume of this arbitrage. We sent consultants to airports on both coasts and had them interview people waiting to board flights to Europe and Asia (airport security was much lighter before 9/11). We asked them if they'd bought Levi's while in the U.S., how many pairs, and what they planned to do with them. It turned out that a staggeringly high percentage of them had Levi's in their luggage, and many planned to resell them once they got home.

Arbitrage activity makes markets more efficient, as each trade brings a little more information to the market and tightens the link between supply and demand. This is what was happening in the market for Levi's 501s. The arbitrage tourists increased the price in the U.S. via increased demand, and their informal sales depressed prices in their home market by increasing supply. E-commerce made the intentionally inefficient market untenable. Today the base model 501 sells for around $90 all over the world—or about $40 in 1990 dollars.

Capital and the Marketplace of Money

What we've covered so far is the fundamental dynamic of an economy. People exchange time for money and money for goods, the product of other exchanges of money and time. These exchanges take place across many types of markets, from literal markets like Whole Foods to exchanges such as the "labor market," which exists only in the world of statistics but is nonetheless a very real, important market most people participate in at some point in their lives. There's one particular set of markets we need to cover in more detail, however, because these are the markets where most investing activity takes place. These are the financial markets, aka the markets for money.

Financial markets empower money to be more than just a medium of exchange. They are the phone booth in which money changes into its superhero outfit and becomes capital. Earlier I said that capital was money at work. But what does that really mean? At any point in time, an organization—a small business, a large corporation, a government, a charity—has all kinds of assets it uses to carry out its mission. A bar needs liquor, glasses, beer taps, furniture, and cash to buy these things, pay employees, and pay rent. All cost money, but when assembled and managed by a capable bar owner, they are worth more than the money it takes to buy them. And we can measure how much more: the profits the bar will make using those assets. Capital is money charged with making more money.

Just as other markets price the goods that are traded in them, the financial markets price capital. If our bar owner wants to expand to a second location, they will need additional capital. The simplest way to do this is to borrow money from a bank. This is a fundamental financial market transaction. The bar owner gets a large sum of money in exchange for a promise to pay back more money in the future. The difference between those amounts is what we call "interest," but it's really the price of money (or, in a deeper sense, the price of time). Interest is typically priced on a percentage basis, from which we get "interest rates." If the bank charges the bar owner 8% interest on a $100,000 loan, the bar owner has to pay $8,000 annually to rent that $100,000. This works out for the bar owner, however, provided they can make enough with their expanded location to pay the $8,000 in interest, and still collect a profit on top of that.

Simple bank loans like this are just one example of the myriad money-for-money transactions that take place in the financial markets. But all of them operate on the same basic principle. Money is provided in exchange for a promise of future repayment of some larger amount. When the transaction is a loan, the difference between the two amounts is called interest, but the more general term is "return." An "investment" is a transfer of money that "returns" a profit to the party that puts up the money (the "investor"). And the party on the other side of the transaction is willing to pay that profit because they believe they can put that money to use as capital, making even more money than the return they owe the investor (e.g., the bar owner who makes more than the $8,000 in interest the loan costs). When it works, and in a healthy economy it works most of the time, these transactions generate value for both sides, and the economy grows. That's a critical point. Investing is not a zero-sum game—it makes the pie bigger.

By this point, you can probably see where we are headed. Investing is a good gig. You give someone money, and then a little while later, they give you back more money. You do this over and over again, and your money grows exponentially. It does so constantly, steadily. In the words of Oliver Stone's *Wall Street* icon Gordon Gekko, "money never sleeps."

Occasionally, however, it doesn't wake up (i.e., you don't get your money back). This is where "credit quality" comes into play. The lender must make an assessment of the probability the borrower will be able to pay back the loan or provide collateral the lender can seize should the borrower be unable to pay back the principal and interest. Loaning money is easy, it's assessing the credit quality that's hard.

To invest wisely, however, we need to understand more than just the basic mechanics of capital. Investments happen within the context of the financial markets. There are three broad categories of entities that act in the financial markets: corporations, banks and other financial institutions, and the government.

Organizing Labor: The Corporation

When we think of investing, we typically think first about buying stock in corporations. That's natural, because corporations are the primary users of capital in our economy, employ large swaths of people, and manufacture most of our goods and deliver most of our services.

For most of human history, private enterprise was small scale: family farms, blacksmiths, and cobblers. Anything more ambitious—like a military campaign or a road network—was typically the domain of a government, or sometimes a religious institution. With the rise of industrial production in the nineteenth century, private enterprise needed more scale. Factories required dozens or hundreds of workers, more than a family or close-knit group of people could provide. So ambitious entrepreneurs needed a way to pool their resources. But pooling resources, especially among large groups of unrelated people, raises a host of questions. If a venture is successful, how do you allocate the profits? If it's unsuccessful, who is responsible for providing more capital? Most crucially, who is in charge? Over time, what evolved to resolve these challenges was the corporation.

A corporation is a legal construct. It has no physical existence—it's not a building or a group of people. But it has legal personhood. It can own property, it can enter into contracts, it can borrow money or lend it, it can sue and be sued in court, and it has to pay taxes. It's not entirely the same as a person—corporations can't vote, for example, and they can't marry or take custody of a child.

But for nearly anything a business needs, the corporation can take the place of the individual business owner.

A corporation has internal rules, written down in what are called bylaws, that determine who makes decisions. These rules are enforceable in court, though it rarely comes to that. They empower corporate officers to delegate decisions to managers, to hire and fire workers, and to allocate the corporation's capital. And they provide for layers of oversight and accountability. This makes corporations *unlike* a person—much more predictable, more transparent in their decision-making, more rational. At least in theory. Just as banks turn short-term deposits into long-term loans, corporations take human emotions and—via the wisdom of crowds—turn them into considered decisions and actions. And it makes sense. Corporations do dumb things every day. However, individuals do crazy things every minute.

The measured characteristics of a corporation, its legal status and its organizational structure, are essential to its mission and give it the capacity to put large amounts of capital to work. Providing capital to corporations is one of the main purposes—arguably *the* main purpose—of the financial markets. I'll get to the mechanics of how that's done when I talk about stocks and bonds a bit later in this chapter.

Organizing Capital: Banking

Operating entities (both corporations and individuals) don't participate in the financial markets directly—we use the services of banks and other financial institutions. There are four major types: retail banks, investment banks, brokerages, and investment companies. The lines between these are not distinct, however, and the largest banks, such as JPMorgan Chase and Bank of America, operate in all four categories.

DIVERSIFICATION

The elemental business is a traditional bank, or what's often called a retail bank. In (very) simplified terms, a retail bank borrows capital from one set of customers and loans capital out to another set of customers. The bank's profit comes from the spread between the interest it offers the first group and the interest it charges the second group (plus all those fees).

Most of us initially encounter retail banks as a member of the first group of customers—we lend capital to the bank in the form of deposits, in part to earn interest, but mainly, as a place to keep our money safe. There's a reason that the classic image of a bank is an imposing marble building with a large vault inside—its basic value proposition to depositors is that it is a safer place to keep money than a shoebox. Since they are holding the money anyway, and to make their money-holding service more attractive, banks also handle the mechanics of financial transactions: they provide and process checks, make electronic payments, and accept electronic deposits. These services are continually being reconfigured and fought over by new entrants—PayPal and its imitators have seized a piece of the transaction business, for example. Cryptocurrency enthusiasts claim that technology will allow us to be our own banks. Holding money securely and conveniently is a foundational element of any economic system, and is largely done by retail banks.

Most of us are also members of the second group of customers, those who borrow from banks. Interest on these loans is primarily how banks make their profits, and the loans themselves are how new money is added into the economy. Loans can take many forms, from a simple unsecured loan, in which the money is loaned out purely on a promise of future repayment, to complex agreements with various obligations and promises over time. A home mortgage is a bank loan, known as a secured loan, because if you don't make your payments, the bank can sell your house to get its money back. Credit card accounts are a type of bank loan, known as a revolving loan, that you can dip into and pay back on your own schedule.

In addition to retail banks, there's also an entirely different kind of bank, known as an **investment bank**. Investment banks, such as Goldman Sachs and Morgan Stanley, combine financial consulting services with capital management. They advise clients on large, complex financial transactions and help facilitate those transactions by deploying their own capital (mostly on an interim basis until other investors can be found). They also trade their own capital and their clients' capital in the financial markets.

Brokerages facilitate clients' more run-of-the-mill financial transactions; buying and selling stock is the headline transaction, but brokers make a market in many financial assets. Both retail and investment banks often offer brokerage services, and there are large standalone brokerage firms, including traditional firms such as Charles Schwab and online start-ups like Robinhood and Public (I am an investor in Public).

Finally, **investment companies** pool their clients' money and invest it themselves, taking a portion of the profits realized on investments where the manager was able to discern an imbalance of risk and return. There's a wide variety of investment companies, and much of the financial capital in the world is invested through them. You may very well hold investments through some of them already—401(k) assets, for example, are invested by investment companies such as Fidelity.

Some investment companies specialize in a specific type of investment: venture capitalists specialize in start-ups, for example. Others specialize in a certain type of investor: Vanguard and Fidelity service individual, small-dollar-volume investors by pooling their capital and investing it in various ways. Hedge funds service wealthy individuals and institutions, making bold, focused bets with different risk and potential return profiles. Some investment companies specialize in a technique or philosophy of investing:

Berkshire Hathaway applies the principles of its founder, Warren Buffett, and makes large, long-term investments in what it believes are stable, enduring businesses. High-frequency traders use huge amounts of computing resources and complex algorithms in an attempt to make money on tiny price changes over very short periods.

One of the major stories of the past few decades has been the increasing importance of "private" capital—sources of financing besides selling stock to the public. Certain types of investment companies have become much larger and more numerous. Venture capital, for example, was a niche field just a generation ago but has ballooned into a marketplace that deploys hundreds of billions of dollars per year. Accessing the wealth creation opportunities in these areas is more difficult for individual investors, who do not have millions of dollars to invest, but markets are innovative. I'll touch on this a bit more in the asset classes discussion.

The Role of Government

There is another important player in the financial markets: the government. Government plays two profoundly important roles.

First, it provides many of the ground rules the markets operate under, and enforces those rules through regulatory action, litigation, and in rare cases physical seizures and prison sentences. It also shapes the course of investment decisions through tax policy. Many in financial services would like to believe that the industry is in a distinct sphere from government, a more efficient, more admirable sphere. This is a myth.

The reliable functioning of financial markets is 100% dependent on the authority of the government to establish and enforce the rules of the game. Absent government authority, markets devolve into a quagmire of scams, broken promises, and outright theft (e.g., crypto, circa 2022). No government performs this function perfectly, and many do so poorly, but every market relies on government regulation to create the requisite trust to encourage market participants.

A more controversial aspect of this regulatory role is shoring up struggling market participants. Most observers agree that some level of assistance is required. For example, the FDIC insures savings and checking account deposits (up to $250,000 as I write this, but it may be increased) and has the authority to seize struggling banks to reduce the risk of destabilizing bank runs. That's widely seen as a good thing. In 2008 and 2020, however, government "bailouts" of banks, airlines, auto companies, and more banks were more controversial. Like it or not, no elected official wants to preside over an economic catastrophe, and so there's always an impulse to intervene. And increasingly, the people being bailed out are overrepresented in DC.

The second role of government is as a major participant in the financial markets. The U.S. government is *by far* the largest single pool of financial capital in the world. As of this writing, nearly $25 trillion has been invested in the U.S. government by holders of Treasury securities. That's roughly the same amount of capital invested in all the corporations on the New York Stock Exchange combined. This makes the government among the most important players in the market for money, a whale whose every move disturbs the currents for miles around.

The most active arm of the government in the financial markets is the central bank, which in the U.S. is the Federal Reserve. The Fed is the government's bank (handling its deposits and facilitating its payments). It regulates commercial banks, it provides much of the critical data on which investors rely, and it borrows and lends money in the banking system itself. The Department of the Treasury issues the government's debt, and a slew of agencies, including the Securities and Exchange Commission, the Department of Labor, and the Commerce Department, regulate and assist various aspects of the financial markets.

Measuring the Economy

There is one more foundational aspect to the financial markets that investors should understand: how we measure the economy. Individual investment decisions (should you buy a stock, how much can you afford to spend on a house) depend in part on the unique circumstances of that investment. But they also should be made in the context of the economy as a whole, and we have developed a set of metrics that are widely followed for that purpose. Incidentally, this is a critical function of the government, which uses its legal authority to collect the massive amounts of data that feed these metrics, and then capital supplied by investors and taxpayers to process the data and release it to the public for free. Several U.S. government websites are indispensable resources for investors, notably the Bureau of Labor Statistics (www.bls.gov), the Department of Commerce (commerce.gov), and the Federal Reserve's Economic Data repository (fred.stlouisfed.org).

There are dozens of widely followed measures and thousands of niche measures. The following are the categories and specific metrics that are both useful to understand and frequently mentioned in the financial press.

Gross Domestic Product (GDP). The mother of all metrics. It is a total value of all the finished goods and services produced in a country over the course of the year. It is not the value of an economy, but a measure of its *output per year*, roughly similar to a corporation's revenue.

There are various ways to measure GDP, and the actual data collection and analysis is complex, but these details rarely matter for investors. In fact, GDP itself isn't what matters so much as the rate of change. When GDP is flat or shrinking, then investments made within that economy are not generating a positive return—which discourages future investment, suppressing growth. When GDP declines for several quarters and other economic indicators are weak, an economy is considered to be in a "recession." On rare occasions, as in the 1930s, years of GDP decline are termed a "depression."

Consumer Price Index (CPI). This is the standard measure of prices across a "basket of goods," and attempts to capture the relative change in prices over time—usually their increase, aka "inflation." Inflation is typically reported on an annual percentage, so when the media reports that inflation is at 4.5%, that means that the CPI is 4.5% higher than it was 12 months earlier. (As I discussed in the last chapter, however, not all goods and services change price at the same rate, and economists dissect the CPI into different categories to get a more nuanced view.)

Consumer prices are a key indicator for several reasons. Consumer spending is the main driver of economic activity, and rapid increases in prices can throttle spending, slowing economic growth. But the more immediate and practical concern for investors is that inflation is one of just two measures that the Fed is charged with influencing (the other is employment, discussed next). The Fed's inflation target is 2%, and when inflation begins to tick much higher than that, the Fed typically responds by taking action to increase interest rates—that is, to make money more expensive. This can have profound ripple effects across the economy.

Unemployment Rate. This is a depressing way to measure employment—we could just as easily report and discuss the employment rate; that would be much more positive—but what we are getting at either way is the pressure of supply and demand on the labor market. When unemployment is low, that means the supply of labor is low relative to the demand, and so the price of labor—wages—will tend to rise.

The misleading term "full employment" refers to the unemployment rate consistent with a supply and demand balance in the labor market. There's no magic number, but somewhere around 5% is what economists usually identify as "full employment." It makes sense that there will always be some unemployed people looking for work—people who have recently quit or who have been let go from their jobs, people coming into the labor market for the first time, or those returning after not seeking work.

Low unemployment is intuitively preferable, and it can be a source of economic strength in the short term, since workers have more money to spend. But when unemployment gets too low (somewhere south of 5%) jobs go unfilled and wages go up, which tends to increase prices, which can cause inflation and reduced economic output. High unemployment can be good (in the short term) for companies with a lot of low-skilled and semiskilled workers in their cost structures, like fast-food and some retail businesses, because a high supply of labor will decrease its price, reducing those companies' operating expenses. But high unemployment ultimately depresses consumer spending, slowing economic growth. As with inflation, the Fed (and the central banks of other countries) is charged with keeping unemployment within a preferred range and will respond with changes to interest rates when it sees the need.

Interest Rates. I've mentioned interest rates several times already, in the context of the cost of money or, more specifically, the cost of a loan. But investors don't just care about the interest rate they are charging or paying on their own investments. They care a great deal about the interest rates everyone else is paying, too. Interest rates are like gravity—they affect everyone and everything all the time, and the higher they are, the stronger they push against growth and profits.

There is no single, aggregated "interest rate" like there is for unemployment or GDP. Instead, analysts and the financial press report dozens of rates on a bewildering array of financial products: 30-year fixed and 7/10 ARM mortgages, 3-month commercial paper, 10-year Treasury bills, certificates of deposit, etc. Most of these specific rates don't matter so much to you, unless you're in the market for the products they are associated with (start shopping for houses and expect to become *extremely* interested in mortgage rates). It's more important to appreciate how they are connected, and in particular how they all piggyback on one specific interest rate, set (sort of) by the Federal Reserve.

The Fed holds the government's money and provides transaction services and the like. But recall how the government is the largest participant in the economy and also its referee—having a special relationship with the government gives the Fed (and the central banks in other countries) banking superpowers. Every day, banks process billions of dollars in transactions, and to ensure they have enough capital, they borrow money from one another and from the Fed itself on very short terms, typically overnight. Through a combination of persuasion and economic inducements, the Fed guides banks toward a target rate for these loans, known as the federal funds rate. When the media reports that the Fed is "raising interest rates," that means the Fed is increasing the federal funds rate.

So why does that matter? Because the federal funds rate is the floor on which all other interest rates rest. Not by government fiat, incidentally, but due to a higher power: the law of supply and demand. Imagine you are a bank president, and you've got $1,000 you want to loan out. Your safest possible investment is putting the money in the Fed's vault or loaning it to a bank the Fed supports. Investing in the Fed is investing in the U.S. government, which has 300 years of history paying its debts, the right to tax the world's largest economy, and if push comes to shove, a $700 billion per year military budget. Loaning money to Uncle Sam is effectively risk free. If the U.S. is offering you, for example, an interest rate

INTEREST RATE LADDER

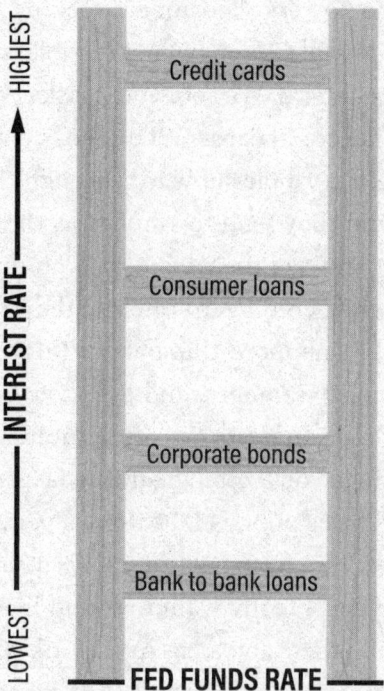

of 3.5%, there's no rational reason to loan money to anyone else for a lower rate, since they are by definition a riskier debtor. That 3.5% is known as the risk-free rate. When a customer comes in the door seeking a $1,000 loan, you'll charge them an interest rate higher than the risk-free rate based on how much risk their loan entails. If the Fed raises the federal funds rate to 5%, then nobody else gets a loan for less than that.

Every loan sits somewhere on a ladder of risks, and the Fed sets the bottom rung. After the government and large banks, big, profitable corporations without a lot of debt are the least risky creditors. So they can get rates close to the federal funds rate on their loans. Then there are corporations with less stellar financials; they have to pay a bit more. These loans are sometimes called junk bonds, which is a colorful but misleading term—these are still relatively good credit risks, just not as good as more stable corporate borrowers. Consumers seeking loans secured by houses and cars are still riskier, but not terrible, since they've got assets to put up as collateral. Way out at the risky end are unsecured consumer loans, like credit cards. When the Fed moves that rate up a half point, the effect ripples upward through the ladder. Its effects are not even, and they tend to amplify as they reach the top, so big companies might see their loan rates go up by less than a percentage point, while credit card rates might jump a few percentage points.

One more thing about interest rates. Because they tend to be small numbers, and even very small changes can have large effects, analysts are often interested in fractional changes. So the lingo you'll often hear is measuring interest rates in "basis points." A basis point is 1/100th of a percent, or 0.01%. Increasing an interest rate from 1.5% to 1.8% is a 30-basis-point increase. Sometimes, when I really want to sound like I know what I'm talking about, I call them "bips," as in "I think we'll see the Fed take rates down 25 to 50 bips tomorrow." Coincidentally, bips is also Latin for "I blew my first annual bonus on a BMW, and I don't regret it."

Market Indexes. The last measure are the stock indexes: the Dow, the S&P 500, and the Nasdaq are the headliners, but there are many more.

The oldest, and also the weirdest, is the Dow Jones Industrial Average, often just called the Dow. For decades, the Dow was *the* average, which really tells you something about first mover advantage. Originally created by Charles Dow in 1896, it was the sum of the stock prices of a few dozen large manufacturing companies, multiplied by the "Dow Divisor," a factor Dow invented to account for nuances in how stock prices are calculated. It's a quirky way to evaluate the state of the stock market. The S&P 500 is arguably more rational; it's a weighted average of the total value of 500 of the largest public companies. The Nasdaq Composite is even broader, in that it is a weighted average of all the stocks traded on the Nasdaq exchange, and also skewed, since the Nasdaq, which rose to promi-

NASDAQ, S&P 500, AND DOW JONES PERFORMANCE

Indexed to 100

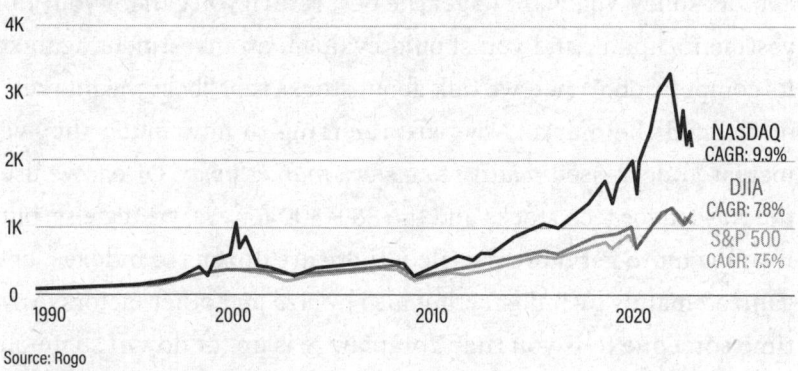

Source: Rogo
Note: CAGR = Compound Annual Growth Rate

nence in the 1980s and '90s, features a disproportionate number of tech companies.

In practice, however, despite the significant differences in how they are calculated, the three indexes tend to move similarly to one another, though the Nasdaq is somewhat more volatile and has outperformed the other two over the past few decades, due to the rapid growth in tech stocks.

A few observations about these indexes. First, they are important in that they gauge investor confidence in the growth potential of large corporations, but they are not nearly as important as the amount of coverage they get in the media would suggest. Most notably, they are only partial measures of the stock market, and not measures of the economy itself. The bulk of economic activity is conducted by companies not included in these indexes, and no single measure can capture as complex a concept as the economy. Think of the stock market as a dog on a leash, and the economy as the person holding the leash. Over the course of a walk, they both end up in the same place. But the dog (market) is going to zig back and forth quite a bit and send out a lot of false signals about what direction the walk is taking.

Second, a valuable function these indexes provide for investors is that they offer a benchmark for investment returns. In the market for money, you want to get the best return you can for your investment capital, and you should evaluate an investment against its competition. When we talk about stocks that "beat the market" or "lagged the market," we are referring to how much they've increased/decreased *relative to a stock market index*. Often, we use the Nasdaq for tech stocks and the S&P 500 for everything else, but if you want to get more detailed, there are dozens of indexes, organized mainly by industry, but also by size and other factors. Any time someone tells you that Company X is up (or down) so much percent on the year, your first instinct should be to compare that with the broader market. Note that over the long term, market indexes perform substantially better than the "average" individual company, because of survivorship bias—as companies falter, they drop out of the index, to be replaced by a more successful company. Remember, over time, few beat the market.

Valuation and the Time Value of Money

The market indexes reflect the value of the companies they cover. Valuation is at the heart of every investment decision. Each investment opportunity is a chance to buy an asset: a share of stock, a bar of gold, a three-bedroom home in a good school district. The investor's challenge is to buy it for a price less than or equal to its value.

PRICE VS. VALUE

Price and value are not the same thing. An asset's price is generally easy to see. It's the amount of money it sells for on the market. Stock prices are reported moment by moment from the exchange, and house prices are recorded in tax records. An asset's value, on the other hand, is how much money it can be expected to produce in the future.

Assets may have different values to different buyers. A house in a good school district is worth more to a family with young kids than a retired couple with grown children. A niche shoe company with a rabid customer base and patent portfolio of manufacturing techniques is likely worth more to Nike than to McDonald's. Many things benefit their owners in non-monetary ways (though they can still be valued). A good-looking pair of sunglasses won't produce income, but they have value: they protect your eyes from the sun, make you more attractive to potential mates, give you a sense of confidence, etc.

In an efficient market, price and value are aligned. Truly efficient markets are rare, however, and no investment market is completely efficient. Prices are tied to underlying value but typically don't match it precisely because of psychology, current events, political dynamics, and incomplete information. Over time these chaotic factors are transient, and the price of most assets tends to converge with their value. Legendary investment guru Benjamin Graham is credited with putting it this way: "In the short run, the market is a voting machine. In the long run, it's a weighing machine." Value investing, which Graham pioneered, is the strategy of identifying investments where the price is below the value, making the investment, and waiting for the price to foot to (i.e., rise) the value.

Valuation has principles applicable to nearly any asset, and specific considerations unique to each asset class. I'll cover the general principles here and the specifics in the next section, where I talk about asset classes.

THE BASIC VALUATION EQUATION

Valuation is prediction and, specifically, predicting three things: income, terminal value, and risk.

First, what income will the asset generate while you own it? For some assets, this is easy. I can tell you with absolute certainty that a $100 bill will generate zero income. On the other hand, a $100 in a savings account paying 4% interest will generate $4 per year. A lot of assets offer predictable income streams. A corporate bond tells you right on its face how much the company that issued it will pay you. Others are harder to predict. A house can generate significant income, either by renting it out or by living in it (and thus, saving on rent), but the value of that income is harder to predict. And some assets, including houses, also have costs associated with them, which you need to predict to accurately determine the net income they will generate.

Second, what will you be able to sell the asset for in the future? In valuation terms, this is typically known as the terminal value. Again, the difficulty of this prediction varies. Both the $100 bill and the $100 in a savings account will be worth precisely $100 tomorrow, ignoring inflation. A house? That depends on the economy, the dynamics of your particular neighborhood, how well you maintain the house, etc.

Third, risk. Which in this context could be termed uncertainty. How likely is it that your first two predictions will be correct? If you have two investment opportunities that offer the same expected future cash flow and terminal value, you want to take the one in which you have greater confidence in those predictions—i.e., the lower risk. The more risk, the higher the return required to make the investment worthwhile.

The fundamental valuation equation puts these three predictions together:

VALUE =
(Future income + Terminal value) × Deduction for risk

That's not strictly how you'd calculate the math—and there's another important component—but, in principle, this is how you want to think about any financial purchase. What money will it earn while you own it, how much can you sell it for in the future, and how confident are you in those two predictions?

A sports team (usually) has zero or negative income/cash flows, as all the revenue is reinvested on the field (i.e., players), but extraordinary terminal value as the market value of the franchise increases. And as long as there is income inequality, we will continue to produce more billionaires who, during a midlife crisis, want to pay billions to host their fourth wife and friends in a team's owner's box. Hertz gets decent income from a car it purchases to rent out, but the terminal value decreases over time. Residential rental real estate has created a great deal of wealth over the last fifty years as the asset class has registered increasing income streams (rents), increasing prices (terminal value), and (relative to other assets) decent surety that both future rents and future sale values will continue to appreciate.

TIME'S ARROW

The "other important component" of valuation is that money tomorrow is worth less than money today. And because of the power of compounding, money several years from now is worth quite a bit less than money today. This is known as the time value of money, and it's a fundamental principle of investing.

Even if you are 100% certain of a future payment, there are still two things that reduce the value of money promised in the future: inflation and opportunity. Inflation I discussed in the previous chapter: because prices tend to rise over time, money is effectively worth less over time. A hundred dollars in a year won't buy you the same quantity of goods then that $100 will buy now.

The other reason that future money is worth less than present money is opportunity cost. Money you have *now* can be invested for a return. That potential return is not available until you get the money, however, rendering future money less valuable by the amount you would expect to make if you had that money now.

Since the value of an asset depends on the money returned to you in the future (it's cash flow), we have to take the time value of money into account. We've already got a reduction in value in our basic equation, taking the riskiness of the investment into account (that is, our uncertainty about our projections), so we can add on to that. The combination of the riskiness of the investment and the reduction in value, based on how long you must wait to receive the cash flow, is what's referred to as the "discount rate." Accordingly, we can update our formula:

VALUE =
(Future income + Terminal value) × Discount rate

Investors often talk about "discounting" an expected return. This means they are applying a discount rate. ***All future cash flows should be discounted to the present.*** Even a hypothetically risk-free future cash flow carries opportunity cost.

The baseline discount rate is the risk-free rate, which is the rate you can earn on capital that carries no risk. In theory there is no such thing, but as I discussed above, loaning money to the U.S. government comes pretty close. Banks use the federal funds rate as a risk-free rate in making loan decisions, but that's not available to investors. So professional analysts typically use the rate on 90-day Treasury bills in their valuation models. As a retail investor, however, a more practical risk-free rate to rely on is the best rate you can get on a simple and safe investment in a savings account or money market fund.

Whatever you use for your risk-free rate, the point is that you can always get at least that return, so you should never settle for anything less. The riskier the opportunity, the greater the anticipated rate of return *over the risk-free rate* has to be to justify your investment.

To recap: wealth comes from converting as much of your current income as possible to investment capital. You choose your investments based on what offers you the greatest return (future cash flows), adjusted based on risk (your confidence in those cash flows). Now we'll turn to your investment options: the major categories of financial assets.

ASSET CLASSES AND THE INVESTING SPECTRUM

Investing doesn't require a deep knowledge of finance. Capitalism on autopilot has just three steps. This isn't the *only* approach to successful investing, but if you apply the advice offered, this approach has proven to be a dependable way to build economic security. Note: this still isn't easy, as it requires the skill and grit to make money and the discipline to save and invest.

1) Keep your long-term funds (aka your investment capital) with an established broker, like Fidelity or Schwab, in a standard account with no fees.
2) Invest this capital in a half dozen low-cost, diversified exchange-traded funds (ETFs) that put the majority of your money in U.S. corporate stocks.
3) Continue adding capital to your investment account until you've hit your number (i.e., it's enough that you can live off your passive income alone).

This is a solid strategy, but it lacks nuance. Thus many successful investors will occasionally divert from it. Two reasons. First, life throws curveballs, good and bad, and there will be times when you should diverge from this strategy, either to protect yourself from downside or to optimize for upside: buying your first house, facing unexpected medical bills, having children, a compelling investment opportunity. When should you diverge from this core approach? How to make that decision?

Second, whatever your career and lifestyle choices, they exist within the framework of capitalism, and you want to understand how that larger system works so you can best navigate it. Maybe even change it. Putting your own money to work as a capitalist—investing—provides insight into not what should be but what is. Not just intellectual knowledge, either, but an instinctual feel for price and value, for market dynamics, and for your own ability to assess and respond to risk.

Most of us are not fortunate enough to have a mentor like Cy Cordner in their lives. But everyone can and should cultivate this knowledge, whatever your other interests or politics. Andy Warhol once said, "Being good in business is the most fascinating kind of art." Friedrich Engels ran his father's textile mills while he and Karl Marx wrote *Das Kapital*. You want to develop an intuitive understanding of interest rates and tax deductions before you step up to buy your first house. And if you're raising capital for your start-up, it's not enough to know your product, your market, and your strategy. You need to understand the investor's point of view, why they are in the room, what they want from you, and what you can get from them: valuation, dilution, governance, liquidity preference, etc.

The Balanced Approach

There is no single best investment for you or anyone else. You will make a wide range of investments over your lifetime, matching risk, return, and other considerations against your needs.

DIVERSIFICATION

In the last chapter, I suggested you think about your money in three buckets: consumption, intermediate spending, and long-term spending. Money in your consumption bucket won't stick around long enough to be invested, but your intermediate and long-term buckets should be treated as investment capital.

If you've started an emergency buffer, that's money in your intermediate bucket. And if you anticipate large expenses, such as grad school or a home, then you've got some additional goals for your intermediate bucket. Keep these needs in mind as you fund your long-term bucket—you don't want money you expect to need in the next year or two tied up in highly variable or illiquid investments. The better asset classes for that money offer stable prices and are easy to get in and out of: high-yield savings accounts are the easiest, but also consider Treasury bonds and high-grade corporate bonds.

If you have a 401(k), any money in it is included in your long-term bucket. You may not have much choice about how to invest it, as plans typically limit you to a few investment vehicles. But learning about those options and making the right allocation is educational and will have a real impact on your long-term returns. Once you've read this chapter, sit down with the 401(k) brochure you've been ignoring and see if you can make sense of the options it offers. (Again, a best practice is, to the extent you can, max out all matching and tax-advantaged opportunities such as a 401(k).)

As you start to save money beyond your retirement plan contributions, you'll have long-term capital—an army under your command. For many people, this comes when you get a bonus or other windfall. If you've got what you need for your emergency cushion, and you are maxing your tax-deferred savings and making progress on your intermediate bucket goals, then you can start your hands-on finance education. Again, if this sounds intimidating, don't worry.

Your ability to begin pouring capital into the second and third buckets is a function of your discipline around living below your means. And this will take time. Q: How do you eat an elephant? A: One bite at a time. Be patient but start now.

Adjust to taste, but I suggest that up to the first $10,000 in cash you save for your long-term budget—your cash savings, not 401(k) contributions—you should split it 80/20 as follows:

The majority goes into passive investments (mainly exchange-traded funds, which I explain in the "Funds" section below). You are going to buy these and hold on to them for years, maybe forever (recall: capitalism on easy mode). These are passive investments.

Twenty percent of the money you save (up to your first $10,000 in savings), you should actively invest. A couple thousand dollars is enough to trade with. It's enough that when you lose, you'll feel the pain, but it's not so much that you're putting your future economic security at unnecessary risk. The goal isn't to get rich quick but to learn the markets, learn about risk, and, most important, learn about yourself—actively managing your investments over the long term isn't for everyone. Active investing takes time (and, especially when you're young, you have this). Brace yourself, it can be emotionally disruptive and cognitively exhausting.

So why do it (active investing) at all? My colleague Aswath Damodaran says the best regulation is life lessons. Most of us, probably all young people, are under the delusion they can beat the market. Fine, have at it. You will likely find you can't, and your active investments over the long term will underperform the passive ones. However, some people enjoy it (consumption), and you will learn. And there will be opportunities to make larger investments in things where you have better access and a better sense for the value than the market does (e.g., the run-down house with great bones next door goes into probate; your mom's friend is retiring and selling her business that you know well, as you worked for her in high school). Ideally, that's not the first direct financial investment you make.

Put the active money into a brokerage account that offers fractional share purchases and zero-commission trades on most investments. You may want to use a different firm than where you keep your passive investments, to reinforce the distinction and to discourage "borrowing" from the passive side to support the active side (don't do this). If you do keep it all at one firm, however, use separate accounts.

Once you're able to save more than $10,000, put all or nearly all of the additional savings in your passive investments. What you can learn actively managing $20,000 in the market isn't any more than what you'll learn with $2,000. If you decide to put more than $2,000 into your active investments, draw up an allocation plan ahead of time and follow it, so you aren't topping off your losses. Track your *true* returns—accounting for losses, net of taxes, fees, etc. If you don't have the discipline to keep good records (you'll need them for taxes anyway) then this is not a hobby for you.

Before we get into active investing, a quick recap of where you should be economically before you YOLO your savings on two-week, out-of-the-money GME call options (don't do that). Before you start making active, individual investments, you should:

a) Be following a waterline budget that reflects your actual spending and includes a savings category.
b) Be maximizing your tax-sheltered retirement plan contributions.
c) Have saved up an emergency cushion appropriate to your circumstances and be on track to fund any intermediate bucket expenses you are planning.
d) Have begun to accumulate additional cash savings (third bucket). These are the funds you'll invest into the asset classes described below, subject to the 80/20 passive/active division.

Once you've checked these boxes, you're ready. So, where to put your money?

The Investment Spectrum

The simplest way to invest your capital is to loan it to your bank by putting it into an interest-bearing savings account. You let the bank use your money, mostly to make loans to other banking customers, and in exchange, the bank pays you a (very) modest interest rate. If you are willing to promise not to withdraw the money for a period of time, such as six or twelve months, the bank will pay you a (slightly) higher interest rate—an investment typically called a certificate of deposit or CD.

Returns on savings accounts and CDs are very low, however, and not enough to build real wealth. For that, you'll need to invest your money with someone who is going to be more aggressive with it (i.e., take more risk), and who will pay you more in return. The classic way to do this is to invest in operating businesses, companies including Microsoft or McDonald's that use the money they get from selling stock to buy raw materials, pay salaries and rents, and cover the costs of producing their products. Since selecting which companies to invest in can be a lot of work and require specialized knowledge, there are a variety of investment companies who will take your capital, pool it with the capital of other customers, and then invest the combined sums into a mix of companies the investment company deems good bets. Mutual funds are the classic example of this for consumers (and the newer exchange-traded funds, or ETFs) and this is also the basic idea behind hedge funds and venture capital.

Besides investing in corporations, either directly or through investment companies, you can also invest directly in the inputs of our economy: land and raw materials.

At the far end of the spectrum, some investors choose to invest in derivatives, which is essentially betting on the financial markets. Put and call options, short selling, and futures are all tools of the derivatives market. Derivatives serve an important function in the economy and in the market for money, but as a side effect, they also offer higher risk and potentially higher return.

CONSUMER INVESTMENT VEHICLES

Savings accounts	Money market/ CDs	Corporate and government bonds	ETFs and mutual funds	Individual stocks	Options

LOW ——————————————— RISK ——————————————→ HIGH

I'll cover these asset classes in some detail because they're important to our financial system, and I think a basic understanding of them is valuable, even if you never invest in them. Indeed, the more you know about some of these asset classes, the more convinced you may become that you *don't* want to invest in them directly. For most people, and that probably means you, and for most of your investment capital, the ultimate answer comes at the end of this section. Your long-term bucket, the money you plan to live off one day, should largely be invested in low-cost, diversified exchange-traded funds. We're going to take the long way around to get there (and I'll explain more about what an exchange-traded fund is when we do), but keep this principle in mind as we tour the major asset classes.

Stocks

Stocks are the investment headliner, no doubt. Financial media including CNBC and *The Wall Street Journal* devote most of their coverage to corporate performance and the price of their stocks, investment social media is obsessed with stocks, and it's our go-to when we think about investing.

Why? Because stocks are your most direct access to the raw wealth-generating power of the economy, and the greatest wealth-generating machine in history, the U.S. corporation. The virtues of a system where corporations can and do amass such economic might is subject to debate, but in the world as it is, your best chance of obtaining economic security is to hitch your wagon to their rocket. Or something like that.

Understanding why stocks are a direct line into the veins of the economy means understanding how stock and stock ownership work. You can buy and sell stock without ever really understanding what it is you are putting your money into, but stocks are likely to be the largest or second-largest (after real estate) asset class in your portfolio, and it's worth a few minutes to understand the basics of a pillar of your pursuit of economic security.

I explained above that a corporation is a legal construct designed to enable multiple parties to pool their resources. Stock is the mechanism by which that pooling takes place.

EQUITY

Stock ownership, also referred to as equity, has two dimensions: control and economics. Control is of less interest to us as retail investors, so I'll cover it quickly. Corporations are run on a day-to-day basis by the CEO, and the CEO answers to the board of directors. Stockholders (or shareholders, the terms are interchangeable) vote, usually once a year, and elect directors to the board. Typically, each share of stock counts for one vote. There has been a recent trend, unfortunate in my view, toward "dual-class" share structures, where some stock gets more than one vote per share, giving the holders of that stock (typically the company's founders and early investors) effective control over the company. But whatever the voting rules, the basic structure is the same: shareholders determine who sits on the board, the board makes major decisions including hiring and firing the CEO, and the CEO runs the company quarter to quarter. Certain momentous decisions, such as the sale of the company, remain subject to shareholder vote.

The economic dimension of stock ownership is what matters to most investors. A share of stock represents an economic interest in the corporation. Concretely, this means two things. First, stockholders have the "residual claim" on the company's assets. Corporations do not expire, but in the dynamic market of capitalism, nothing lasts forever. And when a corporation is extinguished, either because it is bought by someone else (usually another corporation) or because it goes out of business, and once all of the company's debts are paid, any remaining value is divided up among the shareholders. Each share of stock receives a corresponding share of those assets.

But for the most part we don't buy stock in companies we expect to disappear, we buy stock in companies we expect to prosper. And just as with residual asset value, each share of stock gives us a claim on a corresponding share of future profits. Corporations are money-making machines, and stock is how the profits get distributed. In most corporations this doesn't happen directly. Shareholders don't get together at the end of each day, or even each quarter or year, and divide up the cash in the company's bank account. Instead, the company's managers (the CEO and the board) decide when and how much of the profit to distribute to shareholders. Often, especially in young, fast-growing companies, management decides the use of profits is to reinvest and grow the business—i.e., hire more people, open new factories or sales offices. If management is smart with its investments, the company's prospects will improve so even though stockholders don't get a share of the cash profits right away, the value of the stock itself increases, as the market anticipates greater cash flows in the future.

DISTRIBUTION OF PROFITS

Eventually, most successful corporations reach a point where they can't realistically put all of their profits to good use—the company's "mature," if you will—and they start to distribute some of the profits back to the shareholders. This can be done through dividends, which are direct cash payments, or via stock buybacks, where the company uses its profits to buy its own stock.

Dividends are the traditional approach, and many large, stable corporations pay dividends today. It's important to understand that dividends are not free money or some sort of gift. The money was always the shareholder's money, it's just being transferred from one type of ownership, stock, to another, cash. In fact, when a corporation pays a dividend, the market value of the stock typically goes down by the value of the dividend, reflecting this transfer of value out of the stock. Share buybacks are a roundabout way of returning profits to the shareholders—they work by increasing the value of the shares rather than paying cash dividends. Share prices increase after a buyback because there are fewer shares "outstanding" to divide up the total value of the company, so each share of stock claims a larger share of the company's assets and future profits.

Share buybacks are supplanting dividends as the preferred means of distributing profits to shareholders. Historically, the advantage of dividends was that they allowed investors to enjoy some of their investment earnings in cash without having to sell stock. Back in ancient times (before 2020, and even more so before 2000) selling stock came with high fees, especially when selling less than 100 shares at a time. With the availability of low- or no-commission stock trades and fractional shares, however, dividends offer little practical benefit to investors. Now, if an investor wants cash from a stock holding, they can create "synthetic dividends" by selling a few shares, or even a portion of a single share. As long as the price of the stock is going up, shareholders can continue to sell smaller and smaller share amounts to receive a steady cash flow. Meanwhile, buybacks offer shareholders an important tax-related benefit: they allow the shareholder to control the timing of their tax liability. When you receive a dividend, it's taxed (in most cases, at capital gains tax rates) the year you receive it. When the company buys back stock and increases the value of your stock, you don't pay taxes on that increase until you sell the stock, which might be many years later, enabling your investment to grow tax-deferred.

As most of a company's profits are not actually distributed to shareholders in cash, the most consequential return for shareholders is through an increase in the price of a company's shares. Buying a stock is a bet that the price is at or, ideally, below the true value of the stock, and that the market will eventually realize this and bid the share price up to its true value. Which brings us back to the essential question of valuation. How do we gauge the true underlying value of a stock? The short answer, see above, is that it is the present value of all future cash flows the stock will receive. But that begs the question, how do we know the present value of the future cash flows? That requires a brief introduction to the tool corporations use to report on their operations to shareholders: financial statements.

FINANCIAL STATEMENTS

Corporations keep vast records internally, but they distill them down to three primary documents when reporting to shareholders: the income statement, the cash flow statement, and the balance sheet. Companies with stock that trades in the public markets produce these reports every quarter and file them with the Securities and Exchange Commission, where they are available to the public through the SEC's EDGAR service: sec.gov/edgar.

I'll briefly cover the balance sheet and cash flow statement, then turn to the income statement, which is the most interesting and important for investors in most companies. The **balance sheet** lists the company's assets and liabilities and some basic information about its stock. Assets are mostly money, whether in cash or investments, and things, like factory equipment and buildings. Intellectual property, like patents and copyrights, are assets, as are loans owed *to* the company. Loans the company owes somebody else (i.e., debt) are liabilities, as are other claims on the company. Some common liabilities are obligations to make future pension payments, and reserves for potential costs management has identified that might occur, like losses due to lawsuits. In a healthy company, the total asset value is greater than liabilities, and the difference between the two is known as shareholder's equity. Confusingly, the balance sheet value of the shareholder's equity is *not* the market value of the company's stock—that's typically worth far more, because it represents a claim on future profits, not just the company's assets at that moment.

The **cash flow statement** is just what it says—it tracks the movement of cash in and out of the company. Corporations need a cash flow statement because they typically rely on something called accrual accounting to track their operations. (If reading that sentence put you to sleep, you have my permission to skip the rest of this paragraph.) Accrual accounting ignores actual cash paid and received in favor of recording when *value* changes hands. For example, if a company using accrual accounting sells a widget for $100 on December 31, 2023, but doesn't get paid until January 31, 2024—a common arrangement in commercial transactions—the company reports the revenue from the sale as occurring in 2023, even though the cash doesn't arrive until 2024. The cash flow statement reconciles the claim that the company made $100 in revenue with the fact that the $100 doesn't appear in the company's bank account. As with the balance sheet, the cash flow statement includes important information that can be useful for detailed analyses but isn't the main way we understand a company's business.

DIVERSIFICATION

For that, we look at the **income statement**. Sometimes called the statement of operations or the profit and loss (or P and L), this gives us the best picture of how a company makes its money, and how much profit it can be expected to make in the future.

Read from top to bottom, the income statement portrays a river of money, flowing through the business, watering its operations. The headwaters of the river are revenue: the money the company has made selling its goods and services. If a company sells widgets, and it sells 10 widgets for $10 each, that's $100 in revenue. As we go down the income statement, the mighty river of revenue is diverted to feed the components of the business. The first and often largest culling of the river comes right at the outset, in the cost of goods sold. That's the cost of the raw materials used to make the company's products, and the labor that can be directly attributed to production. What's left after paying for the cost of goods is known as a company's gross margin, or gross profit. Next comes operating expenses, the various costs of running the business. Typically, these include a line for selling, general, and administrative expenses, or SG&A. This is mainly salaries for the sales and marketing departments, senior management, and other support

THE INCOME STATEMENT RIVER

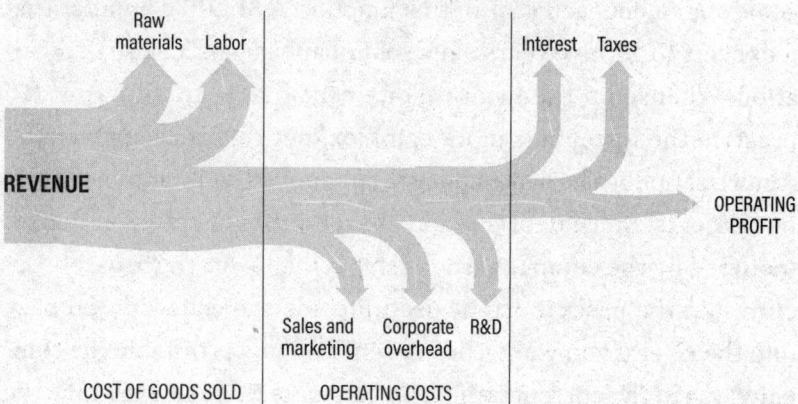

staff. Research and development is sometimes included in SG&A, and sometimes listed separately. Once enough water has been taken from the river to cover operating expenses, what remains in the river is operating profit.

Operating profit is an important number, because it shows how much money the company makes as a function of its operations, before the impact of financing and taxes comes into play. Financing and taxes are real costs, of course, but they're also distinct from the fundamental questions about a business: Do customers want the product and are they willing to pay highly for it? Can the company make and sell the product for less than customers will pay for it? Is the company investing in its future through new product development? Analysts sometimes use the technical term **EBIT** for operating profits, which stands for "earnings before interest and taxes."

A variation on EBIT that also gets a lot of attention is called **EBITDA**. This stands for "earnings before interest, taxes, depreciation, and amortization." Depreciation and amortization is another artifact of the accrual method of accounting. When a company buys an asset that it intends to use for more than a year, it doesn't record the cost of that asset as an expense on the income statement. Instead, it divides the total cost of the asset over the number of years it expects to use it, and then takes depreciation on the income statement each year in that amount. A $1,000 computer that it expects to get five years of use out of appears as a $200 depreciation expense on the income statement five years in a row. (In practice the formula is more complex, but this is the principle.) Amortization is the same concept but applied to intangible assets like patents. Since depreciation charges are not actual expenses incurred by the company (the cash payments for those assets occurred in the past), it can be useful to add the water it used back into the river if you want a better sense of how profitable the company was in the current period. To calculate EBITDA, you take the

GROSS PROFIT =
Revenue − Cost of goods

OPERATING PROFIT ("EBIT") =
Gross profit − SG&A (Selling, general, and administrative expenses)

NET INCOME =
Operating profit − Interest − Taxes

operating profit from the income statement and add depreciation and amortization expense (found on the cash flow statement).

CEOs like to emphasize EBITDA for the simple reason that it makes their business look more profitable. When I was selling L2, EBITDA was the number I featured in my pitch decks. Its use is controversial, however, because while depreciation is not a cash expense, companies still need to make capital expenditures (i.e., buy equipment and invest in research), and EBITDA effectively excludes those very real costs from the company's financial picture. Warren Buffett is famously critical of EBITDA for this reason, once asking, "Does management think the tooth fairy pays for capital expenditures?"

In recent years, there has been a trend toward even more aggressive metrics, especially among early-stage companies, usually described as "adjusted EBITDA," where costs such as marketing and even employee compensation are removed. The dubious justification for these metrics is that the excluded costs are specific to the company's growth stage and shouldn't be considered part of its future operating model. Be wary: most of these metrics feel like a car salesman telling me the miles per gallon a car would get driving downhill.

Below operating profit (EBIT) on the income statement come the costs of financing—mainly interest payments on debt—and taxes. Sometimes a little water gets added back into the river at this point, such as if the company invested some of its own cash, received tax rebates, or had other unusual sources of income. Note that the principal of a loan—the money borrowed—doesn't appear on the income statement, just the interest expense (or income). Loans are not part of the river of revenue since they don't come from the company's actual operations.

Whatever water is left in the river is profit, typically called net income or earnings. Public companies report this as an absolute dollar value, and then also as "earnings per share." They calculated it by dividing net income by the number of shares of stock outstanding. Often abbreviated EPS, earnings per share is the bottom-line measure of a company's profitability—how much profit each share of stock has a claim on (though most of the money will stay with the company).

EQUITY VALUATION

The simplest way to estimate the value of a share of stock is to apply a "multiple" to the earnings per share. This is a rough way to estimate the value of the company's future cash flow based on its most recent earnings. The higher the expected growth, the higher the multiple of current earnings you apply. For publicly traded companies, you can gauge the market's assessment of the company's prospects based on the ratio of a stock's trading price to the company's earnings per share. This is what's known as the price to earnings (P/E) ratio. The higher the P/E ratio, the more the market believes a company will grow its earnings in the future. P/E ratios above 30 typically indicate a high-growth company, whereas mature, slower-growing companies have a P/E closer to 10.

The P/E ratio is what's known as a market multiple. It's the most commonly seen, but not the only one, or even the most useful. Investors frequently look at multiples of each of the major line items on the income statement. A company whose market capitalization is $1,000, which recorded $100 in revenue, $50 in gross profit, $25 in EBIT, and $10 in net income, has a revenue multiple of 10, a gross profit multiple of 20, an EBIT multiple of 40, and a net income multiple of 100.

You can calculate a multiple based on any number in the financial statements. Subscription businesses are sometimes evaluated based on their value per subscriber. Dividend-paying stocks can be valued based on their dividend yield: the total annual dividends divided by the share price. Analysts also look at the ratios of other numbers besides the market value: the gross margin percentage is the share of revenue converted to gross profit, which tells you about the company's pricing power, while inventory turnover (cost of goods sold divided by inventory) tells you how efficiently the company is producing and selling its products.

EQUITY VALUATION MULTIPLES

	INCOME	MARKET CAP	MULTIPLE
REVENUE	$100	$1,000	10
GROSS PROFIT	$50	$1,000	20
EBIT	$25	$1,000	40
NET INCOME	$10	$1,000	100

By themselves, multiples don't tell you much, though if you are familiar with an industry, you come to learn typical multiples in that industry. They are primarily useful as a means of comparison. If you have two companies in the same industry, and one has an EBIT multiple of 20 while the other's is 35, that tells you the market is more optimistic about the second company. We often say the first company is "cheap" and the second "expensive" based on those multiples. But it's all relative.

Generally, multiples based further down the income statement are more meaningful, as they reflect a company's true profitability. But because earnings can be affected by nonoperational factors (tax and financing activities), sophisticated investors often focus on the EBIT multiple as the best gauge of a company's valuation. But for high-growth companies, or for companies that are being considered as takeover targets, a revenue multiple can be the best gauge of value.

When calculating a multiple, it's important to understand the distinction between market capitalization and enterprise value. Market capitalization is the price of a company's stock times the total number of shares. This the value of the company's stock.

MARKET CAPITALIZATION =
Stock price × Number of shares

For a company without significant debt or large cash holdings, the value of its stock is equivalent to the value of the company itself. But debt and cash complicate the picture. Counterintuitively, to get to the market value of the company itself, you *add* the company's long-term debt to its market capitalization and *subtract* its cash. The result is enterprise value. It's more accurate to use enterprise value rather than market capitalization when computing a multiple, but again, for companies without much debt or cash, market capitalization is fine.

ENTERPRISE VALUE =
(Market capitalization + Debt) − Cash

Although a single multiple gives you some information (the higher it is, the more growth the market expects) multiples are mainly a relative measure. Which means a multiple needs "comps"—companies that are *comparable* to the subject of the valuation. Selecting comps is not always as easy as it might seem. Some companies have obvious comparables in their competitive set: Home Depot and Lowe's, for example, are similar-sized companies in the same business, and if they're trading at different multiples, that's a sure sign the market believes one (with the higher multiples) is better positioned for growth than the other. But what's a good comp for Microsoft? The company competes fiercely with Amazon in cloud services, but it's not in Amazon's main business of retail at all. Microsoft Office competes with Google's Docs and Sheets, but Google gives those products away—how do you compare the two companies financially when one doesn't charge for its product?

Multiples are relative and limited by available comps; a more direct valuation method is to build a "discounted cash flow model." Building a DCF is a core competency for professional investors, though not something retail investors need to understand in detail. Briefly, a DCF starts with an income statement, but instead of showing the company's results for the recent past, it projects those results into the future. Then, since *all future cash flows should be discounted*, it applies a discount rate, as I discussed above, to those future earnings, and totals them up to arrive at the present value of the company. If you calculate the present value of a public company and it comes out different from the market price, that suggests your assumptions are different from the market consensus—which may mean there's an investment opportunity.

Any means of valuation requires at some level you understand what business the company is actually in. Like finding comps, that can be trickier than it seems. But different kinds of businesses require very different kinds of companies. A global oil company, for example, like Exxon or Chevron, has to invest billions of dollars in oilfield operations that may not pay back the investment for decades. This requires huge amounts of capital up front, but once the oil starts flowing, it generates vast profits. In this sense, oil companies are not unlike some software companies. Both have to invest in years of upfront development, but once they have a product, can ship infinite copies of it for almost no cost. Compare those models to a law firm. From day one, a small firm with a single lawyer and a paralegal can turn a profit, because their overhead costs are negligible—some laptops, malpractice insurance, rented office space, maybe a few nice suits—and they can bill top dollar for every hour they work. Recall in "Focus," however, that I said services firms don't scale well? If the founding lawyer is booked up and wants to double the firm's revenue, they'll have to hire another lawyer. To 10x revenue, they'll have to hire 10x the number of lawyers. And if the named partner can't sell enough work for those ten new lawyers, they are still going to expect their paychecks.

Some companies aren't really in the business they appear to be in. Google, for example, is the leading search engine, but it doesn't sell search engines, it sells advertising. That's its real business. Though it develops and deploys technologically advanced systems, from a business perspective Google looks more like a traditional television network or newspaper publisher than technology companies like

DIVERSIFICATION

Microsoft and Apple, because its core revenue-generating business is creating content that attracts attention, then selling access to that attention to advertisers. Understanding how a company actually generates revenue, and what it costs, is critical to understanding its finances, growth prospects, and, ultimately, value.

STOCK INVESTING

For the most part, shareholders don't buy stock directly from a corporation. Most stock sales take place in the "secondary market"—third parties selling stock to one another. And the money you spend to buy stock doesn't actually go to the company but to the shareholder you bought the stock from. You're still investing in the company; however, you're taking over an investment previously made by someone else. Even though a company doesn't receive the money that is spent on its stock in the secondary market, management still focuses intently on the share price. Because that's typically an important part of their compensation and how they attract employees, it can be used to buy other companies, and additional stock sales are a potential source of capital for the company. Just as they sometimes buy stock in the market, corporations sometimes sell stock to raise fresh capital. The first time they do this is generally known as the company's initial public offering, or IPO, and it's a significant event in the evolution of the corporation. Subsequent sales are known as secondary offerings and happen with much less fanfare.

Buying and selling stock in specific companies is a good way to get skin in the game and give yourself motivation to learn about companies and investing. I own individual stocks, and I am in favor of informed, prudent retail investors generally owning individual stocks. What I strongly advise against, and what the data confirms doesn't work, is jumping in and out of stocks. The more you trade, the more you lose. It's cognitively and emotionally exhausting, and it doesn't work. It's not tax efficient, either, as assets held less than a year don't qualify for capital gains tax treatment. Don't day trade.

There's a good chance that at some point in your career, you won't have a choice but to own stock in an individual company, because you work there and your compensation is partly in stock (these days, that usually means restricted stock units, or RSUs). My advice in that situation is to sell your stock as soon as you can in the most tax-advantaged way possible. Tax considerations may justify holding on to stock you receive in compensation, but otherwise, it rarely makes sense to keep stock in the company where you work. Why? Because you are already massively exposed to that company, and you want to diversify your risk, not further concentrate it. You are exposed to that company because your future compensation, your reputation in the labor market, and your psychological rewards from work are all dependent on that company's success. Stock is highly liquid, so don't treat your compensation differently because it comes in stock rather than cash. Think of it this way: If you didn't get any stock compensation, but instead you received the equivalent value in cash, would you have used that cash to buy your company stock? I doubt it.

Who might, nonetheless, want to keep company stock? Founders or early employees and investors have to be careful with stock sales because aggressive selling can signal doubt about the company's prospects to the market (and worse, to employees). Don't overvalue this consideration, however. Venture capitalists and bankers always tell founders to leave their money in the company. That's in their interest because they want the share price as high as possible, and the founder as dependent on the business as possible. I always tell founders to take some chips off the table, because the founder's interest is to achieve economic security for their family, and growth stocks are risky stocks. For long-term small business owners (i.e., the Main Street economy I described in Focus), an existential concern should be to gradually convert corporate assets into personal assets, so that economic security is not dependent on a single event like a sale or passing the business to an heir.

Some employees are deep experts in their industry and may have a better understanding of their company's potential than outside analysts. If you have good reasons to believe that your company is going to grow profits faster than the current share price would suggest, that can be a reason to increase your exposure to your company by holding on to (or even buying) company stock. Be careful that your natural affinity for your own work, your colleagues, or the products you've developed are not obscuring your view, however. And be sure you are not trading on "insider information" such as non-public knowledge that a drug has been approved or a large customer signed. People can and do go to jail for that.

Besides being an employee, there are other ways you might develop deep knowledge of a company or an industry. Major customers sometimes have insight into companies that nobody else gets. Academics and scientists may have a unique understanding of certain industries. By the mid-2000s, I had spent twenty years working closely with some of the best companies in retail as they managed the transition to online commerce, and I founded several online commerce companies, including one that went public. I'd developed a deep understanding of the potential in that area, and what it would take to achieve it. It was clear to me that the market was greatly undervaluing Amazon, and I bet a significant portion of my net worth on Jeff Bezos and his team. That investment has returned twenty-five times over the past two decades. That was not an investment I made lightly, but one based on two decades of experience.

A trend that has gained momentum in recent years is policy-driven investing, and in particular so-called environmental, social, and corporate governance (ESG) investments. For individual retail investors, I am not a fan. Your individual investments are not going to shape the decisions of the corporations you buy stock in, but they will determine your future economic security. I understand if you'd rather not share in the profits of a short list of companies that you think are destructive to society—I owned Facebook stock for many years but eventually sold the stock when I became convinced that the company was causing real damage to young people and our broader society. But I urge you not to orient your entire portfolio around your policy preferences. Vote, lobby your representatives, take action in your community. But your capital means far more to you than it does to your investments. The ESG label in particular has been weaponized by corporate PR and means nothing. (Policy investing presents a different calculus for large institutions, whose investment choices have real impacts—but that's a different book.)

Bonds

Both corporations and governments issue bonds, and the bond market is massive: over $120 trillion. Bonds are a kind of debt, but instead of a loan between just two parties, they are debt that has been turned into a "security." A security is a claim on some under-

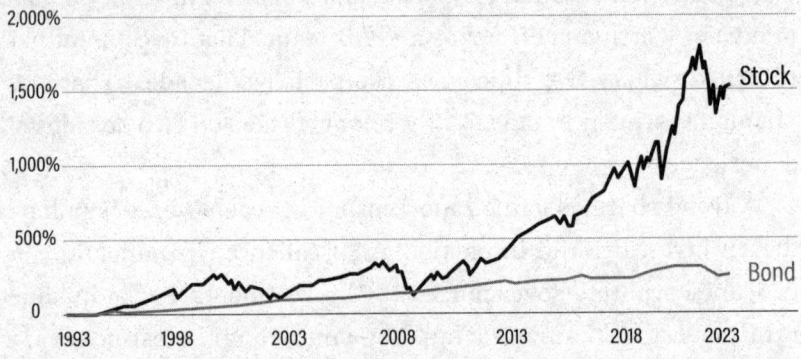

Source: Morningstar, Bond = Vanguard Total Bond Market Index Fund, Stock = Vanguard Total Stock Market Index Fund

lying asset that can be bought and sold independently of that asset. Corporate stock is a type of security—it's a claim on the equity of a corporation, but it changes hands on the market without the involvement of that corporation. Yet it's a binding, legal claim on that corporation nonetheless. Bonds are the same idea but applied to loans.

Here's how a bond works, in a simplified example. Say Amazon wants to borrow $100. It goes to a bank, like Wells Fargo. Wells looks at Amazon's books, decides the company's a good credit risk, and offers it a loan at 6%. Amazon comes back and says, "Hey, we're the dominant online commerce and cloud company, we've got incredible cash flow, so how about 4%?" Eventually, the two sides negotiate a loan at 5%—meaning Wells gives Amazon $100 now, in exchange for a promise to pay $105 in a year. Instead of just holding on to Amazon's promise of $105, however, Wells chops it up into 100 little promises, each one a promise to pay $1.05 in a year (5% interest on $1.00). And then Wells Fargo sells those 100 little promises on the open market. Those are bonds. The investors who buy them might hold on to them until the year is up and collect their $1.05, or they might sell them again to other investors, just as stocks trade in a secondary market.

Something curious happens to bonds once they become securities and trade in the secondary market. When Wells and Amazon negotiated the original terms, the primary variable was the interest rate—Amazon wanted 4%, Wells preferred 6%, and they settled on 5%. For an investor thinking about buying a bond, however, that 5% rate is irrelevant. The bond is a promise from Amazon to pay $1.05 in a year to whoever shows up with a bond in hand. In the secondary market, bondholders don't care how much Amazon originally borrowed, or what interest rate they were charged. All bondholders care about is the value of a promise from Amazon to pay $1.05 in a year. That's the price at which they will buy and sell the bond.

If Amazon starts having serious business issues—supply chain problems, management turnover, data breaches—investors might start to get worried that the company won't be able to make that $1.05 payment, and so they'll value the bond lower. The projected cash flows from the bond haven't changed, but the risk, and hence the discount rate, has gone up, so the present value of the bond goes down. Maybe it was worth $1.00 when Wells negotiated it, but a few months later, the company is in trouble, and its promise is only worth $0.90. The risk that this will happen is known as credit risk or default risk.

Bond prices can change even if investor perceptions of the company don't. When interest rates go up, buyers have better options for their money and won't pay as much now for $1.05 in a year. If an investor can pay the U.S. government $1.00 now for the promise of $1.06 in a year, they aren't going to pay Amazon $1.00 for a promise to pay just $1.05 in a year. No matter how solid a debtor Amazon is, it isn't more reliable than the U.S. government. Thus, the price of Amazon bonds will drop below $1.00. On the other hand, if interest rates go *down*, then that promise of $1.05 in a year from Amazon looks better (since the U.S. government is now offering less than $1.05), and the price of the bond will rise above a dollar. The potential for bond prices to change due to broader interest rate shifts is called interest rate risk.

Regardless of what's going on with Amazon or the broader market, as we get closer to the repayment date, the bond price will approach $1.05 because of the time value of money, and because less can go wrong in less time. A promise from Amazon to pay you $1.05 tomorrow is worth $1.05 unless Amazon is in very serious distress.

Some terminology: the amount a bond will pay out at the end of the term is known as the face value or par value. In our example, the face value is $1.00. The rate of interest as originally negotiated is the coupon rate—here that was 5%. Most bonds are for longer than one year, and so the issuer will make interest payments along the way. In our example, there's just one, for $0.05 at the end of the year. The time when a bond comes due (i.e., when the principal is repaid) is known as its maturity date. Here, that's also the end of the year, when Amazon repays the $1.00 principal, along with that single $0.05 interest payment.

The most important term, however, is "yield." Yield refers to the *effective* annual interest rate you will get if you buy the bond at the market price. For our Amazon example, if you buy the bond one year from maturity for $1.00, the yield is 5%, because it will pay $1.05 in a year. If you buy it for $1.00 just six months from maturity, the yield is 10%, because you will make a 5% return in just six months, which is a 10% *annualized* return. A bond's yield changes daily based on the market price of the bond, and measures how attractive that issuer's promise to pay is to the market. In general, but not always, the bond market and the stock market move in opposite directions, because when stocks are doing well, investors are less inclined to buy bonds, which tend to have lower but more stable returns. This pushes down prices, thereby increasing yields, until risk-adjusted bond returns are competitive with stock returns. Getting your head around these relationships takes some practice, and the best way to internalize the mechanics is to buy some bonds and track their price (and yield) over time.

Governments also issue bonds. In fact, much of the bond market is made up of government bonds, with the U.S. federal government a major issuer. Most U.S. bonds are issued by the Treasury in increments of $100 and with maturities varying from 4 weeks to 30 years. (Shorter-duration bonds are known as T-bills while longer durations are called bonds, but they are functionally the same.) The Treasury issues new bonds every week and sets the interest rate based on an auction to investors. Once in the market as a security, however, they offer a fixed stream of payments, just like a corporate bond, and trade at whatever price the market dictates. A notable advantage of Treasury bonds is that the interest they pay is exempt from state income tax.

Bonds provide an alternative way to invest in corporations, and the only way to invest in governments. They are less risky than stocks, with a more predictable return, and in most cases, there's very little risk that you will lose money, if you hold them to maturity. The trade-off, however, is that they offer only modest returns, and there is very little upside potential. No matter how successful the issuer is, they never have to make *more* than the designated payments on a bond. The most a bondholder ever receives from the company is what's printed on the bond. Any extra profits above and beyond the bond payments go to the stockholders. Risk, as always, is paired with reward.

Real Estate

Real estate is the emperor of the asset classes. Although the price of individual parcels can go up and down, over the long term, it's bulletproof. Land (and buildings) can produce income (through rents or development, or by using it yourself) and it has a nearly guaranteed terminal value: we aren't making any more of it. Plus, real estate enjoys favorable tax treatment in a number of ways. For investors who can afford it, real estate is unmatched as a long-term investment.

As with every investment, however, there's a catch. Two, actually. First, real estate is less liquid than almost any other investment. It's hard to find a buyer, and the transaction costs are high. In fact, when you buy a piece of land, you typically start out at a loss on your investment, because you have to pay brokers, assessors, sometimes surveyors, and a slew of government agencies with their hands out, plus you'll have to make another round of payments when you want to sell it. Second, real estate costs money just to own it: property taxes, insurance, maintenance. Even unimproved land can have maintenance costs: fencing and security, fire and flood abatement, the risk a prior owner dumped waste, or any number of other ways that land can cost you. Though, on the bright side, you might find oil or gold. Just be sure you obtained the mineral rights when you bought the property.

The short of it is that real estate can be an incredible investment, but like most great investments in a capitalist system, it takes money to make money. Investing in real estate requires you to have a lot of capital that you can afford to keep tied up in the land for potentially years, plus enough liquid cash to maintain your ownership. Assuming you are not a billionaire real estate tycoon, there are only a few ways you might encounter viable opportunities to invest in real estate.

The most important real estate investment for most people is their home. For most readers of this book, their home will be the largest component of their investment portfolio for much of their lives. For nearly everyone, it's the largest purchase you will ever make, the largest loan you will ever take out, and the largest expense on your monthly budget. That kind of investment can be a powerful stabilizing force in our lives, and so buying a home is often seen as a major stepping stone to economic security. That perception has shaped tax and economic policy in the U.S. and elsewhere, encouraging home ownership. Today there's more debate around the virtues of owning versus renting, and there are absolutely situations in which buying a home is unwise. But for most people, my strong advice is to make purchasing a home a central component of your plan for achieving economic security. Like much of this book, my advice regarding home ownership is rooted in two domains: the economic and the personal.

First, the economics. Historically, residential real estate has been a good investment over the long term. Comparing home values to other investments is complicated by differing tax treatments, by the costs and benefits of real estate ownership (see above: avoiding rent, paying property tax), and by real estate being highly localized. Homes in established neighborhoods with a history of price appreciation in desirable areas (due to weather and other natural resources, proximity to employment, etc.) are a better investment in this regard. The low-cost starter home in a new, partially built subdivision miles from anything is a low-cost home for a reason. Fringe region real estate investments wrecked many families' financial security when house prices collapsed in 2008. But over the long term, real estate is tax-advantaged and reliable in ways that no other asset class enjoys.

The first $250,000 in *gains* ($500,000 for married couples) you make on the sale of your home is tax free (plus you can reduce the amount counted as a gain by excluding the cost of improvements you've made to the home), and anything above that is taxed at capital gains rates. So if you buy a house for $400,000 and sell it five years later for $500,000, you pay no income tax on the sale, since your gain is only $100,000. Investment real estate (i.e., you don't live in it) has its own array of tax deferral and minimization provisions. There are also numerous federal and state programs for first-time and low- to middle-income buyers, and you may be able to withdraw some (not a lot) of capital from retirement accounts like IRAs and 401(k)s penalty free to put toward your down payment.

Price appreciation is not the only economic benefit of owning a home. It's the only investment *you can live in*, and you have to live somewhere. Millennials are paying upward of 50% of their income on rent in higher cost urban areas. Rent savings are offset by property taxes, insurance, and maintenance costs. The true cost of owning a home is something many first-time home buyers underestimate, but unless you are extremely unlucky or foolish, the money you save in rent will nonetheless exceed the money you have to spend to maintain your home.

For most people, buying a home means taking out a mortgage, and interest payments are substantial. Throughout the 2010s, low interest rates made home buying even more attractive, and while rates went up after the Covid-19 pandemic, it doesn't appear that we're likely to return to the double-digit mortgage rates of the 1970s. Because a mortgage is a "secured" loan (meaning, if you don't make your payments, the bank can take/sell your house) the interest rates are low relative to other forms of consumer credit, reflecting the lower risk to the lender. Even if you can afford to buy a home without a mortgage, that capital can't be invested elsewhere—investment always carries opportunity cost—so if the rate on the mortgage is less than what you can get on other investments, a mortgage might still be the economically sound choice.

U.S. tax policy offers another significant bonus to home buying, though it has been reduced in recent years. Since income taxes were introduced in 1913, homeowners have been allowed to deduct mortgage interest from their income for tax purposes. This is still true, but due to changes in the tax code, the deduction only makes economic sense for a minority of homeowners. The 2017 Tax Cuts and Jobs Act (aka the Trump tax cuts) doubled the "standard deduction" (from $6,000 to $12,000, and twice that for married couples), which neutralized the benefits of the home mortgage interest deduction unless you have a very large mortgage or other large deductions. The impact was dramatic. The year before the change, 21% of taxpayers took the mortgage deduction. In 2018, only 8% took it. Among taxpayers with household incomes between $100,000 and $200,000, the percentage who took the mortgage deduction plummeted from 61% to 21%.

I've emphasized the changes to the mortgage interest deduction because we have over 100 years of experience in a world where the deduction was an important component of the decision to buy a house. Accordingly, that history is reflected in the advice you'll hear from friends and family and in anything published before 2018 (and plenty published after). The mortgage deduction *may* still apply to your situation, but don't assume it will just because your Uncle Carl told you it will—or your Uncle Scott. Tax laws change often, so look into how the current rules apply to you before you buy a home. If you're at the point of being ready to buy a home, you are likely at the point when professional tax advice becomes worth the cost.

All that said, the mortgage deduction was never the main reason to buy a home, and the economics of home ownership still make sense for a lot of people. But in addition, there are personal factors. A mortgage payment is a form of "forced savings." What this means is that you are *highly* motivated to make your mortgage payment, and thus will almost certainly do so. Despite your best intentions, it's hard to take $1,000 a month out of your income and put it in an investment fund. Mortgage payments gradually pay down the amount you owe the bank, and thus, increase your share of the home's value.

Owning a home is a commitment to economic security and stability. A home's lack of liquidity can be a virtue, since you are committed to a neighborhood, perhaps even a job, once you buy one. Constraints encourage focus, and focus will get you where you want to go faster than flexibility. Recall my observation in "Time" that you will change. One of the ways you will change is you will likely become more settled, more interested in roots and stability. So even if a house seems like an impediment to your freedom now, you are highly likely to see it as refuge in another decade. If you're young, don't assume you'll want to live in an apartment and be ready to move on thirty days' notice for the rest of your life.

As with the economics, there are countervailing factors here,

DIVERSIFICATION

too. Roots are great, until you want to move. Selling a home is expensive at the best of times, and if you are forced to sell in a down market, it can be brutal. So if you buy a home, you may have to forgo a job opportunity or quality of life improvement because you can't pull up your roots. (Note: renting out a home you own can solve this riddle and even make you money in some market conditions, but it's a risk and it takes careful management.) Finally, homes require maintenance, they carry a tax obligation, and, I promise you, you'll end up spending more on furnishings and upgrades than you plan.

Beyond your own home, you can invest in other types of real estate. Owning investment properties directly can be an *excellent* way to convert income to capital and build economic security. The challenge is that it comes with a lot of overhead. As "passive" income goes, it's pretty active. That's why I discussed my own experiences with owning investment properties in the "Focus" chapter, because it's more like having a second (or first) career. If you are disciplined and detail oriented, handy and/or comfortable dealing with contractors, tough enough to negotiate with tenants and enforce your agreements, and have deep knowledge and contacts in a regional market and, above all, have the time to do it right, seriously consider buying investment properties to rent or resell. Start small, grow incrementally.

You can also invest in real estate through financial companies. Real estate investment trusts are (often) publicly traded real estate holding companies, and there are many, many private groups that own real estate all over. They range from small consortiums formed to back a single development, such as a mall or office building, to multinational holding companies with many billions in assets. Publicly traded REITs are more highly regulated, which offers some additional safety, whereas private real estate investments require more due diligence on your part. In general, however, these investments are more like stock investments than real estate investments, in that you are investing in a management team and a business model that happens to be in real estate rather than software or sneakers.

Commodities, Currency, and Derivatives

On the fringes of where you might invest, there are asset classes that are more removed from economic activity. Commodities and currencies themselves are real assets. Commodities are raw materials like oil, gold, or corn, and currency is money. And they change hands in (mostly) liquid markets. Commodities prices are largely influenced by real-world considerations: weather has a huge influence on the price of natural gas and many agricultural commodities, for example. Changes in global manufacturing patterns move raw material prices.

Currency prices tend to reflect economic conditions in the countries that use them, in particular interest rates—higher interest rates make a currency more valuable, since investments in that currency are generating higher returns. Cryptocurrencies, the most well-known of which is Bitcoin, trade largely on the market's sentiment toward crypto as an asset class and have been highly volatile throughout their history. It's possible that crypto will ultimately establish itself alongside government-issued currencies as a stable, durable medium of exchange or store of value, but as of 2023 at least, significant technical and societal hurdles remain.

As an investor in most of these assets, you typically won't encounter the underlying asset directly. Rather you will trade in derivative *securities* designed to capture the risk of future price changes in those assets. "Futures" are derivative securities based on commodities, while we call those based on stocks "options." You are essentially betting on future price movements.

Derivatives play an interesting role in the financial markets, because they are a tool for both reducing and increasing risk. Their primary purpose is that they allow businesses and investors to "hedge" their exposure to specific markets. The classic example is a producer of a single commodity, like a soybean farmer or a gold miner. That producer's livelihood depends on the price of their commodity, and if it goes down dramatically, they could be wiped out. Derivatives offer highly leveraged bets that companies with this kind of risk exposure make *against* the outcome they want, so if prices move against them, the payoff from the derivative bet offsets the costs in their operating business. A gold miner can bet that gold prices will go down, hedging their exposure to gold prices, while a company that buys a lot of gold can bet that prices will go up. It's essentially insurance. Likewise, companies that do business in multiple countries are exposed to currency price fluctuations—if you pay your employees in dollars but sell most of your goods to customers paying in euros, it's very bad for you if the dollar strengthens significantly against the euro (i.e., you can buy fewer of the dollars you need to make payroll for each euro you get in revenue). So you bet that the dollar *will* get stronger, hedging your risk.

Someone has to take the other side of these bets, and so many purely financial players operate in these markets, looking for opportunities to essentially buy risk, and the potentially high returns that come with it. Derivatives can get very complicated, and the more extreme examples are sometimes described as "exotic." Exotic derivatives played a major role in the Great Financial Crisis of 2008: banks trading in "collateralized debt obligations" that even they didn't understand found themselves facing billions of dollars in losses when the housing market declined.

A derivative security that retail investors are likely to encounter are options on stock. (These are different from stock options you might receive in compensation from your employer.) You buy the option to either buy or sell a specific stock at a set price (known as the strike price) for a set period. An option to buy stock is a call option and it's essentially a bet that the stock price will go up. An option to sell a stock at a specified price, on the other hand, is a put option, and is a bet that the stock price will go down.

Options trading is tempting to the retail investor because it offers high leverage. A few hundred dollars in call options can produce a profit of many thousands of dollars in a short period. But depending on the type of contract, it's also possible to suffer astronomical losses far exceeding the initial investment. There's not a lot of ways you can lose *more* than you wager, but you can trading options

The options market, and all derivatives markets, are dominated by sophisticated professionals whose full-time job is knowing the tiniest details of their market. These traders typically don't make their money on individual contract purchases, but by linking together a set of contracts with different terms, creating structures with fanciful names like "straddle," "strangle," and "iron butterfly." Retail investors buying individual contracts are minnows who these big fish swallow up for easy profit.

There are situations where individuals can use derivatives the same way institutions do, to hedge risk. If you live and work in different countries, for example, you may be exposed to currency risk. Illiquid stock in your employer might expose you to undue risk in an industry or a region, or your other investments might expose you to significant interest rate risk. In these circumstances, derivatives operate as insurance—you pay a small amount on a highly leveraged basis to protect you from a potential loss. I have used options to create an income stream off a large single stock investment I wanted to hold long term.

There are an endless number of ways market participants use derivatives, including stock options, to fine-tune their investing activities. But one-off options trading at retail isn't really investing in the rigorous sense of the word, or in any sense of the word. It's gambling. And gambling can be a fun diversion, a crippling addiction, or something in between—but it's not investing.

Funds

The final category of financial assets relevant to the retail investor isn't so much a specific asset class as it is a means of accessing the other asset classes. And it should be the primary means you access these assets as well. **Your long-term bucket, the money you plan to live off one day, should largely be invested in funds.** I've put this discussion at the end of the discussion of asset classes because funds are a roll-up of other assets, and I believe in the importance of understanding our financial system. But for the practical purposes of long-term investment, this is the most important category.

Although there are several variations, the basic model of a fund is a pooling of small investor capital that is then invested in larger blocks by a team of professional investors, typically pursuant to a published investment strategy. Funds vary by the mechanics of how you buy into them, what kind of fees they charge, and how they make their investments.

The classic fund model is the mutual fund. More recently, exchange-traded funds (ETFs) have streamlined the process, and they generally offer a more cost-effective way of accessing a diversified investment portfolio through a single security. Besides being easier to buy and sell, ETFs can offer a tax advantage over mutual funds, as some mutual fund trading will generate taxable income for investors even if you are passively holding the fund shares.

Funds pursue a variety of trading strategies. "Actively managed funds" are (usually) complex and dependent on human analysis—these most likely carry higher fees and probably should be avoided. "Passive funds" are allocated based on an algorithm, and the simplest strategy is to match a popular index, like the S&P 500. Numerous investment companies offer an S&P 500 ETF, in fact, with very low fees. The most famous of which (though not quite the cheapest) is the original ETF, SPDR (ticker symbol: SPY), which has been offering investors a single security to track the S&P 500 since 1993. There are ETFs that track other indexes, such as the Russell 3000, encompassing nearly the entirety of publicly traded stocks, ETFs that pursue various defined trading strategies, and ETFs that invest in currencies and commodities.

All funds charge fees, and often these fees are multilayered and difficult to parse. Mutual fund fee structures can be more complex than ETF fees, another point in favor of ETFs. The primary number you care about is the **expense ratio**. This should be low, well under 1%, and the lower the better. Mutual funds sometimes charge for buying and selling or other services, whereas ETFs trade like a stock, and these days, that's usually free of any commission.

Another recent innovation are "robo-advisor" funds, where you keep your money in a dedicated account, and the investment company invests it according to an algorithm. While fees are typically very low, even low fees add up over time, thanks to compounding. And all that most robo-advisors do is allocate your money into several ETFs or mutual funds. If you've taken the time to get this far into a book about investing, you are probably informed enough and interested enough to handle the basics of buying ETFs without paying the fees of a robo-advisor.

In the discussion of valuation, I explained the concept of the risk-free rate. That's the baseline return you demand from any investment; it has to do better than your savings account. If that's the baseline, however, an S&P 500 ETF should be the benchmark for your long-term investments. What I mean by that is that you aren't going to create wealth with the return of a savings account. Your investment money has to take on more risk to get more return. Tracking the returns of the S&P 500 is a proven way to get

DIVERSIFICATION

true investor returns (around 11% since it was created in 1957, and 8% over the past 20 years). In the short term, it's a risky investment. Don't put $10,000 you need to make your mortgage payments this year in the S&P 500. That's what your risk-free savings account is for. But for long money, the money you want to beat inflation and turn into wealth, an S&P 500 ETF is your benchmark. Evaluate any alternative against it from a risk-return perspective. If an investment offers over 8%, how much additional risk are you taking on? That can be worth it to add some upside potential to your long money. If it offers less, how much safer is it? You will want that additional safety for money you are likely to need sooner than decades from now, but for long-term money, bias toward risk.

There are a variety of approaches to allocating your long-term investments across different asset classes. Economists have argued for every conceivable approach, but financial advisers typically recommend you invest mainly in corporate equities when you are younger, with a minority of your assets in lower-risk investments such as corporate bonds, and then to shift the allocation toward lower risk as you get close to retirement. One approach is the "100 minus age" rule, which means you should have the percent of your assets in stocks equal to 100 minus your age (so if you're 35, then 65% of your long-term investments is in stocks and 35% in bonds). In 2005, however, economist Robert Schiller (who would later win a Nobel Prize for his analysis of stock prices) analyzed several different strategies and found that the best-performing approach, by a wide margin, was to invest 100% in corporate stock, and that the inclusion of more conservative investments in a portfolio only reduced returns.

If you are on a career track trending toward high income, and you are being disciplined about funding your intermediate expenses, I recommend biasing your long-term investments toward risk when you are young: more high-growth stocks, few or no low-risk investments like bonds.

INVESTING'S FINAL BOSS: THE TAXMAN

There is probably no entity with which I have a more conflicted relationship than the IRS. The men and women of the IRS do the thankless hard work of securing our nation's revenue. Cicero described taxes as "the sinews of the state" because they fund our security, infrastructure, and social investments. Patriotism is out of fashion these days, and that's another talk show, but if there's anything you think the U.S. government does well, whether it's predicting the weather or commanding aircraft carriers or investing in green energy (and I think all those things are great), remember it's only doing those things because the IRS is out there collecting taxes. God, I love the IRS.

But the IRS is also out there collecting taxes from me. Every time I make a smart investment decision, every time I've sold a company, every dollar I've ever earned, not to mention every dollar I've ever paid to the hundreds of outstanding people who've worked hard for my companies and helped me get to where I am—there's the IRS looking over my shoulder, wetting its beak. God, I hate the IRS.

The only way through this is to minimize your tax burden through all legal means and write those checks with the satisfaction of knowing you are paying your share. U.S. soldiers serving as prisoners of war have an obligation to try to escape. I believe citizens likewise have a dual obligation, to their country and to their family, to pay the minimum legal taxes. Did I just compare the government to an enemy in a war? I told you I'm conflicted.

Anyway, my precious feelings aside, how can you legally minimize your tax burden? There are three basic steps, the "stop, drop, and roll" of tax strategy: awareness, understanding, and assistance.

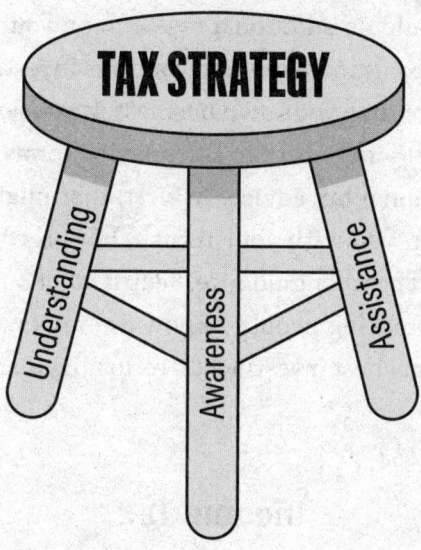

You need to be acutely **aware** at all times that taxes pervade earning, investing, and spending. Every financial decision you make—and that includes decisions *not* to do something—has tax implications. Some are obvious, many are not, and they can radically change your long-term outcomes. Foster awareness bordering on paranoia.

To direct that awareness, you need a basic **understanding** of how taxation works generally and the major moving parts of our tax system. This understanding should inform decisions you make throughout the year, not just when you prepare your tax returns—the game is largely won or lost by that point. My experience and understanding is mainly in the U.S., so that's what I'll focus on here, but many of these issues are universal.

I discuss the basic concepts you need to understand below, but briefly, the third step is that you do not want to face these issues alone. Early in your career, especially if you are a salaried employee, your taxes are likely straightforward and your options limited. What I explain below should get you most of the way there, though you should do additional research on your specific situation. As your income increases and you start investing, if you work as a freelancer or own your own business, if you buy real estate or other complex assets, expect to start paying for **assistance** in the form of professional tax advice. At first, that might just be a tax preparer to help you with your return, but pretty quickly you'll realize you need broader guidance. Seek it out. Some of the smartest, most hardworking people I know are my tax lawyers. They are also one of my best investments, returning many times what I pay them.

Income Tax

The big daddy is income tax. In the U.S. you'll pay both federal and (in most states) state income tax *and* (in a few areas, including New York City) local income tax. (Living in a state without income tax can be a *massive* wealth generator, more on that later.) Federal taxes take the largest bite, and state income taxes are mini-versions of the federal system, so I'll focus on federal here. If you've been paying your own income taxes for several years, most of this is probably familiar to you, but as with the financial markets generally, it can be helpful to step back and see the bigger picture.

Income tax does what it says, it takes a percentage of your income. There are two parts to that equation: the percentage and the income. Political talk about taxes often focuses on the percentage, which is the easy-to-understand, visible element of taxes. But consider that the tax code encompasses over 2,600 pages, but the rates for personal income tax are described in a few tables that take up less than one page. (They are right at the front, U.S. Code Title 26,

Subtitle A, Chapter 1, Subchapter A, Part 1.) Much of the rest is devoted to calculating income.

In the tax world, "income" doesn't mean how much money you made. Instead, it's a number (usually quite a bit less than how much money you made) used as the basis for your tax obligation. I don't pay my tax lawyers to figure out my tax rate. I pay them to minimize the amount of money that counts as taxable income. You should do the same.

The first line of defense against taxation is money that doesn't count as income at all. The largest non-income source of money is borrowed money, which is not income, and thus, not taxed. When you use a mortgage to buy a house, you don't have to pay taxes on the money you borrow. The same applies if you take out a home equity loan, meaning the bank gives you cash. It's not free money, since you'll pay interest and have to pay it back, but it's tax free. This is one of the main ways the super wealthy avoid paying taxes—tech founders such as Jeff Bezos and Elon Musk, for example, rely largely on stock for their compensation, but they rarely sell that stock. Instead, they use it as collateral for large loans at very low interest rates and fund their lavish lifestyles with tax-free loan proceeds (and deduct the interest costs). This has the ancillary benefit that they maintain their voting power at their companies. Owners of private companies often rely on the company's operations to supplement their lifestyle—such as having the business pay for travel and entertainment. The owner ultimately pays either way, since the costs come out of the profits of the business, but doesn't pay income tax on the money, as it reduces the business's profits. Overly aggressive use of this strategy, however, can cross over into tax fraud and put the owner's personal assets at risk for liabilities incurred by the business.

Another way to keep money from even showing up in the income calculation is to make sure someone—or something—else earns it. Some investors and entrepreneurs are able to create corporate entities that receive revenue from various activities rather than the individual. Doing this in low-tax jurisdictions, like the Cayman Islands, can be part of this strategy, but not necessarily. In some circumstances, family members can be installed to receive money. Professional partnerships such as law firms and doctors' offices use their firms to hold their fee revenue and minimize and delay taxable income.

Most of the money we receive, however, is taxable. There are two major types of income for tax purposes: current income and capital gains. Current income is mainly wages. Capital gains are profits from selling assets like stocks and houses. Although the relative rates have changed from time to time, in the U.S. capital gains are taxed at lower rates than current income.

Capital gains tax rates vary by income and jurisdiction. Federally, capital gains taxes range from zero for lower-income households, to 23.8% for the highest earners. At the state level, capital gains range from 0% to 10% or more.* Capital losses (when you sell an asset for less than you paid for it) can be deducted from your income, though currently only up to $3,000 in losses per year (you can roll over additional losses to future years).

Obviously, then, it's better to make a dollar in capital gains than a dollar in current income. However, you typically can't change the classification of income from one category to the other after you've earned it—so you can and should take the difference into account when making financial plans. The favorable tax treatment of capital gains is one of the reasons that investing generally is so important to building wealth. It also advantages careers where the money is made buying and selling assets: e.g., hedge funds, private

---

* Two important limits to know about, however: One, you have to hold an asset for at least a year to get the lower rate. And two, investment profits made within a tax-deferred program like a 401(k) or IRA are not taxed when they are earned, but *all* your withdrawals are taxed at ordinary income rates, even profits made from asset sales.

equity, real estate. A lower tax rate is still tax, however—it's easy to forget about taxes when your stock portfolio shoots up in a bull market, or if you buy a rental property in a rising market. But the IRS won't.

That leaves current income. The main way to reduce this is with deductions. Deductions are primarily expenses that Congress has decided should reduce your taxable income. They've been created for many reasons, or no discernable reason at all—the policy justifications for deductions range from inarguable to patently absurd.

Deductions are much less of a tax minimization tool for most people than they used to be, however. In fact, just 10% of taxpayers utilize anything besides the default option, known as the standard deduction. In 2023, it's $13,850 per adult (so double for married couples). A single person with a current income of $100,000 has a taxable income of just $86,150, simply by operation of the standard deduction. There's a catch, however, which is that if you apply the standard deduction, you can't take most other deductions. (Contributions to retirement plans like a 401(k) and IRA are still deducted.) In practice, this means your so-called itemized deductions have to add up to more than the standard deduction, or it's not worth it. That's not the case for nine out of ten taxpayers.

For the 10% who itemize, the two largest deductions are typically state income taxes and interest paid on a home mortgage. Not the mortgage *payments*, just the portion that goes to interest (early in a mortgage, that's most of the payment). Medical expenses, most charitable donations, some educational expenses, and retirement plan contributions are also important tax deductions. Many deductions, such as those for student loan interest, are phased out at higher income levels.

It's important to appreciate the role of the standard deduction and the nature of what tax deductions actually do when presented with the promise that something is "tax deductible." Most deductions, including charitable donations, only benefit you if you are itemizing rather than taking the standard deduction—remember, that's something 90% of taxpayers don't do. It's highly unlikely you'll have enough itemized deductions to eschew the standard deduction unless you have a home mortgage. Even then, many deductions, such as those for student loan debt, are subject to income limits, mostly in the neighborhood of $100,000. Finally, if you can deduct it, it's a deduction from your *income*, not from your taxes—so it will only save you somewhere around a third of the amount of the deduction, depending on your tax rate.

There are also different kinds of tax "credits," which mostly benefit lower-income taxpayers, a few of which can even result in payments from the government, where they reduce a taxpayer's income below zero. The earned-income tax credit and the child tax credit are both major social safety net programs that are delivered through the income tax system as credits.

Self-employed individuals (aka freelancers) face a more complex tax situation. The good news is that expenses related to their work, such as travel and equipment, are deducted from their income (even if they take the standard deduction). The bad news is that they are subject to additional taxation, which captures the taxes their employer would have paid if they had an employer. They also need to make estimated tax payments during the year rather than just a single payment on April 15. If you have substantial self-employment income, then it's highly likely you'll benefit from the guidance of a tax adviser.

Once all these calculations are made, your taxable income determines your tax rate. It's not determined as a single number, however. Income tax rates are "graduated," meaning rates go up as your income goes up, but you only pay the higher rate on the incremental income. In 2022, a single filer paid 10% on the first $10,275, 12% on the *next* $31,500, 22% on the *next* $47,300, and so on, until reaching the top rate of 37% on income over $539,900. That's important because while earning more money does increase your overall tax rate, it doesn't change how much you were taxed already—you aren't punished for making more, but the more is taxed higher.

The High-Income Trap

Tax systems that increase with income are known as progressive. (It's an economic term, not a political one.) Progressive income taxes are widely adopted because they account for the marginal utility of income. For someone making $30,000 per year, every incremental dollar in taxes takes a significant bite out of their quality of life. For someone making $300,000, a dollar in taxes is much less onerous, and for someone making $3 million, it's irrelevant. So progressive tax systems take lightly from those who can least afford to pay and draw more heavily on those with more. Note that only income taxes are progressive. Sales tax, property tax, car registration, and just about every other form of taxation is "regressive": everyone pays the same regardless of their income. These weigh more heavily on low-income people.

The U.S. rate system is progressive to a point but flattens out

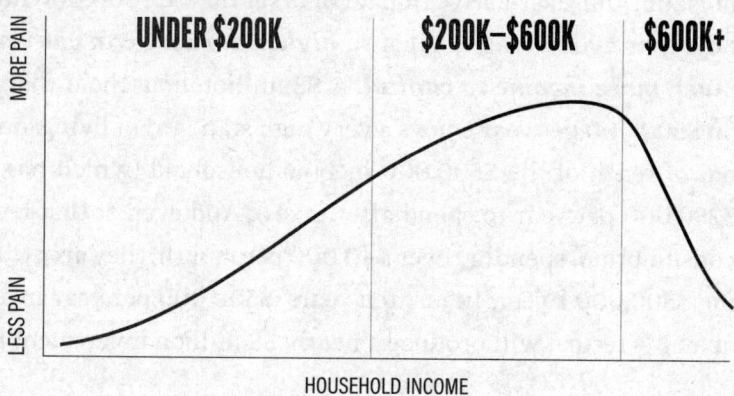

INCOME TAX IMPACT

once you reach the top bracket (currently $539,900 in income). As a result, the *impact* of income taxes is greatest on high-income earners: doctors, lawyers, engineers, senior managers—those whose compensation puts them *near* the top tax rate but not higher. And that's before you consider the means the truly rich have to keep their taxes down. Warren Buffett has famously said that his tax rate is lower than his secretary's.

Consider two households, one with $500,000 in annual income, one with $2 million. The second household will pay a *slightly* higher tax rate (if they don't have Warren Buffett's tax lawyers), but assuming they both live in high-tax states, both will pay *about* 50% of their income in taxes. The rate is the same, but the impact on quality of life will be far greater for the lower-income household. This is because of the declining marginal utility of money, but also because the expenses of prosperity—private school tuition, retirement savings, car and mortgage payments—all live in the sub-$500,000 zone. Capitalism never runs out of things to sell us, but once you have more than $500,000 or so in *after-tax* income, what's left are luxuries in every sense. Taxes turn the $500,000 household into a $250,000 household, which is a much more significant change than turning a $2 million household into a $1 million household.

That's not even half the story, however. Lengthen the time horizon, and the relative impact of taxes on the $500,000 household gets even greater, because **higher earners can convert so much more income to capital**. A $2 million household that lives on $500,000 per year enjoys a very high standard of living, one far out of reach of the $500,000 income household (which has only $250,000 per year to spend after taxes). And even at that level of consumption, spending over $40,000 per month, they are still saving $500,000 a year. In just ten years, $500,000 per year invested at an 8% return will produce a nearly $8 million investment fund, generating more than $600,000 per year in investment income (taxed at capital gains rates). Very high earners typically do pay high income tax rates, but it barely dents their quality of life or slows their rapid wealth creation, because they are able to convert so much income into capital.

It's called "capitalism" and not "laborism" for a reason. Wealth comes from capital investment, not labor wages. Once you are able to convert significant amounts of your wages to investment capital, you make the jump to light speed.

Payroll Taxes

Payroll taxes are a form of income tax, but they are much simpler in principle and in execution, especially for salaried employees, who have them taken out of their paycheck automatically. They can be a nasty surprise for self-employed workers, however.

There are two federal payroll taxes: Social Security and Medicare. Social Security is 12.4%, but half is "paid by the employer," so you only see a 6.2% tax on your pay slip. I put that in quotes though because, don't be fooled, your company was well aware it would be paying that other 6.2% when it hired you. Social Security payroll taxes are capped, however. In 2023 the cap is at $160,200 in wages—if you make more than that in a year, the Social Security tax goes away for the rest of the year. Medicare is 2.9% and split the same way. There is no cap on Medicare taxes, and the tax rate goes up slightly for high earners. Most states have payroll taxes as well, though they are generally very low and capped at low levels.

If you have wages, there's no escaping payroll taxes—there are no deductions and they even apply to money you contribute to a 401(k). It's easy to overlook payroll taxes if you're self-employed, but they take a large bite, since you have to pay both the employer and the employee portion, totaling over 15% on the first $160,000 of income.

Effective vs. Marginal Tax Rates

The combination of graduated income tax rates and capped payroll taxes means that not every dollar of income is taxed at the same rate, and for some people, this difference can be substantial enough to influence life decisions.

The key concept is the difference between your "effective" tax rate and your "marginal" tax rate. This is wonky but bear with me, it matters. Your effective tax rate is what you paid overall. But your marginal tax rate is what you pay on the next incremental dollar. Consider a married couple in which one spouse made $200,000, while the other was full-time at home with children. If they have a mortgage and some sensible tax planning, their taxable income is just $130,000 and federal income and payroll tax will be about $32,000, for an effective federal tax rate of 16%.*

But what happens if the second spouse returns to work? That 16% effective rate already takes advantage of the couple's deductions, the first spouse's Social Security tax cap, and the graduated nature of income tax. Incremental money is taxed at a much higher rate. If the second spouse takes a job for $100,000, it's all taxable income and results in an incremental $30,000 in federal taxes, or a *marginal* tax rate of 30%. That's $14,000 more in taxes than you'd get if you just assumed the effective tax rate of 16% would apply to additional earnings. In a high-tax state, the delta can be even greater.

These sorts of uneven outcomes are all over the tax code, and

---

*Assuming enough mortgage interest and other deductions to itemize, plus a maximum 401(k) contribution, their taxable income is $130,000, making their federal income tax $19,800, plus payroll taxes of about $12,800, and an effective federal tax rate of 16%: ($19,800 + $12,800) / $200,000. Though keep in mind that the tax code changes every year, and these specific numbers will get increasingly out of date.

they make it risky to extrapolate from your current circumstances. Increases in income can trigger various taxes and eliminate savings in surprising ways. Likewise, small changes in the tax code can render some strategies obsolete and expose new ones. All of this makes *timing* a crucial aspect of tax planning.

Defer? I Hardly Even Know Her!

Timing is the most important tax planning dynamic. The basic idea is this: you want to spread your income over time so your lifetime effective tax rate is as low as possible. For ordinary income, this typically means deferring income out of your highest earning years (or highest earning locations, if you foresee a move in or out of a high/low tax jurisdiction). Years when you have high income, your marginal tax rate will be high—37% at the top federal bracket (which kicks in at $540,000 in taxable income), plus another 10% or more in high-tax states. For every dollar of income you defer out of a 47% marginal tax rate year to one when your marginal tax rate is just 20%, you're saving 27¢. A 27% return just on the tax effect alone is incredibly powerful. When you add the power of compounding interest by investing that extra 27%, the tax savings alone could double your money.

This is the benefit of 401(k) and IRA retirement plans. They give you control over when you pay taxes on some of your income. There are two different kinds of these plans, the traditional and the Roth, and the best one varies by person and situation.

The simpler distinction is between 401(k) plans and IRAs. A 401(k) is offered by an employer, who withholds your contributions from your paycheck and deposits them on your account into the plan. An IRA you set up yourself. Also, 401(k) plans allow for much higher annual contributions, but your employer has to offer one. (Self-employed people can set up their own.)

The more complex distinction is between the traditional and Roth variations. When you contribute money to a *traditional* plan, the amount is deducted from your taxable income the year you make the contribution. So if your income tax rate is 30%, and you contribute $1,000 to an IRA, then your taxable income is reduced by $1,000 and you save $300 in taxes. And you pay no taxes on investment gains that money makes while it is in the plan. Eventually, when you withdraw the money, you pay income tax on those withdrawals. The money is illiquid until you are 59.5, because you can't withdraw before then without paying both taxes and a fee, and you must start withdrawing your money by age 73.

Roth plans are the inverse. You don't get to deduct contributions from your taxes when you make them, but when you start withdrawing money later, it's all tax free. Plus, you can withdraw money contributed to a Roth plan at any time (though not investment income it has earned), and you are never required to withdraw money. Roth IRAs are limited to middle- and lower-income earners, whereas Roth 401(k)s are not.

In your peak earning years, you likely want to max out traditional 401(k) and IRA contributions, because you won't pay taxes on the money at your current high-tax rate. But early in your ca-

TRADITIONAL 401(k)	**TRADITIONAL IRA**
ROTH 401(k)	**ROTH IRA**

Traditional:
- Tax break now
- Penalty for < age 59.5 withdrawal
- Mandatory withdrawals at age 73

Roth:
- Tax break later
- No penalty for < age 59.5 withdrawals
- No mandatory withdrawals

• Employer • High contribution limit   • Self • Low contribution limit

reer, if your income is low, you are probably better off contributing after-tax money to a Roth IRA or Roth 401(k), because your tax rate is low now, and likely will be higher in retirement, when you have built up wealth. Plus, Roth plans offer the added benefit that you can access some of the money sooner if you need to.

There are also specific savings and tax plans for certain situations. The 529 college savings plan can help families save for college and reduce taxes. Health savings accounts (HSAs) can be used to avoid taxes on income you expect to need for health care expenses. These sorts of plans are the meat and potatoes of deferring income, the concept at the heart of all kinds of tax strategies. One of the advantages of capital over labor is the simple ability to time returns: you can hold on to appreciating assets until you need the money, thus deferring taxes, whereas income you earn gets taxed when you earn it.

Between retirement plans and other vehicles, you need to be thinking about your income as something you can slide around in time—take it when your marginal tax rates are low, defer it when they are high. In your peak earning years, deferral is usually your objective, but the right answer for you in any given year may change. The objective is to minimize your taxes over your lifetime, not in any specific year. That said, taxes you pay early in your career are more expensive than those you pay later because of the opportunity cost associated with not investing that money.

ADVICE FROM A LIFETIME OF INVESTING

Zig When Others Zag

When everyone is barking up the same tree, we get stupid and lose money. Zig when everyone else is zagging. Initially, money pouring into a sector can create a market, as a certain amount of capital is required to get traction. But soon, the more money, the greater the entry price and the lower the return. When everyone is buying condos in Miami, or when everyone can borrow money for student loans, the price of condos and education increases (inflation) and the return decreases. With student debt, the more you pay, the less your degree is worth. Over the last eighty years, college certification offered an enormous ROI. However, my higher ed colleagues and I have been asking ourselves every day for decades: "How do I increase my compensation while reducing my accountability?" The resulting pursuit of luxury positioning and massive tuition increases has drained much of the ROI from a college degree. Approximately a third of people can't pay their loans back as over-investment has hammered returns.

Don't Trust Your Emotions

Anything riskier than a savings account will have down days. Know this is part of the process, don't overreact. Ultimately, your tolerance for losses determines how far up the risk scale you should go.

When you suffer a loss, learn from it. Learn first about yourself. How heavy was the psychological hit, and how long does it take you to shake it off? This is the indicator of your suitability for active investing. Learn also about your strategy. Billionaire investor Ray Dalio is obsessed with learning from losses. His book *Principles* is a 500-page lecture about rigorously analyzing your mistakes and learning from them. He preaches writing down your decision-making process in detail and reviewing it with the benefit of hindsight to understand where you went wrong and how to avoid that mistake in the future: "The most common mistake I see people make is dealing with their problems as one-offs rather than using them to diagnose how their machine is working so that they can improve it. . . . A thorough and accurate diagnosis, while more time-consuming, will pay huge dividends in the future." I don't have Ray's discipline—few do—but when I've taken the time to think seriously about where I went wrong in an investment, a business decision, a relationship, it has always, as promised, paid "huge dividends."

This has implications for up days as well. Be willing to take profits. If an investment spikes, whether because you guessed right on a meme stock or your start-up went public, take a healthy piece of the growth out of that asset and diversify. Psychology will fight this—if you won yesterday, you'll begin to believe that winning is a habit, and you will win again tomorrow. But gravity and reversion to the mean are iron laws of the financial universe. For every story you hear about an entrepreneur who mortgaged their house to buy company stock and became mega-wealthy, there are hundreds who did the same and went bust. I kept doubling down on Red Envelope (the firm I started in 1997), and it left me near broke at 40. Take profits—you earned them—and hope you were wrong to sell.

Don't Day Trade

The line between active investing and gambling-adjacent day trading is thin, but clear once you've crossed it. Likely, you won't be the only one. In bull markets, conflating luck with talent and dopamine with investing goes viral. And trading houses are only too willing to service your addiction. Diabetes, high blood pressure, and sharing a screenshot of your Robinhood gains are maladies of industrial production that exceed our instincts. Trading—distinct from "investing"—can feel like work and productivity. It's not. It's gambling, but with worse odds and no free drinks. One study found that over a two-year period, only 3% of active retail traders made any profit at all. During the most recent day-trading epidemic, millions of (mostly) young men, trapped inside by Covid, discovered apps such as Robinhood, with its dopamine-triggering confetti, and twenty-four-hour-a-day, volatile crypto trading became their drug of choice.

Most day traders will be fine, suffering affordable losses . . . most. However, for many there are darker outcomes. Young men are especially vulnerable, as they are more risk aggressive. Nine out of ten day traders are men, and 14% of young men who gamble become addicted (as opposed to 3% of women). Most of us can gamble without becoming addicted, just as most of us can drink without becoming an alcoholic. Again, most of us.

Move

One of the most powerful wealth building tools at your disposal is to allocate your most important resource (your time), especially when you are young, to markets that offer greater returns. One of the reasons the U.S. economy has grown faster, and more consistently, than any economy over the past two centuries is it's in our DNA to move. "Go west, young man." When you are young, let geographic flexibility be an advantage relative to your older peers, who likely have more roots and less flexibility. Whatever your age, keep half an eye over the horizon scanning for opportunity.

The arbitrage recognized moving from a high-tax to a low-tax state can be life-altering. Several states, including Florida, Texas, and Washington, have no income tax. (Washington recently enacted a capital gains tax, but with a high deductible.) Income tax is not the only consideration—something has to pay for government services, so often there are higher sales taxes or property taxes in states with lower income taxes. But the total tax burden varies substantially from state to state, and depending on your income and spending profile, the differences could be significant.

Moving out of notoriously high-tax states like New York and California can save 10+% of your gross income each year. If you are able to maintain your income trajectory, and have the discipline to invest the tax savings, you will be on your way re: your long-term investment goals. Obviously, where you live has economic consequences beyond taxes, and significant personal consequences. But at a minimum, if you're considering different employment offers, housing prices, and other factors between different opportunities, consider the tax implications.

CHAPTER REVIEW

ACTION ITEM BULLETS

- **Convert your income into capital.** Capital is money put to work, creating value. Investing is providing capital in exchange for a share of that value. Wealth is achieved through investing, not income alone.

- **Learn about the economy.** From the operations of individual businesses to the Fed's interest rate moves, the economic ecosystem affects all of us. It should inform your decisions in all areas.

- **Diversify to maximize returns, not upside.** Your objective is to generate steady, long-term gains so that compound interest can work its power. This means diversifying your capital into different investments rather than concentrating it all on the one you think will give the highest return.

- **Think of money as a means of exchanging time.** Time is our baseline asset, and we sell it in exchange for money, which we use to buy the fruits of other people's time. When you make an investment, value the time you spend on it just as you value the money you put into it. When you make a purchase decision, consider the cost in terms of the hours it took to earn that money.

- **Risk is the price of a return.** Risk is a measure of probability, the likelihood of gaining or losing money. There is no investment without risk, so be sure the potential return justifies the level of risk.

- **Value returns based on probability and time.** Money you have today is worth more than money promised tomorrow. Money promised tomorrow is worth more than money promised in a year. Money promised from a reliable source is worth more than money promised from an unknown or unreliable source.

- **Invest mainly in passive, diversified, low-cost securities.** Exchange traded funds (ETFs) are the retail investor's best friend. They provide passive diversification and transparent risk.

ACTION ITEM BULLETS

- **Set aside a small portion of your savings for active market investing.** I recommend 20% of the first $10,000 you save. Buy and sell individual stocks, take positions in commodities, "play" the market. Learn by doing, and get a feel for wins and losses. Keep accurate records of your investments, fees, gains, losses, and taxes.

- **Buy a home when it's the right time in your *life*.** Real estate is the emperor of asset classes, and owning a home is the way most people invest in real estate. It's forced savings, an investment you get value from every day, and can be the anchor of your portfolio. But an anchor is no good when you want to set sail. Home ownership is a life-stage decision first, an investment decision second.

- **Be wary of fees.** Financial markets run on fees, little slices taken off your capital as it moves from place to place. Often buried in the fine print and calculated from misleadingly small numbers, fees can add up to material reductions in your returns.

- **Be aware of taxes.** The largest fee of them all, taxation can significantly alter your investment returns. You don't understand an investment unless you understand the tax implications.

- **Time your taxes.** Investing through a traditional IRA or 401(k) boosts your returns by delaying taxation, potentially for decades. Investing through a Roth version, on the other hand, takes the tax hit now in exchange for tax-free income in the future. The right choice for you depends on your current and expected circumstances.

- **Discount your emotions.** Emotions are valuable and essential to good decision-making. But investing stirs up strong emotions that can overwhelm the calculations required for success.

- **Don't day trade.** If you want to trade securities on a daily basis, then make it your full-time job. It can be a great career if it suits your talents. But if it's a hobby, don't let it become an obsession. You will lose not only money, but also something more valuable: time.

EPILOGUE
THE WHOLE SHOOTING MATCH

EVERYTHING MEANINGFUL IN LIFE is about others. Your ability to support and love others and your willingness to let them love you. Nothing profound is achieved in isolation.

When my mom was diagnosed with cancer for the third time, we knew this was "it." The last week of her life she would become uncontrollably cold, shivering. No matter how much we turned up the thermostat, or how many blankets we put on her, she still shivered. Finally, out of instinct, I held my mom in my arms, as a father would hold a child who'd fallen asleep before the end of dinner. Her shivers subsided. Riddled with cancer and barely 80 pounds soaking wet, this woman could only find warmth in her son's arms. For the first time, the success and relevance I had been chasing for so long had meaning. I was a man. A man people could depend on.

This past weekend, I gave the weekend to my son: "Whatever you want to do." This meant a Chelsea football game and two separate sojourns to the Battersea Power Station Mall and the Coal

Drop Mall. Malls . . . go figure. Shopping for Nike football cleats, waiting in line for gelato and the "chimney lift" that takes you to the top of Battersea Station. Spoiler alert: all kids must go to the top of any structure that has a "top" where you can look out on what surrounds you.

My ability to care for my mom and spoil my son (who bears her name as his middle name) is a function of humanity and paternal instincts. And the ability to let these instincts find greater purchase is afforded by my economic security. I could take a leave from work and coordinate the substantial resources required so my mom could die at home and not under bright lights surrounded by strangers. The ability to be the child or parent you envision is possible without money, but it's more likely you can be present and not distracted by the immense stress with which a capitalist society burdens you if you have some economic security.

Find something you're good at that people will pay you for and go hard, really hard, at it. Spend less than you make so you can deploy a platoon, then a division, then an army of capital that fights for you and your loved ones while you sleep. Diversify so you can endure the unknown that surrounds us. And have a long-term perspective: embrace the wisdom to recognize time will go faster than you think.

All of this can get you to the profound more quickly and let you be in the company, in the moment, of the profound . . . others. This is the whole shooting match.

Life is so rich,

SCOTT

ACKNOWLEDGMENTS

BOOKS, SIMILAR TO WEALTH, are not created alone.

Recognizing that greatness is in the agency of others and spending the capital (time and money) to attract and retain people, vendors, and relationships is a superpower.

The entire team at Prof G Media made this book possible. The following people had their hands on it directly:

EXECUTIVE PRODUCERS:	Jason Stavers
	Katherine Dillon
RESEARCH AND FIRST READERS:	Ed Elson
	Claire Miller
	Caroline Schagrin
	Mia Silverio
GRAPHIC DESIGN:	Olivia Reaney-Hall

ACKNOWLEDGMENTS

I've had the same agent, publisher, and editor since we first pitched *The Four* several years and books ago:

Jim Levine

Adrian Zackheim

Niki Papadopoulos

Thanks also to my good friend Todd Benson, my NYU Stern School of Business colleague professor Sabrina Howell, and Joe Day of Bear Mountain Capital for their thoughtful suggestions throughout the book. Tyler Comrie created the cover art.

I told the story of Cy Cordner in Chapter Four, a stockbroker who took an interest in me when I was 13. Mentors are uniquely valuable. Not just for practical advice and support but also for the human connection they offer. Forty years after Cy helped me buy my first shares of stock, I register prosperity every day thanks to him and the many other people who planted trees, the shade of which they would never sit in. Of all the blessings I've enjoyed, an abundance of mentors was singular. Cy was the first.

Professor David Aaker inspired me to start a brand strategy firm and was instrumental in its success. Warren Hellman brought me to my first corporate board meetings and taught me when to speak and when to listen. Pat Connolly believed in me and our budding firm, Prophet, engaging us at Williams-Sonoma in the 1990s. The list goes on through the present day. This book is a nod to the many people who helped me build economic security and focus on being a good citizen and father.

NOTES

INTRODUCTION: WEALTH

4 **"having what you want":** Sheryl Crow and Jeff Trott, "Soak Up the Sun," *C'mon, C'mon*, A&M Records, 2002.

5 **"Money doesn't talk":** Bob Dylan, "It's Alright, Ma (I'm Only Bleeding)," *Bringing It All Back Home*, Columbia Records, 1965.

5 **six times the median annual income:** Eylul Tekin, "A Timeline of Affordability: How Have Home Prices and Household Incomes Changed Since 1960?" Clever, August 7, 2022, listwithclever.com/research/home-price-v-income-historical-study.

5 **share of first-time buyers:** Ronda Kaysen, "'It's Never Our Time': First-Time Home Buyers Face a Brutal Market," *New York Times*, November 11, 2022, www.nytimes.com/2022/11/11/realestate/first-time-buyers-housing-market.html.

5 **Medical debt is the leading cause:** Erika Giovanetti, "Medical Debt Is the Leading Cause of Bankruptcy, Data Shows: How to Reduce Your Hospital Bills," Fox Business, October 25, 2021, www.foxbusiness.com/personal-finance/medical-debt-bankruptcy-hospital-bill-forgiveness.

5 **Marriage rates among all but the wealthiest:** Janet Adamy and Paul Overberg, "Affluent Americans Still Say 'I Do.' More in the Middle Class Don't," *Wall Street Journal*, March 8, 2020, www.wsj.com/articles/

NOTES

affluent-americans-still-say-i-do-its-the-middle-class-that-does-not-11583691336.

5 **making more than their parents:** "The American Dream Is Fading," Opportunity Insights, Harvard University, opportunityinsights.org/national_trends, accessed August 31, 2023.

5 **Twenty-five percent of Gen Z'ers:** "How the Young Spend Their Money," *Economist*, January 16, 2023, www.economist.com/business/2023/01/16/how-the-young-spend-their-money.

11 **higher blood pressure:** Gary W. Evans, "Childhood Poverty and Blood Pressure Reactivity to and Recovery from an Acute Stressor in Late Adolescence: The Mediating Role of Family Conflict," *Psychosomatic Medicine* 75, no. 7 (2013): 691–700.

CHAPTER 1: STOICISM

16 **A study of UK consumers found:** John Gathergood, "Self-Control, Financial Literacy and Consumer Over-Indebtedness," *Journal of Economic Psychology* 33, no. 3 (June 2012): 590–602, doi.org/10.1016/j.joep.2011.11.006.

21 **reviewed the literature:** Stephen R. Covey, *The 7 Habits of Highly Effective People: Powerful Lessons in Personal Change*, 30th anniversary edition (New York: Simon & Schuster, 2020), 18–19.

22 **a survey of 121 studies:** Long Ge et al., "Comparison of Dietary Macronutrient Patterns of 14 Popular Named Dietary Programmes for Weight and Cardiovascular Risk Factor Reduction in Adults: Systematic Review and Network Meta-Analysis of Randomised Trials," *BMJ* (April 1, 2020): 696, doi.org/10.1136/bmj.m696.

27 **"Your identity emerges out of your habits":** James Clear, *Atomic Habits: An Easy & Proven Way to Build Good Habits & Break Bad Ones* (New York: Avery, 2018), 36.

30 **lottery winners were no happier:** Philip Brickman et al., "Lottery Winners and Accident Victims: Is Happiness Relative?" *Journal of Personality and Social Psychology* 36, no. 8 (August 1978): 917–27, doi.org/10.1037/0022-3514.36.8.917.

30 **Subsequent studies of different groups of lottery winners:** Erik Lindqvist et al., "Long-Run Effects of Lottery Wealth on Psychological Well-Being," *Review of Economic Studies* 87, no. 6 (November 2020): 2703–26, doi.org/10.1093/restud/rdaa006.

NOTES

33 **higher incomes *are* associated with greater happiness:** Daniel Kahneman and Angus Deaton, "High Income Improves Evaluation of Life but Not Emotional Well-Being," *Proceedings of the National Academy of Sciences of the United States of America* 107, no. 38 (September 2010): 16489–93, www.pnas.org/doi/full/10.1073/pnas.1011492107; Matthew A. Killingsworth, "Experienced Well-Being Rises with Income, Even Above $75,000 Per Year," *Proceedings of the National Academy of Sciences of the United States of America* 118, no. 4 (2021): e2016976118, www.pnas.org/doi/full/10.1073/pnas.2016976118; Matthew A. Killingsworth, Daniel Kahneman, and Barbara Mellers, "Income and Emotional Well-Being: A Conflict Resolved," *Proceedings of the National Academy of Sciences of the United States of America* 120, no. 10 (March 2023): e2208661120, www.pnas.org/doi/full/10.1073/pnas.2208661120. *See also* Aimee Picchi, "One Study Said Happiness Peaked at $75,000 in Income. Now, Economists Say It's Higher—by a Lot," CBS News Money Watch, March 10, 2023, www.cbsnews.com/news/money-happiness-study-daniel-kahneman-500000-versus-75000 (summarizing 2023 paper).

33 **50% of our happiness level:** Espen Røysamb et al., "Genetics, Personality and Wellbeing: A Twin Study of Traits, Facets, and Life Satisfaction," *Scientific Reports* 8, no. 1 (August 17, 2018): doi.org/10.1038/s41598-018-29881-x.

36 **their biggest regret was worrying too much:** Karl Pillemer, "The Most Surprising Regret of the Very Old—and How You Can Avoid It," *HuffPost*, April 4, 2013, huffpost.com/entry/how-to-stop-worrying-reduce-stress_b_2989589.

36 **Ryan Holiday put it this way:** Ryan Holiday, *The Obstacle Is the Way* (New York: Portfolio, 2014), 22.

38 **"effectiveness of workplace physical fitness":** Maryam Etemadi et al., "A Review of the Importance of Physical Fitness to Company Performance and Productivity," *American Journal of Applied Sciences* 13, no. 11 (November 2016): 1104–18, doi.org/10.3844/ajassp.2016.1104.1118.

38 **the more we exercise, the stronger:** Ayse Yemiscigil and Ivo Vlaev, "The Bidirectional Relationship between Sense of Purpose in Life and Physical Activity: A Longitudinal Study," *Journal of Behavioral Medicine* 44, no. 5 (April 23, 2021): 715–25, doi.org/10.1007/s10865-021-00220-2.

39 **exercise is 50% more effective:** Ben Singh et al., "Effectiveness of Physical Activity Interventions for Improving Depression, Anxiety

NOTES

and Distress: An Overview of Systematic Reviews," *British Journal of Sports Medicine* 57 (February 16, 2023): 1203–09, doi.org/10.1136/bjsports-2022-106195.

39 **"Exercise is nonnegotiable for peak performance":** Steven Kotler, *The Art of Impossible: A Peak Performance Primer* (New York: Harper Wave, 2023), 47.

39 **resistance work improves mood and memory:** Regarding flexibility, see: Thalita B. Leite et al., "Effects of Different Number of Sets of Resistance Training on Flexibility," *International Journal of Exercise Science* 10, no. 3 (September 1, 2017): 354–64. For other benefits, see: Suzette Lohmeyer, "Weight Training Isn't Such a Heavy Lift. Here Are 7 Reasons Why You Should Try It," NPR, September 26, 2021, www.npr.org/sections/health-shots/2021/09/26/1040577137/how-to-weight-training-getting-started-tips.

47 **Being kind reduces stress hormones:** Rollin McCraty et al., "The Impact of a New Emotional Self-Management Program on Stress, Emotions, Heart Rate Variability, DHEA and Cortisol," *Integrative Physiological and Behavioral Science* 33, no. 2 (April 1998): 151–70, doi.org/10.1007/bf02688660; Kathryn E. Buchanan and Anat Bardi, "Acts of Kindness and Acts of Novelty Affect Life Satisfaction," *Journal of Social Psychology* 150, no. 3 (May–June 2010): 235–37, doi.org/10.1080/00224540903365554; Ashley V. Whillans et al., "Is Spending Money on Others Good for Your Heart?" *Health Psychology* 35, no. 6 (June 2016), 574–83, doi.org/10.1037/hea0000332.

47 **People even eat more:** Yao-Hua Law, "Why You Eat More When You're in Company," BBC Future, May 16, 2018, www.bbc.com/future/article/20180430-why-you-eat-more-when-youre-in-company.

47 **Humans are exceptional mimics:** Nicola McGuigan, J. Mackinson, and A. Whiten, "From Over-Imitation to Super-Copying: Adults Imitate Causally Irrelevant Aspects of Tool Use with Higher Fidelity than Young Children," *British Journal of Psychology* 102, no. 1 (February 2011): 1–18, doi.org/10.1348/000712610x493115.

47 **modeling their financial habits on those of their friends:** Ad Council, "New Survey Finds Millennials Rely on Friends' Financial Habits to Determine Their Own," PR Newswire, October 30, 2013, www.prnewswire.com/news-releases/new-survey-finds-millennials-rely-on-friends-financial-habits-to-determine-their-own-229841261.html.

NOTES

49 **Married individuals are 77% wealthier:** Jay L. Zagorsky, "Marriage and Divorce's Impact on Wealth," *Journal of Sociology* 41, no. 4 (December 2005): 406–24, doi.org/10.1177/1440783305058478.

50 **Married people also live longer:** Life expectancy: Haomiao Jia and Erica I. Lubetkin, "Life Expectancy and Active Life Expectancy by Marital Status Among Older U.S. Adults: Results from the U.S. Medicare Health Outcome Survey (HOS)," *SSM—Population Health* 12 (August 2020): 100642, doi.org/10.1016/j.ssmph.2020.100642; Lyman Stone, "Does Getting Married Really Make You Happier?" Institute for Family Studies (February 7, 2022), ifstudies.org/blog/does-getting-married-really-make-you-happier.

50 **a divorce in America reduces your wealth:** Zagorsky, "Marriage and Divorce's Impact on Wealth."

50 **Money is the second-most-argued-about topic:** Taylor Orth, "How and Why Do American Couples Argue?" YouGov, June 1, 2022, today.yougov.com/society/articles/42707-how-and-why-do-american-couples-argue?.

50 **Half of Americans struggling with financial tension:** "Relationship Intimacy Being Crushed by Financial Tension: AICPA Survey," AICPA & CIMA, February 4, 2021, www.aicpa-cima.com/news/article/relationship-intimacy-being-crushed-by-financial-tension-aicpa-survey.

50 **divorce rates are significantly higher:** Nathan Yau, "Divorce Rates and Income," FlowingData, May 4, 2021, flowingdata.com/2021/05/04/divorce-rates-and-income.

CHAPTER 2: FOCUS

56 **study of 233 millionaires:** Thomas C. Corley, "I Spent 5 Years Analyzing How Rich People Get Rich—and Found There Are Generally 4 Paths to Wealth," *Business Insider*, September 3, 2019, www.businessinsider.com/personal-finance/how-people-get-rich-paths-to-wealth.

61 **20% of people younger than 26:** Bill Burnett and Dave Evans, *Designing Your Life: How to Build a Well-Lived, Joyful Life* (New York: Alfred A. Knopf, 2016), xxiv–iv.

61 **Researchers studying the aspirations:** Sapna Cheryan and Therese Anne Mortejo, "The Most Common Graduation Advice Tends to Backfire," *New York Times*, May 22, 2023, nytimes.com/2023/05/22/opinion/stem-women-gender-disparity.html.

NOTES

62 **avocations than careers:** Oliver E. Williams, L. Lacasa, and V. Latora, "Quantifying and Predicting Success in Show Business," *Nature Communications* 10, no. 2256 (June 2019): doi.org/10.1038/s41467-019-10213-0; Mark Mulligan, "The Death of the Long Tail: The Superstar Music Economy," July 14, 2014, www.midiaresearch.com/reports/the-death-of-the-long-tail; "Survey Report: A Study on the Financial State of Visual Artists Today," The Creative Independent, 2018, thecreativeindependent.com/artist-survey; Mathias Bärtl, "YouTube Channels, Uploads and Views," *Convergence: The International Journal of Research into New Media Technologies* 24, no. 1 (January 2018): 16–32, doi.org/10.1177/1354856517736979; Todd C. Frankel, "Why Almost No One Is Making a Living on YouTube," *Washington Post*, March 2, 2018, www.washingtonpost.com/news/the-switch/wp/2018/03/02/why-almost-no-one-is-making-a-living-on-youtube.

63 **high match quality:** Yi Zhang, M. Salm, and A. V. Soest, "The Effect of Training on Workers' Perceived Job Match Quality," *Empirical Economics* 60, no. 3 (May 2021), 2477–98, doi.org/10.1007/s00181-020-01833-3.

64 **rewarding neurochemicals improves memory:** Steven Kotler, *The Art of Impossible: A Peak Performance Primer* (New York: HarperCollins, 2021), 157.

67 **the science behind them is limited:** Adam Grant, "MBTI, If You Want Me Back, You Need to Change Too," Medium, November 17, 2015, medium.com/@AdamMGrant/mbti-if-you-want-me-back-you-need-to-change-too-c7f1a7b6970; Tomas Chamorro-Premuzic, "Strengths-Based Coaching Can Actually Weaken You," *Harvard Business Review*, January 4, 2016, hbr.org/2016/01/strengths-based-coaching-can-actually-weaken-you.

72 **traditional workers and entrepreneurs**: Bostjan Antoncic et al., "The Big Five Personality–Entrepreneurship Relationship: Evidence from Slovenia," *Journal of Small Business Management* 53, no. 3 (2015): 819–41, doi.org/10.1111/jsbm.12089.

72 **correlates with risk propensity:** C. Nieß and T. Biemann, "The Role of Risk Propensity in Predicting Self-Employment," *Journal of Applied Psychology* 99, no. 5 (September 2014): 1000–9, doi.org/10.1037/a0035992.

72 **and is genetic:** Nicos Nicolaou et al., "Is the Tendency to Engage in Entrepreneurship Genetic?" *Management Science* 54, no. 1 (January 1, 2008): 167–79, doi.org/10.1287/mnsc.1070.0761.

73 **"Do you want your 22-year-old self":** Bill Burnett, "Bill Burnett on

NOTES

Transforming Your Work Life," *Literary Hub*, November 1, 2021, YouTube video, 37:11, www.youtube.com/watch?v=af8adeD9uMM.

75 **75% of new molecular entities:** Mariana Mazzucato, *The Entrepreneurial State: Debunking Public vs. Private Sector Myths* (London: Anthem Press, 2013).

79 **Twenty percent of start-ups fail:** U.S. Bureau of Labor Statistics, Business Employment Dynamics, www.bls.gov/bdm/us_age_naics_00_table7.txt.

84 **Eighty-seven percent of journalism majors:** Joshua Young, "Journalism Is 'Most Regretted' Major for College Grads," Post Millennial, November 14, 2022, thepostmillennial.com/journalism-is-most-regretted-major-for-college-grads.

89 **a venomous stowaway:** Derrick Bryson Taylor, "A Cobra Appeared Mid-Flight. The Pilot's Quick Thinking Saved Lives," *New York Times*, April 7, 2023, www.nytimes.com/2023/04/07/world/africa/snake-plane-cobra-pilot.html.

90 **44% of GDP:** Kathryn Kobe and Richard Schwinn, "Small Businesses Generate 44 Percent of U.S. Economic Activity," U.S. Small Business Administration Office of Advocacy, January 30, 2019, advocacy.sba.gov/2019/01/30/small-businesses-generate-44-percent-of-u-s-economic-activity.

90 **15 times more patents:** Anthony Breitzman and Patrick Thomas, "Analysis of Small Business Innovation in Green Technologies," U.S. Small Business Administration Office of Advocacy, October 1, 2011, advocacy.sba.gov/2011/10/01/analysis-of-small-business-innovation-in-green-technologies.

90 **are primarily *electrification* projects:** "Electricians: Occupational Outlook Handbook," U.S. Bureau of Labor Statistics, May 15, 2023, www.bls.gov/ooh/construction-and-extraction/electricians.htm.

90 **half a million plumbers short:** Judy Wohlt, "Plumber Shortage Costing Economy Billions of Dollars," *Ripple Effect: The Voice of Plumbing Manufacturers International* 25, no. 8 (August 2, 2022), issuu.com/pmi-news/docs/2022-august-ripple-effect/s/16499947.

90 **careers in construction:** Ryan Golden, "Construction's Career Crisis: Recruiters Target Young Workers Driving the Great Resignation," Construction Dive, October 25, 2021, www.constructiondive.com/news/construction-recruiters-aim-to-capitalize-on-young-workers-driving-great-resignation/608507.

NOTES

91 **Complexity thrives in large cities:** Pierre-Alexandre Balland et al., "Complex Economic Activities Concentrate in Large Cities," *Nature Human Behavior* 4 (January 2020), doi.org10.1038/s41562-019-0803-3.

91 **Over 80% of global GDP is generated in cities:** "Urban Development," World Bank, October 6, 2022, www.worldbank.org/en/topic/urbandevelopment/overview, accessed August 2023.

92 **A 2022 survey of C-level executives:** Aaron Drapkin, "41% of Execs Say Remote Employees Less Likely to Be Promoted," Tech.Co, April 13, 2022, tech.co/news/41-execs-remote-employees-less-likely-promoted; "Homeworking Hours, Rewards and Opportunities in the UK: 2011 to 2020," Office for National Statistics, April 19, 2021, www.ons.gov.uk/employmentandlabourmarket/peopleinwork/labourproductivity/articles/homeworkinghoursrewardsandopportunitiesintheuk2011to2020/2021-04-19.

93 **writing down your goals:** Dave Ramsey, *The Total Money Makeover Journal* (Nashville, TN: Nelson Books, 2013), 93.

94 **"Focus on your systems":** James Clear, *Atomic Habits* (New York: Avery, 2018), 24.

94 **measures of grit have been shown to be predictive:** Jennifer Bashant, "Developing Grit in Our Students: Why Grit Is Such a Desirable Trait, and Practical Strategies for Teachers and Schools," *Journal for Leadership and Instruction* 13, no. 2 (Fall 2014): 14–17, eric.ed.gov/?id=EJ1081394.

95 **"talent is merely a starting point":** Steven Kotler, *The Art of Impossible: A Peak Performance Primer* (New York: HarperCollins, 2023), 72; see also Mae-Hyang Hwang and JeeEun Karin Nam, "Enhancing Grit: Possibility and Intervention Strategies," in *Multidisciplinary Perspectives on Grit*, eds: Llewellyn Ellardus van Zyl, Chantal Olckers, and Leoni van der Vaart (New York: Springer Nature, 2021), 77–93, link.springer.com/chapter/10.1007/978-3-030-57389-8_5.

97 **Kenny Rogers's signature song:** Don Reid, "The Gambler," by Don Schlitz, performed by Kenny Rogers, United Artists, 1978.

97 **an entire book about quitting:** Annie Duke, *Quit: The Power of Knowing When to Walk Away* (New York: Portfolio, 2022).

98 **the best predictor of a new CEO's success:** David J. Epstein, *Range: Why Generalists Triumph in a Specialized World* (New York: Riverhead Books, 2021).

NOTES

99 **Americans who had changed jobs:** "Wage Growth Tracker," Federal Reserve Bank of Atlanta, www.atlantafed.org/chcs/wage-growth-tracker, accessed June 2023.

99 **the median tenure for workers:** Craig Copeland, "Trends in Employee Tenure, 1983–2018," *Issue Brief no. 474*, Employee Benefit Research Institute, February 28, 2019, www.ebri.org/content/trends-in-employee-tenure-1983-2018.

99 **By 2022, that had declined:** Bureau of Labor Statistics, "Employee Tenure in 2022," U.S. Department of Labor, September 22, 2022, www.bls.gov/news.release/tenure.nr0.htm.

100 **Members of Gen Z are switching jobs:** Cate Chapman, "Job Hopping Is the Gen Z Way," LinkedIn News, March 29, 2022, www.linkedin.com/news/story/job-hopping-is-the-gen-z-way-5743786.

101 **"hobo syndrome" to describe:** Sang Eun Woo, "A Study of Ghiselli's Hobo Syndrome," *Journal of Vocational Behavior* 79, no. 2 (2011): 461–69, doi.org/10.1016/j.jvb.2011.02.003.

102 **mentorship has been shown:** Lisa Quast, "How Becoming a Mentor Can Boost Your Career," *Forbes*, October 31, 2012, www.forbes.com/sites/lisaquast/2011/10/31/how-becoming-a-mentor-can-boost-your-career.

102 **"I have always had a policy":** James Bennet, "The Bloomberg Way," *Atlantic*, November 2012, www.theatlantic.com/magazine/archive/2012/11/the-bloomberg-way/309136.

105 **MBAs coming out of the top schools:** Ilana Kowarski and Cole Claybourn, "Find MBAs That Lead to Employment, High Salaries," *US News & World Report*, April 25, 2023, www.usnews.com/education/best-graduate-schools/top-business-schools/articles/mba-salary-jobs.

106 **"you need quick wins to get fired up"**: Ramsey, *Total Money Makeover*, 107.

CHAPTER 3: TIME

113 **"Time is the fire in which we burn":** Delmore Schwartz, "Calmly We Walk Through This April's Day," *Selected Poems (1938–1958): Summer Knowledge* (New York: New Directions Publishing Corporation, 1967).

120 **"menu of illusions":** Brittany Tausen, "Thinking About Time: Identifying Prospective Temporal Illusions and Their Consequences," *Cognitive*

NOTES

Research: Principles and Implications 7, no. 16 (February 2022), doi.org/10.1186/s41235-022-00368-8.

120 **When asked to evaluate:** Tausen, "Thinking About Time."

121 **recollection of past performance is positively biased:** Daniel J. Walters and Philip Fernbach, "Investor Memory of Past Performance Is Positively Biased and Predicts Overconfidence," *PNAS* 118, no. 36 (September 2, 2021), www.pnas.org/doi/10.1073/pnas.2026680118.

124 **A study of happiness:** Alex Bryson and George MacKerron, "Are You Happy While You Work?" *Economic Journal* 127, no. 599 (February 2017), doi.org/10.1111/ecoj.12269.

128 **"What gets measured gets managed" (attributed to:** Though Drucker strongly believed in measuring results, there's no evidence he ever actually said this. See Paul Zak, "Measurement Myopia," Drucker Institute, September 4, 2013, www.drucker.institute/thedx/measurement-myopia.

130 **people underpredicted their spending:** Ray Charles Howard et al., "Understanding and Neutralizing the Expense Prediction Bias: The Role of Accessibility, Typicality, and Skewness," *Journal of Marketing Research* 59, no. 2 (December 6, 2021), doi.org/10.1177/00222437211068025.

130 **fail to account for "exceptional" expenditures:** Adam Alter and Abigail Sussman, "The Exception Is the Rule: Underestimating and Overspending on Exceptional Expenses," *Journal of Consumer Research* 39, no. 4 (December 1, 2012), doi.org/10.1086/665833.

137 **Research on savings:** Leona Tam and Utpal M. Dholakia, "The Effects of Time Frames on Personal Savings Estimates, Saving Behavior, and Financial Decision Making," SSRN (August 2008), doi.org/10.2139/ssrn.1265095.

143 **56% of American adults:** Carmen Reinicke, "56% of Americans Can't Cover a $1,000 Emergency Expense with Savings," CNBC.com, January 19, 2022, www.cnbc.com/2022/01/19/56percent-of-americans-cant-cover-a-1000-emergency-expense-with-savings.html.

149 **Consumer Financial Protection Bureau offers a guide:** "What Is Credit Counseling," Consumer Financial Protection Bureau, www.consumerfinance.gov/ask-cfpb/what-is-credit-counseling-en-1451.

150 **"exaggerate the degree to which their future tastes":** George Loewenstein, T. Donoghue, and M. Rabin, "Projection Bias in Predicting

NOTES

Future Utility," *Quarterly Journal of Economics* 118, no. 4 (November 2003): 1209–48, doi.org/10.1162/003355303322552784.

150 **Twenty percent of "retired" Americans:** Brent Orwell, "The Age of Re-retirement: Retirees and the Gig Economy," American Enterprise Institute, August 3, 2021, www.aei.org/poverty-studies/workforce/the-age-of-re-retirement-retirees-and-the-gig-economy.

150 **who divorce after 65:** "The Nation's Retirement System: A Comprehensive Re-Evaluation Is Needed to Better Promote Future Retirement Security," U.S. Government Accountability Office, October 18, 2017, www.gao.gov/products/gao-18-111sp.

151 **the lesson to take from surprising events:** Morgan Housel, *The Psychology of Money* (Hampshire, UK: Harriman House, 2020), 127–28.

CHAPTER 4: DIVERSIFICATION

168 **Buffett offered to bet:** Warren Buffett, Berkshire Hathaway Letter to Shareholders 2017, www.berkshirehathaway.com/letters/2017ltr.pdf.

169 **Buffett was so far ahead:** Mark Perry, "The SP 500 Index Out-Performed Hedge Funds over the Last 10 Years. And It Wasn't Even Close," American Enterprise Institute, January 7, 2021, www.aei.org/carpe-diem/the-sp-500-index-out-performed-hedge-funds-over-the-last-10-years-and-it-wasnt-even-close.

169 **three out of four crypto traders:** Raphael Auer et al., "Crypto Trading and Bitcoin Prices: Evidence from a New Database of Retail Adoption," BIS Working Papers, No. 1049, November 2022, www.bis.org/publ/work1049.htm.

169 **94% of all large-cap funds:** Burton Malkiel, *A Random Walk Down Wall Street* (New York: W. W. Norton & Company, 2023), 180.

169 **In that same period:** Malkiel, *A Random Walk Down Wall Street*, 176.

169 **only half of actively managed:** Brian Wimmer et al., "The Bumpy Road to Outperformance," Vanguard Research, July 2013, static.vgcontent.info/crp/intl/auw/docs/literature/research/bumpy-road-to-outperformance-TLRV.pdf.

173 **Ten men in a factory:** Robert L. Heilbroner, "The Wealth of Nations," *Encyclopedia Britannica*, www.britannica.com/topic/the-Wealth-of-Nations, accessed June 2023.

NOTES

174 **Cristiano Ronaldo's contract:** Fabrizio Romano, "Cristiano Ronaldo Completes Deal to Join Saudi Arabian Club Al Nassr," *Guardian*, December 30, 2022, www.theguardian.com/football/2022/dec/30/cristiano-ronaldo-al-nassr-saudi-arabia.

184 **nearly $25 trillion:** "Debt to the Penny," FiscalData.Treasury.Gov, fiscaldata.treasury.gov/datasets/debt-to-the-penny/debt-to-the-penny, accessed April 7, 2023.

193 **Legendary investment guru:** "Did Benjamin Graham Ever Say That 'The Market Is a Weighing Machine'?" *Investing.Ideas's Blog*, Seeking Alpha, July 14, 2020, seekingalpha.com/instablog/50345280-investing-ideas/5471002-benjamin-graham-ever-say-market-is-weighing-machine.

198 **"the most fascinating kind of art":** Dina Gachman, "Andy Warhol on Business, Celebrity and Life," *Forbes*, August 6, 2013, www.forbes.com/sites/dinagachman/2013/08/06/andy-warhol-on-business-celebrity-and-life.

211 **"Does management think the tooth fairy":** Warren Buffett, Chairman's Letter, February 28, 2001, www.berkshirehathaway.com/2000ar/2000letter.html.

227 **only 8% took it:** Ben Casselman and Jim Tankersley, "As Mortgage-Interest Deduction Vanishes, Housing Market Offers a Shrug," *New York Times*, August 4, 2019, www.nytimes.com/2019/08/04/business/economy/mortgage-interest-deduction-tax.html.

234 **Tracking the returns:** J. B. Maverick, "S&P 500 Average Return," Investopedia, May 24, 2023, www.investopedia.com/ask/answers/042415/what-average-annual-return-sp-500.asp.

235 **the best-performing approach:** Robert J. Schiller, "The Life-Cycle Personal Accounts Proposal for Social Security: An Evaluation," National Bureau of Economic Research, May 2005, www.nber.org/papers/w11300. See also Dale Kintzel, "Portfolio Theory, Life-Cycle Investing, and Retirement Income," Social Security Administration Policy Brief No. 2007-02.

241 **just 10% of taxpayers:** Laura Saunders and Richard Rubin, "Standard Deduction 2020–2021: What It Is and How It Affects Your Taxes," *Wall Street Journal*, April 8, 2021, www.wsj.com/articles/standard-deduction-2020-2021-what-it-is-and-how-it-affects-your-taxes-11617911161.

244 **Warren Buffett has famously said:** Chris Isidore, "Buffett Says He's Still

NOTES

Paying Lower Tax Rate Than His Secretary," CNN Business, March 4, 2013, https://money.cnn.com/2013/03/04/news/economy/buffett-secretary-taxes/index.html.

250 **"The most common mistake":** Ray Dalio, *Principles* (New York: Simon and Schuster, 2017).

251 **only 3% of active retail traders:** Fernando Chague, R. De-Losso, and B. Giovannetti, "Day Trading for a Living?" June 11, 2020, papers.ssrn.com/sol3/papers.cfm?abstract_id=3423101.

252 **Nine out of ten day traders:** "Day Trader Demographics and Statistics in the US," *Zippia*, www.zippia.com/day-trader-jobs/demographics, accessed June 2023.

252 **14% of young men:** Gloria Wong et al., "Examining Gender Differences for Gambling Engagement and Gambling Problems Among Emerging Adults," *Journal of Gambling Studies* 29, no. 2 (June 2013): 171–89, doi.org/10.1007/s10899-012-9305-1.

BIBLIOGRAPHY

ONE OF THE THINGS my team and I set out to do with this book was to cover the full scope of what it takes to build wealth. It's a whole person project, not a math problem or an optimal set of life hacks. On every topic we covered, however, there's much more to say. The following books helped us refine our own thoughts, and we recommend them if you want to go deeper. Go deeper.

Stoicism and Life Skills

Allen, David. *Getting Things Done*, revised edition. New York: Penguin Books, 2015.

Cipolla, Carlo M. *The Basic Laws of Human Stupidity*. New York: Doubleday, 2021.

Clear, James. *Atomic Habits*. New York: Avery, 2018.

Covey, Stephen R. *The 7 Habits of Highly Effective People*. New York, Free Press, 1989.

Dalio, Ray. *Principles*. New York: Simon & Schuster, 2017.

Duhigg, Charles. *The Power of Habit*. New York: Random House, 2012.

Holiday, Ryan. *The Obstacle Is the Way*. New York: Portfolio, 2014.

Kotler, Steven. *The Art of Impossible*. New York: Harper Wave, 2021.

BIBLIOGRAPHY

Focus and Career Planning

Bolles, Richard N. *What Color Is Your Parachute? 2022*. New York: Ten Speed Press, 2021.

Burnett, Bill, and Dave Evans. *Designing Your Life*. New York: Knopf, 2016.

Mulcahy, Diane. *The Gig Economy*. New York: AMACOM, 2016.

Newport, Cal. *So Good They Can't Ignore You*. New York: Grand Central Publishing, 2012.

Tieger, Paul D., Barbara Barron-Tieger, and Kelly Tieger. *Do What You Are*. New York: Little, Brown and Company, 1992.

Financial Planning and Investing

Aliche, Tiffany. *Get Good with Money*. New York: Rodale Books, 2021.

Damodaran, Aswath. *Narrative and Numbers*. New York: Columbia University Press, 2017.

Graham, Benjamin. *The Intelligent Investor*. New York: Harper & Row, 1949.

Greenblatt, Joel. *You Can Be a Stock Market Genius*. New York: Simon & Schuster, 1997.

Housel, Morgan. *The Psychology of Money*. Hampshire, UK: Harriman House, 2020.

Malkiel, Burton G. *A Random Walk Down Wall Street*, 13th edition. New York: W. W. Norton & Company, 2023.

Moss, David. *A Concise Guide to Macroeconomics*. Boston: Harvard Business School Press, 2007.

Orman, Suze. *The 9 Steps to Financial Freedom*. New York: Crown Publishers, 1997.

Ramsey, Dave. *The Total Money Makeover: A Proven Plan for Financial Fitness*. Nashville, TN: Thomas Nelson, 2003.

Robbins, Tony. *Money, Master the Game*. New York: Simon & Schuster, 2014.

INDEX

Note: Italicized page numbers indicate material in tables or illustrations.

academic careers, 82–83
accountability partners, 136
accountants, 152
accrual accounting, 208, 210
actors, professional, 62, 75–76
advice, asking for, 45–46, 102
advisors, cultivating a group of, 45–46
affirmation, pursuit of, 28
aging, 150. *See also* retirement
agreeableness, 72
AIG, *164*
Airbnb, 74, 76
airline pilots, 88–89
Alden, Lyn, 37
Allen, David, 125
allies and fans, cultivation of, 7
Alter, Adam, 83, 130
Amazon, 219
ambitions, 68
amortization, 210
analysis paralysis, 52
anger, Stoic approach to, 36–37
Apple, 74, 75, 163, 165–66, 168

arbitrage, 175–76
artists, 62
athletes, professional, 63
Atomic Habits (Clear), 25, 27
attention to finances, 127–28, 154
attribution bias, 35

balance, maintaining, 56–60
balance sheets of corporations, 208
bandit people, *42*
bank loans, *189*
Bank of America, 180
bankruptcy, 5
banks and banking, 180–83
    bank-to-bank loans, *189*
    and certificates of deposit, 202, *203*
    and federal funds rate set by U.S. Federal Reserve, 196
    savings accounts, 202
    See also loans
Barton & Gray, 31–32
The Basic Laws of Human Stupidity (Cipolla), 42

INDEX

basis points, 190
battles that are unwinnable, 95–96
behavioral patterns, 16, *17*, 52
Benson, Todd, 102
Berkshire Hathaway, 183
Bezos, Jeff, 219, 239
Bitcoin, *162*, 230
black swan events, 151–52
Block, 75
Bloomberg, Mike, 102
Bolles, Richard, 77
bonds, 199, *203*, 220–24, *220*
bonuses, 131
borrowed money, tax advantages of, 239
Brand Farm, 97
Brickman, Philip, 30
Brokeback Mountain (film), 23
brokerages, 182
Buddhism, 18
budgeting
   and accountability partners, 136
   and after-tax income, 135
   allocating funds, 141–43
   and annual costs, 134
   and baseline spending, 134, 154, 201
   and debt, 147–49
   and emergency funds, 143–45, 151, 201
   gamification of, 133–34, 136
   and investment capital, 199–200, 254
   and liquidity concerns, 142–43
   online tools for, 130
   and "pay yourself first" ethic, 135
   in practice, 146–47
   reframing, 129
   for savings, 135
   setting goals for, 135
   three-bucket model for, 139–43, *140*, 155, 199
   and variability, 142–43
Buffett, Warren
   affluent background of, 1–2
   on EBITDA, 211
   and investing principles of Berkshire Hathaway, 183
   and power of compound interest, 117
   on tax rate, 244
   wager on stock market average, 168–70
Bureau of Labor Statistics, 185
Burnett, Bill, 70–71, 73, 95
burn rate
   definition of, 4
   and formula for economic security, 4–5
   identifying, 8–10
Bush, George W., 39
business school, 104–5

Campbell, Donald, 30
capital expenditures of corporations, 211
capital gains taxes, 240–41
capitalism, 172–97
   and banking, 180–83
   and consumerism, 18–19, 129
   and corporations, 179–80
   and financial markets, 176–79
   fundamental truths of, 1
   and government regulation, 183–85
   and lack of self-control, 23
   and marketplace of supply and demand, 174–76
   and measuring the economy, 185–92
   and talking about money, 49
   and trading time for money, 172–74
   and valuation and time value of money, 192–97
   and working hard, 29
careers, 72–91
   academia, 82–83
   airline pilots, 88–89
   basic considerations for, 73–77, 111
   and changing jobs, 99–101
   and compensation, 98–99
   entrepreneurship, 78–82
   finance, 86–87

INDEX

management consulting, 85–86
and market checks, 98–99
media, 83–84
nonlinear progressions in, 98–101
professional careers, 84–85, 111
real estate, 87–88
in trades and small/regional businesses, 89–91, 111
car purchases, 148
cash, spending, 135–36
cash flow statements of corporations, 208
catastrophizing, 36
Cayman Islands, 240
certificates of deposit (CD), 162, 202, *203*
certified financial planners (CFP), 152
Chanel, 62
character
and aligning behaviors with intentions, 16–17, 52
behavior's relationship with, 16–27, *17*
building a strong, 27–41
as long-term goal, 52
role of, in building/protecting wealth, 43–44, 151
See also Stoicism
charitable donations, 140, 241
Charity: water, 64–65
Charles Schwab, 182
chartered financial analysts (CFA), 152
children
and finding the right partner, 59
in low-income households, 11
money spent on, 31, 122
and tax credits, 242
China, 165–66
Churchill, Winston, 7, 35, 36
Cicero, 236
Cipolla, Carlo, 42–43, *42*
Citi, *164*
city life, value of, 91–93, 111
Clear, James, 25, 27, 93–94

CliftonStrengths by Gallup, 68
commodities, 230
communication skills, 76, 80, 110–11
compound interest
about, 115–17
and investing for the long term, 132, *132*
power of, *115*, *117*, 154
computer science, 84
constraints, value of, 59–60
consulting careers, 85–86
Consumer Financial Protection Bureau, 149
consumerism/consumption, 18–21, 129, 138
Consumer Price Index (CPI), 118, 186
Cordner, Cy, 160–61
corporations, 179–80
bonds, *189*, 199, *203*
capital expenditures of, 211
financial statements of, 207–12, *209*
initial public offerings of, 217
in low-tax jurisdictions, 240
wealth-generating power of, 204
See also stocks
counsel of others, accepting, 45–46
courage, 22–23
Covey, Stephen, 21–22, 42
credit cards, 148, 181–82, *189*
credit counseling, 149
credit quality, assessing, 178–79
Crow, Sheryl, 4
cryptocurrencies, 169, 181, 230
Csikszentmihalyi, Mihaly, 72
currency prices, 230

Dalio, Ray, 67, 250–51
Damodaran, Aswath, 83, 200
Damon, William, 61
day trading, *162*, 163, 217–18, 251–52, 255
debt, 16, 147–49
decision-making, 39–41, 52, 53
democracies, 44

INDEX

depreciation, 210
depressions, economic, 186
derivatives, 203, 230–33
Designing Your Life (Burnett and Evans), 70–71, 95
design skills, 76
desires, 93–94
diminishing marginal utility, 33, 243, 244
discounted cash flow (DCF) model, 215–16
discounting expected returns, 196
diversification, 3, 13, 254. *See also* capitalism; investments and investing
dividends, 206
divorces, 50, 150
doctors, 84
Dogecoin, 169
dogs, benefits of having, 44
Dow, Charles, 190
Do What You Are (Tieger, Barron-Tieger, and Tieger), 77
Dow Jones Industrial Average, 190, *191*
Drucker, Peter, 128
Duckworth, Angela, 94
Duhigg, Charles, 25
Duke, Annie, 97
Dylan, Bob, 5, 6

earned-income tax credit, 242
earnings per share (EPS), 212
EBIT (earnings before interest and taxes), 210, 212, *213*, 214
EBITDA (earnings before interest, taxes, depreciation, and amortization), 210–11
Economic Data repository of the Federal Reserve, 185
economic downturns, 74–75, 186
economic security
  about, 4
  basic formula for, 4–5, 152
  and happiness, 34
  and home ownership, 225
  number required for, 8 (*see also* burn rate)
  obtaining prior to stopping work, 8
  plan for achieving, 12–13 (*see also* diversification; focus; Stoicism; time)
  and relationships, 153, 258
  as result of behavioral patterns, 16
  role of character in building, 151
  as source of options, 8
  vs. economic anxiety, 10–12
  wealth as related to, 4
education
  budgeting for, 139, 140
  and 529 college savings plans, 249
  grad school, 104–5
  return on investment from, 250
  and student loans, 241, 250
  and tax deductions, 241
Einstein, Albert, 115
electricians, 90
emergency funds, 143–45, 151, 201
emotions
  acknowledging, 52
  decision-making based on, 24
  distinguishing wisdom from, 40
  Duke's advice on managing, 97
  and investing, 160, 200, 217, 250, 255
  and tracking finances, 128, 131, 154
employment measurements, 186–87
Engels, Friedrich, 198
enterprise value, 214–15
entertainment, professionals in, 62
The Entrepreneurial State (Mazzucato), 75
entrepreneurship
  and agreeableness in entrepreneurs, 72
  as career option, 78–82
  and side hustles, 103
  and tracking money, 129

INDEX

environmental, social, and corporate governance (ESG) investments, 219–20
Epictetus, 23, 48
equity valuation, 212–17
estimated tax payments, 242
Evans, Dave, 70–71, 95
exceptionalism, belief in one's, 14–15
exchange-traded funds (ETFs), 202, 203, *203*, 233–34, 254
exercise, 38–39, 52, 106
exit strategies, 97
expectations, 6–7
expense ratios, 234
ExxonMobil, *164*

Facebook, 220
failures, 35, 36, 110
families, 5, 44
FDIC (Federal Deposit Insurance Corporation), 184
fear
   combating, with courage, 23
   as driver behind pursuit of wealth, 12
federal funds rate set by U.S. Federal Reserve, 188–89, *189*, 196
Fidelity, 182
finance careers, 86–87, 152–53
finance industry, 73
financial markets, 176–79, 203, 255
529 college savings plans, 249
flexibility, cultivating, 58, 59
flow state, 72, 107
focus, 54–111
   about, 13
   and accepting limitations, 57–58
   in basic formula for economic security, 3
   and benefits of partners, 59
   and city life, 91–92
   and cultivating flexibility, 58, 59
   and desires/goals, 93–94
   and employment (*see* careers)
   and following your talent, 63–72
   and grad school, 104–5
   and grit, 94–95
   and hobbies, 106–8, 111
   and keeping balance, 56–60
   and knowing when to quit, 96–97, 111
   and loyalty, 101–2, 111
   and nonlinear career progressions, 98–101
   and passion pursuits, 60–63, 66, 70–72, 75–76
   and "quick wins" tactic, 105–6
   and side hustles, 103–4
   and unwinnable battles, 95–96
   and value of constraints, 59–60
   and value of mastery, 70–71, 110
4% Rule, 9, 152
401(k) accounts
   and employer match, 145–46, 155
   importance of contributing to, 145–46
   and investment companies, 182
   in practice, 146–47
   and taxes, 241, 247, *248*, 255
   and three-bucket model for budgeting, 199
Frasier (television show), 32
Frankl, Viktor, 24
freelancers (self-employed individuals), 103, 242, 245–46
free-market economy, 174
funding for new ventures, 79, 81
funds, 233–36
future, planning for, 149–53. *See also* investments and investing
futures (derivative securities), 230

Gallup's CliftonStrengths, 68
GE, 81, *164*
Gen Z'ers, 5, 100
Getting Things Done (Allen), 125
gift purchases and budgeting, 140
Gladwell, Malcolm, 71

goals and goal setting, 93–94, 118, 137–38
gold, investments in, *162*
Goldman Sachs, 182
Google, 75, 79, 81, 216–17
government investments, leveraging, 75
government regulation, 183–85
graduate school, 104–5
Graham, Benjamin, 193
gravity problems, 95–96
Great Financial Crisis of 2008, 184, 226, 231
grit, 23, 94–95
gross domestic product (GDP), 185–86
gross margin percentage, 213

Haas School of Business, 104
habit development, 25–27, 52, 141
Haidt, Jonathan, 83
Hallquist, Connie, 64
happiness
 and economic security, 34
 and expectations, 6–7
 genetic predisposition for, 33
 and hedonic treadmill, 30–31, *31*, 33–34
 and income levels, 33
 of lottery winners vs. paraplegic individuals, 30
 and practicing kindness, 47
Harari, Yuval Noah, 30
hard work, 28–30, 56, 66, 110
Harley-Davidson, 166
Harrison, Scott, 64–65
Hawthorne effect, 131
health savings accounts (HSAs), 249
hedge funds, 182, 202
hedonic treadmill, 30–31, *31*, 33–34
helpless people, *42*
high-yield savings accounts (HYSA), 199
hobbies, 106–8, 111
hobo syndrome, 101

Holiday, Ryan, 36
home equity loans, 239
Housel, Morgan, 63
House of Sand and Fog (film), 129
housing and home ownership
 and economic security, 225
 and Great Financial Crisis of 2008, 226, 231
 and home equity, 87
 as investment, *162*, 170–71, 225–29, 255
 and mortgages, 148, 181, 227–28, 239
 rising prices, 5
 shortages in, 87
Howell, Sabrina, 83
How to Win Friends and Influence People (Carnegie), 22

IBM, *164*
income
 and budgeting, 135
 declines in, 5, *6*
 declining marginal utility of, 33, 243, 244
 focusing on maximizing, 165
 and happiness, 33
 patterns of, over a lifetime, 121–22
 and payroll taxes, 245–46
 and stock in lieu of compensation, 239
 and tax rates, 241–45
income statements of corporations, 209–10, *209*
income tax, 238–45
index funds, *162*, 185–92
indifference, 37
inflation, 117–20, 154, 186, 195
initial public offerings (IPO), 217
Intel, 75
intelligent people, *42*, 43
intentions, aligning behaviors with, 16, 52
interdependence, 42

INDEX

interest and interest rates, 177–78, 181, 187–90, *189*
Internal Revenue Service (IRS), 236
introversion of author, 28
inventory turnover of corporations, 213
investment banks, 182
investment companies, 182–83
investments and investing, 159–71, 197–236
  active and passive, *162*, 163, 200–201, 254
  author's introduction to, 159–61
  on autopilot, 197–98
  bonds, 220–24, *220*
  building a habit for, 141
  capital for, 199–200, 254
  and capital gains taxes, 240–41
  and cognitive errors regarding time, 121
  commodities, 230
  and compound interest, 115–17, *115*, *116*, *117*, 154
  consumption expenditures vs., 139–40
  conversations about, 48–49
  currency prices, 230
  day trading, *162*, 163, 217–18, 251–52, 255
  derivatives, 230–33
  and discounting, 196
  diversification as defense strategy, 164–68, 171
  diversified vs. concentrated, *162*, 163–64
  and emotions, 160, 200, 217, 250, 255
  exchange-traded funds (ETFs), 202, 203, *203*, 254
  and expense ratios, 234
  and fees, 255
  funds, 233–36
  and learning from losses, 250–51
  as a long-term exercise, 132, *132*
  and market capitalization rank, *164*
  as means to wealth, 197, 245, 254
  and opportunity costs, 121
  policy-driven, 219–20
  real estate, 224–30
  and recollections of past performance, 121
  remaining rational about, 250, 255
  risks and returns, 161–62, 171, 178, 254
  and robo-advisors, *162*, 234
  spectrum of, 202–3
  taking profits from, 251
  and time value of money, 195–97
  tracking, 131–32
  and variability, 142
  and youth's advantage, 126–27
  See also stocks
IRAs (individual retirement accounts), 145, 241, 247–49, *248*, 255

Jay-Z, 1, 63
Jesus, 18
job changes, 99–101
Jobs, Steve, 32, 60, 61–62
Johnson & Johnson, *164*
journalists, 83–84
JPMorgan, 180
Jung, Carl, 21
junk bonds, 189–90
justice, 22–23, 29

Kahlo, Frida, 40
Kahneman, Daniel, 151
kindness, practicing, 45–47, 53
Kingsley, Ben, 129
kitchen cabinet, cultivating a, 45–46, 96
Kotler, Steven, 39

L2, 74, 94, 128
labor. *See* working/labor
law school, 62–63
lawyers, 84, 152
leveraging money, 147–48
Levi Strauss & Co., 175–76
life hacks, 22

INDEX

lifestyle creep, 30–31, 138
limitations, accepting, 57–58
Lin, Johnny, 69
LinkedIn, 99
liquidity, 142–43. *See also* budgeting
loans
   about, 181–82
   bank loans, 177–78, 181, *189*
   home equity loans, 239
   and interest rates, 177–78, *189*
   and leveraging money, 147–48
   mortgages, 148, 181, 227–28, 239
   short-term, 148
   stock used as collateral for, 239
   and tax strategies, 239
lottery winners, 30
loyalty, 101–2, 111
luck, 34–35, 52

macroeconomic cycles/factors, 74, 96
Main Street economy, 89–91, 111
Malkiel, Burton, 169–70
management consulting, 85–86
Marciano, Sonia, 83
Marcus Aurelius, 18, 24, 42
market capitalization, 214–15
market dynamics, 74, 110
market indexes, 190–92
market multiples, 213–15
marketplace of supply and demand, 174–76
marriages, 5, 49–51, 59
Marx, Karl, 198
mastery, value of, 70–71, 110
Mazzucato, Mariana, 75
measurements of economies, 185–92
media, 36, 83–84
medical bills and debt, 5, 241
medical professionals, 84
Medicare, 245
memento mori, 40
mentors, 92, 101–2
Merck, *164*
metrics for measuring finances, 128

Microsoft, 74, *164*
millionaires, 90
mimicry, 47
Moghadam, Hamid, 38
money
   and diminishing marginal utility, 33, 243, 244
   and financial markets, 176–79
   as a goal, 30–33
   and hedonic treadmill, 30–31, *31*, 34
   leveraging, 147–48
   and lifestyle creep, 30–31
   rational obsession with, 127–28, 154
   talking about, 49, 53, 99
   trading time for, 172–74, 254
   valuation and time value of, 192–97
   See also spending
money markets, *203*
Morgan Stanley, 78, 182
Mormon families, 44
mortgages, 148, 181, 227–28, 239, 241
motivation for pursuing wealth, 12, 52
moving to low-tax states, 252–53
musicians, 62
Musk, Elon, 60, 239
mutual funds, *162*, 202, *203*, 233, 234
Myers-Briggs, 67–68, 77

Nasdaq Composite, 190–91, *191*, 192
Netflix, 168
Newport, Cal, 61
"no," value of saying, 60
No Mercy / No Malice blog, 26, 66
NYU, 28, 66, 82, 98–99

The Obstacle Is the Way (Holiday), 36
offices, value of working in, 91–93, 111
the 1% (world's wealthiest people), 6–7
opportunity costs, 121, 148, 195–96
options trading, *203*, 231–32
Orange County Airport, 122

paraplegics, happiness of, 30
partners, benefits of finding, 59

INDEX

passion pursuits
and careers in media, 83–84
folly of, 60–63, 75–76
pursuing talent instead of, 110
as result of mastery, 70–72
passive income
ability to live off of, 197
active investments vs., 170, 200–201
and classification of investment options, 162–63, *162*
and formula for economic security, 4–5, *5*
funds, 233
prioritizing, 200–201, 254
real estate, 229
PayPal, 181
payroll taxes, 245–46
"pay yourself first" ethic, 135
persistence, 96–97
Personal Capital (app), 130
personality ethic, 21–22
personality tests, 67–68
perspective keeping, 36, 53
Pfizer, *164*
philosophy, purpose of, 18
pilots, 88–89
plumbers, 90
policy-driven investing, 219–20
power, 29, 44
The Power of Habit (Duhigg), 25
president of the United States, 39–40
price to earnings (P/E) ratio, 212–13
pricing, 174–76, 192–97
Principles (Dalio), 250
private capital, 183
professional careers, 84–85, 111
profit and loss (P and L) statements, 209–10
projection bias, 150
promotions, talking about, 99
propagation, humans' hard-wiring for, 20–21
Prophet, 59–60, 64, 69
Protégé Partners, 169

Public (app), 182
purpose, sense of, 38

Qualcomm, 75
"quick wins" tactic, 105–6
quitting a venture, 96–97, 111

Ramsey, Dave, 105
A Random Walk Down Wall Street (Malkiel), 169–70
Read, Ronald, 1
real estate, 74, 87–88, 170, 224–30
real estate investment trusts (REIT), 229–30
recessions, 74–75, 186
recreational activities, 106–8
Red Envelope, 74, 97, 167, 251
regional businesses, 89–91
registered investment advisers (RIA), 152
rejection as secret to success, 80
relationships
and economic security, 153, 258
and loyalty to people, 101–2, 111
and rich friends, 47–49
sacrificed for work, 30
spouses, 49–51, 53
and talking about money, 49, 53
as ultimate objective in life, 7, 257–58
rental properties, 88, 163
resentments, 57, 110
responses, choosing our, 24–25
retail banks, 181–82
retirement
changing notions about, 150
contributing to tax-sheltered plans for, 201, 241
Gen Z'ers pessimism about, 5
and maxing out employers' matches, 145–46, 155
as outdated construct, 7
and three-bucket model for budgeting, 140
See also investments and investing

INDEX

returns, 178
revenge, 38
rich friends, 47–49
risk taking, propensity for, 72
Robinhood, 182, 252
robo-advisors, *162*, 234
Rocket Money, 130
Ronaldo, Cristiano, 174
Roth IRAs (Roth individual retirement accounts), 145, 247, 248–49, *248*, 255
Russell 3000, 234

S&P 500
  about, 190
  as benchmark, 192
  and Buffett's wager, 168–70
  ETFs for, 233–34
  as passive investment, 233
  performance of, over time, 132, *132*, 142, *191*, 234–35
S&P Composite 1500, 169
sales, 74
Sapiens (Harari), 30
saving money
  and budgeting, 135, 142
  building a habit for, 141, 154
  and debt, 148
  and emergency funds, 143–45, 151
  goals for, 137–38, 154
  and managing spending, 131
  reframing, 128–29
  and rounding up purchases, 136
  and savings accounts, 163, 202, *203*
  and tracking money, 127–28, 129
  and youth's advantage, 126–27
scalability in industries, 73–74
Schiller, Friedrich, 43
Schiller, Robert, 235
Schmidt, Eric, 32
Schwartz, Delmore, 113
SEC (Securities and Exchange Commission), 184
securities, 220–21, 230, 254

self-control, 16, 23, 24–25
self-employed individuals (freelancers), 103, 242, 245–46
self-improvement, 21–22
selfishness, 27–28
Seneca, 34, 48
service industry, practicing kindness to people in, 45–47
service to others, 44
The 7 Habits of Highly Effective People (Covey), 42
sexual harassment, 44
Siddhartha Gautama, 18
side hustles, 103–4
signaling status, 20–21
Silicon Valley, 75
Simplifi (app), 130
skilled workers, 89–91
Slack, 74
slowing down, 24–25, 52
small businesses, 89–91
Smith, Adam, 173
Snap, 76
social media, 22, 124
Social Security, 9, 245, 246
software engineering, 74
So Good They Can't Ignore You (Newport), 61
Sonnenfeld, Jeffrey, 83
specialization, 173
spending
  and accountability partners, 136
  baseline levels of, 134, 154, 201
  and burn rate, 4–5, 8–10
  cash used for, 135–36
  on children, 31, 122
  and choosing our responses, 31–32
  and cost of working hard, 29
  developing discipline with, 135 (*see also* budgeting)
  fluctuation in, 139, 154
  and hedonic treadmill, 30–31, *31*
  introducing friction into, 129–30, 135–36

INDEX

investments vs. expenditures, 139–40
and lifestyle creep, 30–31, 138
and online budgeting tools, 130
patterns of, over a lifetime, 121–22
and practicing kindness, 47
prioritizing, over saving, 137
purchases requiring ongoing funding, 138–39, 154
and three-bucket model for budgeting, 139–41, *140*, 155, 199
tracking, 127, 129–31, *130*, 134, 136, 154
underestimation of, 130, *130*
spouses, 49–51, 53, 153
Stanley, Thomas J., 8
start-ups, failures of, 79
state income taxes, 241, 252–53
Stavers, Jason, 69–70
Stern School of Business, NYU, 28, 66, 82, 98–99
stocks, *162*, 203–20
   day trading, *162*, 163, 217–18
   distribution of profits from, 206–7
   and diversification, 166–67
   and dual-class share structures, 204
   equity (ownership) in, 204–5
   equity valuation, 212–17, *213*
   financial statements for, 207–12
   gauging value of, 207
   investing in, 217–20
   in lieu of compensation, 239
   and market capitalization, 214–15
   options trading, *203*, 231–32
   risk associated with, *203*
   selling, 206–7
   and share buybacks, 206–7
   stock indexes, 190–92
   See also investments and investing
Stoicism, 14–53
   about, 13, 18
   and anger, 36–37
   in basic formula for economic security, 3
   and behavior's relationship with character, 16–27
   and belief in one's exceptionalism, 14–15
   and choosing our responses, 24–25
   and consumerism, 18–21, 138
   and decision-making, 39–41, 53
   and discipline with spending, 135
   and exercise, 38–39, 52
   and four virtues, 22–23
   and goal of having money, 30–33
   and habit development, 25–27, 52
   and hard-wiring of humans, 20–21
   and indifference, 37
   and interdependence, 42
   and a kitchen cabinet, 45–46
   and luck's role in success, 34–35, 52
   and memento mori, 40
   and personality ethic, 21–22
   and perspective keeping, 36, 53
   and practicing kindness, 45–47, 53
   and resisting temptations, 22–23
   and revenge, 38
   and rich friends, 47–49
   role of character in building/protecting wealth, 43–44
   and service to others, 44
   and stupidity, 42–43, *42*, 53
   and sympatheia, 42
   and taking action, 21–22
   and talking about money, 49, 53
   and working hard, 28–30
store financing, 148
stress/anxiety, economic, 8, 10–12, 47
student loans, 241, 250
stupidity, 42–43, *42*, 53
success
   and nonlinear career progressions, 98–101
   and perspective keeping, 36
   role of luck in, 34–35, 52
supply and demand, marketplace of, 174–76
surprises, preparing for, 151–52

INDEX

survival, humans' hard-wiring for, 20–21
sympatheia, 42

talent, following your, 63–72, 110
tax advisers, 152
taxes, 236–49
  assistance with, 237–38, *237*
  awareness of, 237, *237*
  and borrowed money, 239
  and burn rate, 9
  and deductions, 241–42
  deferring, 247–49, 255
  effective vs. marginal, 246–47
  and high-income trap, 243–45, *243*
  income tax, 238–45, 252–53
  minimizing, 236–37, 239–43, 247–49
  and mortgage interest deductions, 227–28
  and moving to low-tax states, 252–53
  payroll taxes, 245–46
  progressive/regressive, 243–44, *243*
  and the self-employed, 242
  and share buybacks, 207
  state income taxes, 241
  tax credits, 242
  and tax lawyers, 238
  understanding of, 237, *237*, 255
tax policy, 183
technology, saving time with, 124–25
temperance, 22–23
temptations, keys to resisting, 22–23
Tesla, 75
thinking about money, 127
Thoreau, Henry David, 18
three-bucket model for budgeting, 139–43, *140*, 155, 199
time, 112–55
  about, 13
  in basic formula for economic security, 3
  cognitive errors regarding, 120–22
  and compound interest, 115–17, *115, 116, 117*, 154
  and the future, 149–53
  and goals, 137–38
  identifying thieves of, 123–26
  and inflation, 117–20
  limitations on, 57
  as most valuable resource, 113–14, 122–26, 154
  trading, for money, 172–74, 254
  valuation and time value of money, 192–97
  and youth's advantage, 126–27
tipping well, 45–47, 53
tracking money and spending, 127–32, *130*, 154
trade careers, 89–91, 111
Treasury securities, 184, 196, 199, 223–24
Truman, Harry, 39

Uber, 74
UCLA, 18, 80, 133–34, 161
UC Berkeley, 104
unemployment rate, 186–87
U.S. Department of Commerce, 185
U.S. Department of Labor, 184–85
U.S. Department of the Treasury, 184
U.S. Federal Reserve
  about, 184
  and employment rates, 187
  and inflation, 118, 186
  and interest rates, 188–90, *189*
  online tools, 185
  power of, 96
U.S. Securities and Exchange Commission (SEC), 184
U.S. Small Business Administration, 90

valuation and time value of money, 192–97
values and decision-making, 40

INDEX

Vanguard, 182
venture capital and venture capitalists, 81, 182, 183, 202
visual communication, 76

wages, 98–99, 186–87
walking, 39
Wall Street (movie), 44, 178
Walmart, *164*
Walsh, Bill, 94
Warhol, Andy, 198
wealth
  basic formula for, 3
  changes in standards of, 6–7
  economic security as related to, 4
  investing as a means to, 197, 245, 254
  motivation for pursuing, 12
  outliers with, 1–2
  permission to pursue, 5–7
  role of character in, 43–44
  variety of paths to, 1–2
What Color Is Your Parachute? (Bolles), 77
WhatsApp, 74
willpower, 16
wisdom, 22–23, 24
Wolfe, Tom, 28
working/labor
  and flexibility in scheduling, 58
  hard work, 28–30, 56, 66, 110
  from home, 91
  and trading time for money, 172–74
  and unemployment rate, 186–87
Wozniak, Steve, 61

yields, bond, 223
YNAB (app), 130
youth's advantage, 126–27
YouTube channels, 62